The Uncrowned Queen

A Cassell BOOK

Books by Ishbel Ross

The
Uncrowned
Queen

LIFE OF LOLA MONTEZ

by Ishbel Ross

HARPER & ROW, PUBLISHERS
New York, Evanston, San Francisco, London

FIRST EDITION

STANDARD BOOK NUMBER: 06-013662-6

LIBRARY OF CONGRESS CATALOG CARD NUMBER: 70-181641

Contents

Illustrations

Acknowledgments

The history of Lola Montez, or the Countess of Landsfeld as she preferred to be called, has a wide geographical range, since she traveled across Europe, the United States and Australia in the nineteenth century with a sure sense of the dramatic and a genius for causing trouble. She used a variety of names and at times covered her tracks to the point of total anonymity, thus encouraging many conflicting stories of her importance as a courtesan who mixed sex and politics. But her meddling in the revolutionary events leading up to the great upheavals of 1848, resulting in her exile from Bavaria and the subsequent abdication of King Ludwig I, is well defined. So, too, is the history of her early years in Ireland, India, London, Paris, Bath and Montrose.

Details of her turbulent days as a schoolgirl in the ancient royal burgh of Montrose on the east coast of Scotland were given to me by local residents, and I am particularly indebted to Mrs. Anne Watson who lives in Holly House, the picturesque mansion with an ancient close facing the town steeple, where Lola stayed for a time as the ward of the town provost, Sir Patrick Edmonstone Craigie. His son, Adjutant-General John Craigie, of the East India Army, was Lola's stepfather and she had been sent there from India to be educated and prepared for the conventional social debut of her era.

Mrs. Watson and her son, John Lindsay Watson, known on the air as John Lindsay, Officer for Scotland of the Independent Television Authority, were generous in sharing with me their knowledge of Lola's early history, and in guiding me to others well informed on the subject. There are a number of Craigies around Montrose and Perth, and a few are direct descendants of the Provost. Most of them would just as soon forget that Lola Montez was ever identified with the family name. But Major Colin F. I. Neish, of Tannadice, Forfar, recalled for me stories of Lola told him by his mother, whose grandfather was a Craigie and a doctor with the East India Army. The Major gave his mother's copy of a painting of Lola to Montrose Museum, where it still hangs as a reminder of her early links with the burgh. He had grown up with the image of the famous siren, like John Lindsay, who remembers that Lola's portrait with plumed hat hung in the nursery of Holly House when he was a small boy. It was years before he learned that she had been a world-famous adventuress.

I am much indebted to Miss Mary Smith, County Librarian for Angus and Kincardineshire, for the material she supplied on the history of Montrose, and for introductions to various residents with special knowledge of Lola's life there. She and her associates at the library in Montrose went out of their way to aid me in my quest for fresh material. Files of the Montrose *Standard*, the Montrose *Review* and the Montrose *Chronicle* for the late 1820's proved to be enlightening about the atmosphere in which Lola lived. John S. Richardson, Town Clerk, traced old municipal records for me involving Provost Craigie. Ian Murray was helpful about pictures.

I should also like to express my appreciation of the help and interest shown in my proposed book by Thomas I. Rae, manuscript department, National Library of Scotland, Edinburgh; H. J. H. Drummond, Aberdeen University Library; D. MacArthur, University Library, St. Andrews; J. R. Barker, University Library, Dundee; Peter Pagan, director, City of Bath Municipal Libraries, and Miss Patricia M. Baxendine, director of the Scots Ancestry Research Society. I was most cordially aided in my research at the London Library, thanks to the courtesy of its director, Stanley Gillam, and Douglas Matthews, getting ready access to old files highlighting Lola's career on the stage, and her adventures in Bavaria.

Echoes of Lola Montez are still strong in Munich and I am especially indebted to Dr. Anton Schneiders, director of the Bayerische Staatsbibliothek, and his able assistant, Mrs. Gabriele Hütz, for guiding me to a wealth of material bearing on my subject, and for suggesting other avenues of approach. I am grateful to Dr. Schattenhofer, director of the State Archives, and to his associate, Dr. Ludwig Morenz, for permission to use the text of the handwritten *City Chronicle* compiled by the municipal authorities, detailing the insurrection in Munich that led almost to revolution on February 10 and 11, 1848, and ended with the banishment of Lola Montez from the city. Miss Gabriele Kissling, of the State Archives, was most helpful in supplying me with pictures, scrapbooks and other memorabilia of Lola. I was also generously aided at the Monacensia-Sammlung by Miss Beate Geis, who produced scrapbooks, magazine articles, Lola's memoirs and general material about her days in Munich. Dr. Hans Rall of the Bayerisches Hauptstaatsarchiv gave me a courteous reception and helpful suggestions.

Allan Ottley, director of the California Room of the State Library at Sacramento, was generous in supplying me with manuscript material and documents bearing on Lola's adventures in San Francisco, Sacramento and Grass Valley. Miss Helen D. Willard and Dr. Jeanne T. Newlin, of the Harvard Theatre Collection, provided me with pictures and letters. The scrapbooks and other material at Lincoln Center on Lola's theatrical experiences in America were revealing. Her adventures on both sides of the Atlantic were lavishly chronicled in the contemporary magazines and newspapers. James Gordon Bennett in particular had his reporters follow her wherever she appeared and she was constantly championed in his paper, the New York *Herald*. Few nineteenth-century women reaped as much publicity as Lola Montez. Her doings were chronicled from San Francisco to St. Petersburg, and the London *Times* kept close track of her until she died.

I am deeply grateful to Cass Canfield for having suggested that I write this biography of Lola Montez, and for his interest in its development.

I.R.

The Uncrowned Queen

ONE

A Calvinist Setting

Cool winds from the North Sea blew over the small town of Montrose on a sleepy summer day early in the nineteenth century. Wide, historic High Street, that for hundreds of years had been a highway for warriors, merchants and smugglers, showed few signs of life until a white figure ran out of a dark close, stark naked, her long hair flowing free, the blue eyes that would topple a throne and wreck men's lives burning with anger. Nine-year-old Marie Dolores Eliza Rosanna Gilbert, in a fury of protest over her disciplined life, had torn off her clothes in a tantrum, knowing no better way to provoke her guardians, or stir up the town.

Unconsciously she was setting the key for her own future, when she would be known to the world as Lola Montez, the courtesan who cost Ludwig I of Bavaria his throne, who was cherished by the wits and savants of Paris in the 1830's, who was hissed and applauded in the capitals of Europe as a dancer, but whose distinctive fame lay in her reputation as an insatiable amoureuse. Her loves were legion, and she tired of men more quickly than they did of her, even the

1

romantic Franz Liszt. Alexandre Dumas, who loved her briefly and always admired her, decided that she had a fatal touch. He predicted early in her career that she would bring ill luck to any man who linked his life with hers. He proved to be right. Death and disaster followed Lola Montez like a dark cloud.

She was already aware of both when she arrived in Montrose from India in 1826, for her young soldier father, Edward Gilbert, had died of cholera the year before, and she had been close to the horrors of war. She had come to know the squalor of the cities as well as the palaces and jewels of the maharajahs. Long before she ran wild on the Scottish coast she was difficult to control, hostile to her beautiful mother, spoiled by ayahs and sepoys, and recklessly unafraid of snakes and jungle beasts. As the pet of her father's regiment she was used to adulation, to being waited on, and to having her own way. Lord Hastings, Governor General of Bengal at the time, cast an approving eye on the little beauty, and all showed concern for her when her father died.

From her earliest years she chattered as freely in Hindustani and Bengali as in English. She was exposed to the jangle of many dialects and was alive to differences in rank, creed and color. Her ears were attuned to jungle sounds. Her eyes were accustomed to the blaze of exotic flowers, of gorgeously plumaged birds, and she learned to imitate the slow ritualistic dances of the Indians. Her ayah could scarcely keep up with her restless charge, or gauge her lightning changes of mood.

She was a true child of the tropics when her widowed mother married Captain John Craigie a few months after her father's death. Her reaction was so severe that Mrs. Craigie decided the time had come to send her to Scotland to be educated, disciplined and prepared for a civilized social life. She had reached the age of eight, the usual time for the Anglo-Indian child to be removed from tropical influences and exposed to a brisker climate and well-regulated studies. It seemed to be doubly necessary in her case, both for her health and her conduct. She had loved her father deeply, and had bitterly resented her mother's remarriage, although young Gilbert had consigned them both to his best friend's care in his dying hour. Although known as Eliza in her early years, she was called Dolores or Lola after this, to prevent confusion with her mother, Elizabeth, usually referred to by Captain Craigie as Eliza.

The Captain, one of the most popular officers in the East India Army and destined later to become a major, colonel and finally adjutant general, was a tall Scot of thirty-two with a chestnut beard and grave eyes. He was already on his way up the professional ladder when he married Elizabeth Gilbert, who was noted in army circles for her delicate beauty and her professional style of dancing. Her red hair matched her sparkling disposition, and her cameo face with its widely spaced green eyes and bow mouth was a constant challenge to young officers far from home. She was as coquettish in her manner, and as frivolous in her ways, as her small daughter was intense, but she observed the conventions of army life and built up a substantial position from obscure beginnings. Theirs was a life of regimental functions, dances and parades.

From the start Captain Craigie seemed to understand his stepchild better than her mother did. He saw that she had developed beyond her years, and had seen too much of the feverish social life of an army station. She was not the docile child of her era, and her tempers were so violent that her mother quailed before her and left her entirely to servants. Lola's will was like iron, and she was as unresponsive to the Captain's kindness and understanding as she was to her mother's disapproval.

Strolling in the shade of giant trees in their garden one day her stepfather saw that she was heading into an area forbidden for her because of the snakes that haunted it. Barefooted, she ran along a pebbled path to a small pool that lay blue and shimmering in the heat haze. Before Captain Craigie could catch up with her she had ripped off her clothes and slipped smoothly into the water. A fringe of hibiscus bushes hid her from view but Captain Craigie shouted to her to get dressed at once and return to the house to see her mother. Lola laughed as she kicked her feet and splashed in the water.

Mrs. Craigie was upset, not because she had bathed unclad—that did not surprise or shock her—but because of the danger of cobras, and the fact that she had disobeyed a cardinal rule of the compound about where she could go in jungle territory. The natives had convinced Lola that cobras killed only those who showed fear, so this hazard made no impression on her. Neither did her mother's reproaches, although Mrs. Craigie wound up in tears. Captain Craigie sent his defiant stepdaughter to her room to study a Bible passage on modesty, but when her ayah arrived with her tea she was dancing around with abandon and ignoring the closed Bible that lay on a taboret.

Arrangements were quickly made to send her to Montrose on the east coast of Scotland to stay with the Craigie family. At the age of eight she was already a well-developed rebel, aware that she was unloved and unwanted by her mother, although greatly spoiled as a regimental pet. An ayah accompanied her on the long voyage, and the arrangements were superintended by Sir Jasper Nicolls, retiring from a high command in the Indian Army, who had a daughter, Fanny, going home for the finishing process in London and Paris that Lady Nicolls had not lived to see.

Shaken with sobs, and defiant as she was dragged onto the ship, Lola screamed that she did not wish to leave her soldier friends or the natives in the compound. But when they reached London a new world opened before her eager eyes. Georgian London spread in wide arcs with a sense of order and uniformity. The three- and four-story houses of gray and brown brick were mellow in the late-afternoon sun. Stone belfries rose here and there above the chimney pots. The flagstone pavements were guarded by hitching posts, and iron railings ringed many of the houses. Their polished knockers and heraldic insignia were novel to the child from the tropics who stayed briefly in London before being taken north to Montrose.

She watched the city's dandies and fashionable women with ob-

4

servant eyes, and quickly spotted regimental uniforms among them. For the first time in her life she was away from the roll of drums and the precision of army routine, but Anglo-Indians circulated around Sir Jasper so that she did not develop a sense of isolation until she reached Montrose. Even in London, however, she was visibly alien to her surroundings, and felt confined in the stuffy clothes and frilled pantalettes that she had to wear after the freedom of her Indian cottons and silks.

The soft greens and misty coolness were a new experience as she drove through Hampstead, or watched the ceaseless traffic on the Thames, but the bright life of the streets excited her more. She saw scarlet-coated footmen threading their way through the traffic with mailbags and bells; bakers crying their wares; chimney sweeps with faces black as their circular brushes; news vendors shouting bulletins through horns; and porters scurrying about in a tangle of carts and carriages, ranging from wheelbarrows to the royal coaches.

All this diverted her before she traveled north by stage, but her loneliness became acute in Montrose, when she found herself in an unfamiliar world of family prayers and rigid discipline. She brought passionate resistance into the austere but kindly Craigie household, presided over by Captain Craigie's father, Patrick Edmonstone Craigie, who was later knighted. Fresh from the undisciplined life she had led in India, with servants to wait on her, she shivered in the aqueous atmosphere of the Angus coast after the penetrating sunshine of the tropics. She could find no meeting ground with her new guardian's sister, who believed in the Victorian tradition of the wholly obedient child. Accustomed to cool drinks, curries, and other highly spiced foods she disliked the hearty fare offered her, and at the dinner table she talked a strange jargon that the Craigies found worldly and bewildering. Used to freedom of movement she could not understand the need for decorum.

Her presence in Montrose was noticed at once, since the Craigies were the best-known family in town. Craigie had been Provost of the ancient burgh off and on for nearly a quarter of a century and was always known as Provost Craigie. He had a chemist's shop on High Street when Lola arrived, and he lived in a large house opening off a close directly facing the tall steeple of Town House. Montrose resembled an eighteenth-century Flemish market town, with its gabled houses, its plaza where merchants conducted their business, its gardens with flower circles and tree-lined paths.

The local boys and girls found something exotic in Lola's bearing, speech and dress. Her white skin, glossy black hair and startling blue eyes gave her an alien air unlike their hardy, windblown looks. The ease with which they read, wrote and mastered mathematics hurt her pride, yet in her knowledge of the world, of languages other than Greek and Latin, of manners and fashions, she was years ahead of them. If at times she had trouble understanding their East Coast idiom, it was almost impossible for them to follow her strongly accented English, spiced here and there with comments in Hindustani.

Lola suffered intensely from the cold and damp, missing the burning sun, the familiar fragrance of herbs and tropical flowers, the garrison sounds, the undercurrent of excitement that the natives gave to her life in India. The curlew, the lapwing and the black-headed gulls that rose from the Angus heath were drab after the jungle birds; and the great army of pink-footed geese that came from their Arctic breeding grounds to settle around the basin at Montrose seemed part of the bleak environment. But romantic echoes of the past were strong in this community of fifteen thousand, as noted for the shipment of grain as for its famous fisheries.

Montrose was also Scotland's principal tobacco port and Lola liked to hear of the fierce smuggling operations when soldiers patrolled the coastline night and day. Wines and tobacco, tea, coffee and sugar, figs and currants, guns, playing cards, French window panes and mirrors had brought fortunes into the local coffers. Like the Greek tankers of a later date that skirted their home ports, a Montrose fleet had shuttled back and forth between Portugal and Norway in the seventeenth century, with cargoes of salt for the fishing fleet off Bergen.

A special breed of merchant and smuggler had made Montrose the finest shopping center in the country long before the ill-fated Marquis of Montrose added to its warrior legend in the days of the Covenanters. The affluent citizens had built their Flemish-style mansions behind winding closes that opened through courtyard gates onto High Street. They had made their fortunes on the commerce of the sea. Their salmon was served on the ducal tables of Civitavecchia and Venice. Cork was brought in from Lisbon for the bottlers who worked in wine vaults under the town mansions, one of which remains today in the old Craigie dwelling known as Holly House.

Lola was expected to learn some local history, as well as much else that was taken for granted by the well-taught children of Montrose. The Craigies believed in scholarship as they did in godliness, and she was singularly lacking in both. Although she grasped at the picturesque, Lola refused to parrot arithmetic tables and Latin verbs, and the tight rules of the Craigie household kept the spoiled child from the tropics in a state of chronic rebellion. Because of her mother's indifference she scarcely knew what close family affection was, but in India the petting she had received from everyone else had kept her from the agonizing loneliness that beset her in Montrose. When her life had run its course attempts were made by many commentators to find roots for her fantastic behavior in these early years, and sometimes she dwelt on this herself.

In Lola's autobiography, which blurred the sharp edges of her early experiences, she expressed regret for her behavior in Montrose. She conceded that she quickly saw herself as a public character and began, "even at this early age, to assume airs and customs of her own." Apologizing for the dance she had led the Craigies, she wrote: "This venerable man who had been provost of Montrose for nearly a quarter of a century and the dignity of his profession, as well as the great respectability of the family, made every event connected with his household a matter of some public notice."

French classes for girls were conducted at the local academy, and the prevailing sentiment in the local schools was: "Learn and suffer, thus thy God shall bless thee." The town had its own theater, where a touring company of the Edinburgh Theatre Royal gave performances regularly. But this was a side of life that Lola saw little of while she lived with the Craigies. However, she attended lectures on astronomy and was on belligerent terms with the Montrose Sabbath School Society. She wriggled and yawned in church, and was ingenious in finding ways to dawdle through the hours devoted to study.

After her wild dash into the open without her clothes, she was established in a neighbor's house until arrangements could be made to send her away from Montrose. She did not return to the Craigies. Her conduct had created a crisis that had to be coped with at once. The Provost's sister had roused the utmost defiance in her ward.

Lola, a poor letter writer all her life, kept imploring her mother to take her back to India, although in her autobiography she wrote that she was rescued from Montrose because she was being spoiled and pampered by the Craigies. But at the time more truthful evidence had reached Major Craigie in India from his family that his stepdaughter was totally maladjusted to her surroundings. She was in rebellion, upsetting the household and causing gossip in the town. No one could cope with her tempers. Sir Jasper Nicolls, who now spent his time between London, Bath and Paris, was called on again to intervene and to bring Lola into the same environment as his own Fanny. He had already superintended her return to Scotland from India, and was well aware of her sparkling qualities as well as her sudden furies. His wife, before her death, had been interested in Lola, and had understood her, in so far as anyone could. Sir Jasper accepted the fact that Montrose was not the setting for this alien spirit, and he decided to take her in hand as a companion for Fanny.

Lola left the north without regret, and only once again in her lifetime did she visit the stately old town. By then she was known around the world as Lola Montez, but her memories of her childhood days were sharp and painful. She conceded that Montrose was indeed a lovely burgh, but she left a ripple of hurt feelings behind her by adding that she did not like the people. They, in turn, looked with more interest than admiration at this bright bloom from the tropics who had lived so briefly but conspicuously among them.

The sun shone for her again when Sir Jasper had her stay at his house in London, and took her to Paris to join Fanny in her studies. She was entering yet another world when she viewed for the first time the ancient buildings and great museums of the French capital. It was a setting she would come to know intimately in the future, and to the end of her life she looked back on her school days in Paris with pleasure.

Sir Jasper, popular and worldly, moved in diplomatic and military circles. Most of the English families in Paris settled on the Rue de Rivoli or the Rue Castiglione, and it was customary for the Anglo-Indian girls to be welcomed in the liveliest social circles, although their boarding-school regime was austere. The masters who gave them music and dancing lessons worked under the eyes of their regular teachers, for they were chaperoned ceaselessly. They were trained in the arts and graces of the social world, and Lola found herself again in the company of peers. With her facility for languages, she learned to speak French better than she did any other language except English, and she used it freely all her life.

Even though she promenaded in schoolgirl attire, she was alert to the world of fashion, and she sparkled with excitement over the shops and cafés she saw in passing. She was developing rapidly, her body maturing at an early age. To her contemporaries she seemed exotic, but not to the Anglo-Indian girls, who understood her background and the sort of life that she had led. It was all too apparent to her teachers that on their outings she instinctively drew the attention of men. Far from lowering her long-lashed sapphire eyes she

9

responded boldly and Sir Jasper was relieved to enter his precocious ward with Fanny at a boarding establishment in Bath. This was to be the final step in the polishing process, but it was hastened by his desire to get out of Paris before the storm that had long been threatening broke. At the end of July, 1830, the restored Bourbons were overthrown and the Orléanist Prince, Louis Philippe, assumed power as a constitutional monarch.

Back in England, Lola listened attentively to tales of the first political revolution to touch her own life. She had been close enough to the French scene to know what it meant, and she and Fanny chattered about the excitement they had missed by leaving Paris when they did. Listening to some of her comments Sir Jasper was satisfied that Lola had come a long way from the undisciplined regimental pet he had brought home from India. Yet there was something about her that boded trouble, an ominous resistance to authority that strengthened as she matured.

TWO

From Bath to Simla

Bath in the 1830's provided an education in worldly ways for Lola since she spent this impressionable period of her life in a city noted for its air of sophistication: of letters and of fashion, with echoes of the days of Queen Anne and the Georges, of Beau Nash and Fielding, of Mrs. Siddons and Gainsborough. For eighteen months she and Fanny Nicolls promenaded as a pair, studied together, and were supervised by Mrs. Barbara Oldridge, who took charge of groups of girls, most of whom had been sent home from India for the finishing process before being presented to society.

However confining the school routine, there was no escaping the life of Bath, and Lola eagerly watched the crush of chairs and chariots on the ill-paved streets, the fashionably gowned women with their whiskered escorts, the coaches drawing up at the Bear and the White Hart Inn. She was quick to appraise the stripes and stars of the military men, to laugh at the exaggerated tailoring and eccentric coiffures of London's dandies, to recognize the plain black coats of the Methodists and the quiet gray of the Quakers.

The Wesleyan movement had spread far since John Wesley had first invaded the worldly spa with his gospel message, to the accompaniment of kettledrums and French horns. Lola and Fanny listened attentively to tales of the proselytizing done by the Countess of Huntingdon, otherwise known as the great lady of Bath, who had drawn Horace Walpole, the Duchess of Marlborough, Lord Chesterfield, Lord Chatham, and other nobles of the day into the nonconformist movement.

In some respects the strict rules of Montrose were again in operation but excitement threaded Lola's life as the worldly men of Bath observed her on the daily promenade. Even her plain school uniform could not wholly conceal her developing form and swinging walk. The magnetism of her eyes as she looked back at them, unsmiling but entranced, was not in keeping with schoolgirl decorum. There was further excitement in the visits of the music master who conducted their spinet and harpsichord lessons. By this time Lola sang and played without any self-consciousness. She drew with a touch of humor and became expert in all forms of needlework, an art that soothed her in the midst of revolution in Munich two decades later, and during other crises in her life.

Mrs. Oldridge's teachers found her gifted and brilliant, but as in Montrose she refused to study. She mimicked them mercilessly and let them know that she had seen much more of the world than any one of them. It was a school rule to talk French exclusively except on Sundays, when they were allowed to chatter in English, but this restriction did not hamper Lola who was nothing short of pyrotechnic when it came to languages. There were lectures on the arts and sciences in scholarly Bath, and Mrs. Oldridge's girls were sometimes exposed to these outside adventures, but decorum always prevailed and they were allowed only fleeting glimpses of the worldly pleasures around them. Lola yearned to attend the theater, where London's leading actors appeared for short engagements. In fact, Bath had become a breeding ground for stage figures, and even the great Mrs. Siddons had found it her true home. When Garrick dismissed her at Drury Lane she went to Bath, became a star there, and returned in triumph to London. Lola found this story fascinating. The first twinges of ambition stirred in her, to flower later in her own attempts to find a place for herself in the theater.

The mothers of the boarding-school girls liked to visit Bath, not only as a maternal duty, but because of the life there. When word reached Lola that her mother was coming from India, she did not know what to expect. Separation had widened the breach between them, for Mrs. Craigie had been wholly unresponsive to her repeated appeals from Montrose. Their correspondence had not been revealing on either side. Mrs. Oldridge had sent discreet reports on Lola's progress and scholarship, but Sir Jasper had been a more precise informant. Sometimes the news had not been good. A few of the mothers considered Lola a disturbing element in the school. They cited her wild conversation, her irreverent attitude to her teachers, her feeling for rank, her constant demands for service and her furious temper when aroused. All of these characteristics were well known to her mother, and it did not surprise her to learn that Lola was openly amorous in the presence of the music master. After all, it was not unusual for girls her age to go into raptures over any good-looking master who enlivened their cloistered days.

But when Lola had to be found and brought back to school after breaking a binding rule by joining a youth beyond the barrier of the high garden wall, it was clear that the civilizing process had not been wholly successful, nor had her education flourished. An attempt to return her to the Craigie family in Montrose had been met by Lola with fury, and the time had come for her mother to take her back to India, launch her in society there and hope for an early marriage.

Mrs. Craigie arrived in England with an ailing young subaltern in tow. Thomas James, a lieutenant in the 21st Regiment of Native Infantry, was returning home on sick leave and he had been committed to her care. She nursed him and listened to his talk of the girl he intended to marry, but he was soon infatuated with the doll-faced Mrs. Craigie and went with her to Bath, where he met her sultry daughter. Although she had been told of Lola's rapid development her mother was scarcely prepared for what she found. Mother and daughter made a stunning but quite contrasting pair when they appeared together in Bath. Mrs. Craigie, still young, for she had eloped in her early teens, had an obvious beauty that caught the eye at once. She was dressed in the height of fashion, but it was Lola who all unconsciously had the ripe bloom of maturity and seduction.

In spite of the growing tide of Methodism, Bath was not committed to puritanism, and Mrs. Craigie had seen a good deal of life herself. Like other visiting mothers she decided to enjoy the pleasures of the spa while she had the chance, and to drink the waters. She knew that this would benefit her after the long, hot years in India. They would also invigorate the convalescing young lieutenant, who was only too glad to be her escort to the balls and other entertainments. Lola was introduced to the more worldly aspects of life in Bath as they took her to the Spring Gardens, where the public breakfasts were held, and to the Pump Room, where all manner of people in dishabille sat about and tried to make themselves heard above the band. She studied the strange attire of the bathers and later mimicked the ladies in brown linen costumes and chip hats being borne to the baths in their sedan chairs, carrying wooden dishes designed to keep afloat and to hold their handkerchiefs, nosegays, snuffboxes and gold sovereigns. The spa scene would be a recurrent experience in Lola's future.

She felt that she was seeing life as she had not known it in Paris or Montrose, and she enjoyed attending concerts and having tea in the Assembly Rooms with her mother and Lieutenant James. They watched the fashionable parade before dinner, with women in monstrous flower-laden hats and vast billowing sleeves, and inevitably they attended the drums and routs inseparable from the army tradition. But Lola, who was beginning to feel the fascination of beautiful clothes, was baffled by her mother's wild spending spree on her behalf. At first she thought that she might be making up for the lost years since they had parted in India, but she soon saw that the clothes for which she was being fitted were more suggestive of a bride's trousseau than of a debutante's simpler needs. The frilled and lacy lingerie was entrancing to Lola but the truth came out in the course of an argument.

Warily Mrs. Craigie disclosed that before leaving India she had told Sir Abraham Lumley, a Supreme Court judge and old family friend, that Lola would be his bride on her return from England. He was sixty years old and extremely rich, so that it was purely a marriage of convenience planned by Mrs. Craigie. The explosion that followed was all that she had dreaded. Lola stormed and raged. She dashed a tea service to the floor, tore up the flimsiest of the trousseau garments, and firmly announced that she would never marry Sir Abraham.

Her mother tried to reason with her, but no one had ever succeeded at that. Mrs. Craigie spoke of the Judge's eminence, of the established life she would have in India as his wife, with social standing and a substantial fortune. When Lola did not budge she reminded her raging daughter that she was still a minor and could be forced to go through with the marriage. This led to another outburst in which Lola accused her mother of "throwing her alive into the jaws of death." The friendly relations they had established since Mrs. Craigie's return were shattered and never restored. The bitterness between them over this incident was to have a profound effect on Lola's future.

With a sense of desperation she turned to James for sympathy. He knew Sir Abraham and he did not approve of Mrs. Craigie's insistence on this marriage. Before her mother knew what was happening Lola and James had eloped, repeating her own history almost to the letter. They fled from Bath by coach, heading for James's family home in Ireland. It was his intention to marry Lola at once, but there were obstacles in the way. They could not find anyone willing to conduct the wedding ceremony for a minor with-

15

out parental consent. It was not until James's sister visited Mrs. Craigie in Bath and made clear to her that her daughter was already compromised that she finally gave her consent, but she refused to attend the wedding. James's brother, the Rev. John James, of the parish of Rathbiggen in Meath County, Ireland, agreed to officiate and with his wife and a nephew named Young for witnesses, they were married in the parish church on July 23, 1837. Lola signed the register Eliza Rosanna Gilbert, spinster. She was then nineteen and James was twenty-seven.

On sheer impulse and in fierce rebellion against her mother she had taken her first step into the larger world, and it promised to be exciting when her husband took her to lodgings on Westmoreland Street in Dublin and introduced her to the "Castle Set." Lord Normanby, Lord Lieutenant of Ireland, had served in Lord Melbourne's cabinet and was well known for his interest in beautiful women. When young Mrs. James was presented to him he studied her great sapphire eyes and her graceful curves with attention. He found her conversation animated and witty, too, and she was soon riding and dancing with him at every opportunity. All the men in the viceregal circle, accustomed to their own Irish and English beauties, were won by Lola's sultry charm. Her mother had returned to India and Judge Lumley now knew that he had lost this prize.

Lola, however, was beginning to wonder if James was the husband for her. He became so jealous of Lord Normanby's attentions that he took her to his father's home in Westmeath. He had already discovered that nothing less than a cloister would hold his racy young bride. For eight months she languished in the family home, bored and impatient, once the novelty of her surroundings had worn off. The mists, the rains, the faintly critical attitude of her husband's family discouraged her, although she enjoyed the riding and hunting, showing more dash than any other woman in the field. But religious exercises were prolonged under the stern eye of her father-in-law and, in Lola's own words, she tired of "drinking innumerable cups of tea (medicinal baths for the inside) taken with the most imperturbable gravity at all hours of the day."

It was too reminiscent of Montrose, and once away from Dublin the Irish gentry did not warm to Mrs. James, particularly the women. They saw in her the irresistible quality that threatened their own security, and some were aware of the ruthless drive behind her knowing ways. She was bored and restless and would have shot herself had this life gone on, she later wrote. But her spirits rose when her husband was ordered to rejoin his regiment in India. She was going back to the fabulous land that she had never forgotten, and this gave her hope that her marriage, already foundering, might revive in a more exotic setting.

In running away from her mother's coercive plan Lola had found what she later described as "only the outside shell of a husband, who had neither a brain which she could respect, nor a heart which it was possible for her to love." It would be part of Lola's history that she would always crave intellectual stimulation as passionately as she did physical satisfaction in her men, and seek the combination of both whenever possible.

The journey to India fortified her conviction that James failed to pass muster on both counts, for he passed so much of his time at sea drinking porter and ale that he "slept like a boa constrictor" and paid little attention to his wife, who demanded much. He feared her sudden outbursts of rage and her instinctive zest for flirtation. Her second journey to India brought back memories of her voyage as a child on a troop ship. She was now counting on the gay garrison life that lay ahead, the balls, the riding, the admiration of handsome military men. It was a milieu that she understood. Meanwhile she had long conversations with an English traveler, and an ardent Spaniard who helped her to while away the hours at sea while her husband slept through the day. The Captain, who liked to philosophize, coined a phrase that she never forgot: "Love is a pipe we fill at eighteen and smoke until forty; then we rake the ashes till our

17

exit." He was not blind to the disappointment young Mrs. James was experiencing in her marriage, but he deduced that a wealth of living lay ahead of her.

She had sailed home to Britain in 1826. It was now 1838 but her childhood recollections had prepared her for the life and color of the Calcutta streets, the endless chatter and flat, insidious music. In London she had heard much talk of empire building and of strife in India, but now she saw the picture with more perception. There was something more than the blare of regimental bands and the pleasures of garrison life. Lola had been developing theories of her own, and had absorbed some political sagacity from the men she had met all through her teens. The "Castle Set" in Dublin had made many things clear to her about the game of empire building. She had also taken note of the poverty and hardship that underlay the icing on the cake.

The Jameses were stationed at first in Calcutta, where the social life was brisk, until the regiment moved to Karnal in the Punjab, between Delhi and Simla. Postal service had just been introduced, slavery had been abolished and the Hindu wives were no longer committed to throwing themselves on the funeral pyres of their husbands. The cholera that killed Lola's father in three days was still a threat to the white population and natives alike. Snakebite and the strange fevers of the jungle were ever-present hazards. Tiger shoots were now discussed in Lola's hearing, a new form of excitement in her life. The power of the maharajahs was unlimited. Their wealth, their palaces, their jewels seemed legendary to young Mrs. James. The army officers, who drank so heavily at their clubs, were often handsome men, hard-bitten and reckless in action.

Women were scarce at the stations in the 1830's, and beauties were especially prized. The General's wife usually threw a protective cloak around the young ones, and they were expected to observe the conventions. They were waited on slavishly by willing servants and the ayahs took loving care of their children. They watched eagerly for letters and new novels from home, and they dressed as

18

seductively as they could for garden parties and the evening's gaiety. The Honourable Emily Eden, sister of Lord Auckland, who was Governor-General of India from 1835 to 1841, noted that the women coming out from England had "no gardens, no villages, no poor people, no schools, no poultry to look after," and so felt out of things. The heat was destructive to their health, their looks and their morale. "Very few of them are at ease with their parents; and, in short, it is a melancholy sight to see a new young arrival," Miss Eden added.

Mrs. James was noticed at once, and the fact that her mother made no effort to see her was commented on with disapproval by Miss Eden. By this time Craigie was Deputy Adjutant General, and they were in the top echelon of the army structure. It was well known in gossipy army circles that Lola's conduct in Montrose and Bath had caused much trouble, and that she had openly defied her mother in eloping with young James instead of marrying Sir Abraham Lumley.

With this background Lola was closely observed as she showed up at functions with her handsome but sulky-looking husband. He had a swaggering manner and was given to wearing flashy waistcoats and to riding spirited horses. Women fluttered around him and he danced with style when he was sober. But none could hold a candle to Lola, who was not the usual type arriving at the station from Britain. The peaches-and-cream complexion, the blond hair, so common among them, was not her style. Hair that shone like jet against the opaque whiteness of her smoothly chiseled face gave her an exotic look well suited to the tropical setting. She was of medium height but moved with such grace that she seemed tall. Her eyes alone were unmistakably Irish.

When the first Afghan War broke out James's regiment was moved from Calcutta to Karnal. At that time Miss Eden took a firm stand with Mrs. Craigie, and indicated plainly that she must become reconciled with her daughter for the sake of army discipline. General Craigie had favored this course all along, but he had trouble persuading his wife that they should lend countenance to the young Jameses. Finally Lola and her husband were invited to join the top army brass at Simla, the resort in the hills where social life flourished and the officers went for relief from the deadly heat.

Lola arrived in a palanquin on a September day in 1839, wearing the same dust-resistant brown-and-orange costume as her bearers. There had been some apprehension about Mrs. James's reception at the hill resort, for her mother was extremely popular, but with Lord Auckland's sister backing her all went well. Miss Eden noted in her diary that the new arrival had been talked of all year as a great beauty, and this had driven "every other woman, with any pretensions, in that line, quite distracted."

But Lola's looks were so dramatic that she could not be classed as a mere beauty, and after giving a dinner party in her honor Miss Eden was at a loss to describe her, and underestimated her age. She found her "merry, affectionate, beautiful to look at, and seemingly younger than the seventeen years ascribed to her." She deplored her worldly prospects as the wife of a junior lieutenant in the Indian Army, making one hundred rupees a month and likely to spend his entire life in India. Considering all this, Miss Eden observed that she did not wonder at Mrs. Craigie's resentment of her daughter for having run away from school.

There was little warmth in the reception Lola had from her mother, although Miss Eden noticed how deferential James was to his mother-in-law. The General was his usual kind and hearty self, enjoying the brief triumph that his stepdaughter was having. Although she was not yet the full-fledged enchantress that she later became, she skillfully assumed the role of the charming young matron, as seventeen junior officers who had arrived at Simla for a month's leave soon noticed. She was unmistakably the belle of a Fancy Fair given by Lord Auckland, the largest party of its kind held up to that time at the hill station. The regimental wives whose husbands were then on the march back from Kabul were invited to attend, a novelty in army circles at that time. "Are regimental ladies in India nowadays expected to keep in seclusion while their husbands are on active service—I think not," wrote the spirited Miss Eden, who was more or less the social arbiter and duenna of the station.

Lola wore gypsy costume, the perfect masquerade for her type. Five nights later she danced all night at a large ball given by the Craigies, outshining her graceful mother, who was noted for her style on a ballroom floor. All the important visitors to Simla were present to celebrate a military victory. Transparencies of the capture of Chazni on the Afghan border flickered in the moonlight and Lord Auckland's name was spelled out in arches of flowers. Empire building was gathering momentum.

In October the Sikhs arrived and the Governor-General gave a spectacular ball in their honor. The chiefs, imposing in gold robes, sat bolt upright in their chairs and marveled at the sight of men and women dancing together. Their women never went to parties, or appeared in public, or looked on the face of any man except members of their own family. But the most memorable event of Lola's stay in India was the reception given to Lord Auckland and the officers of the British Army by Ranjit Singh, known as "The Lion of the Punjab," in his palace at Lahore. He had consolidated most of the Punjab into a Sikh kingdom, and was a loyal supporter of the British. By all odds the most powerful and richest of the native princes, he singled out young Mrs. James for special attention during their stay.

The officers' tents were lined with gold and silver trimmings and were hung with cashmere shawls. The walls of the palace, where the visitors were received, were studded with agate, carnelian, turquoise and other semi-precious stones. The officers, servants and elephants belonging to the Maharajah were decked with jewels. Trays of precious stones were brought in for the British officers and were distributed according to rank and office. Mrs. Craigie received a lapful of jewels, all of which had to be turned over to the East India Company.

Ranjit Singh, plainly dressed in white muslin and without jewels except for a dazzling cluster on his turban, sat on a gold throne. Lord Auckland was led to another of the same kind, representing the British throne. The Governor-General's gifts to the Prince and his officers were swords, pistols, and gold and silver ornaments. The ball that followed was unlike anything that Lola had ever imagined. Circassian and Georgian slaves of the Maharajah were presented to the British dignitaries, and then he suggested that the bejeweled girls entertain the guests. Lord Auckland explained to his host that English law did not permit favors of this kind.

In later years Lola Montez liked to recall that she could have married Ranjit Singh, for she was to see him again after her marriage broke up. But the enchanted days and nights at Simla came to an end and she was soon back in dreary Karnal, where Miss Eden decided that she looked "like a star among the others, the women were all plain." She watched her riding an elephant, with Lieutenant James hanging on behind, and this time she wrote in her diary with more perception that Mrs. James was "very young and lively, and if she falls into bad hands she would soon find herself in foolish scrapes. At present the husband and wife are very fond of each other, but a girl who marries at fifteen [sic] hardly knows what she likes."

Miss Eden had not been blind to the admiration Lola had drawn in high places, but she had misread the signs of devotion to her husband, for the James marriage was already shaky. When the Governor's party returned to Calcutta Lola was bored and restless. Karnal was a dreary cantonment, an anticlimax to the gay days at Simla. The Jumna drained its polluted waters, and cholera raged constantly, so that the British were cautioned not to mingle with the natives. Lola resented this, for her early years at Dinapore had given her some understanding of the people of India. She had warmth of feeling toward them, and she had not forgotten the Hindustani and Bengali that she had learned early in life.

By this time she was well aware that she had a philandering

husband who was spending a good deal of time with the worldly Mrs. Lomer, thirty-three years old and the wife of a regimental captain. Jealous and possessive by nature, she watched them leave the verandah and stroll in the grounds during a party, and she soon became suspicious of her husband's early-morning rides. Her fears were confirmed when she went riding with an officer's wife one morning and saw across a stream two figures in an embrace— Mrs. Lomer and her husband, whom she always called Tommy. She sped back to their bleak quarters and waited for his return. He had left before seven, saying that he had to inspect troops.

Shaking with anger Lola clung to a wooden railing on their verandah as she watched him ride up and dismount. She told him that he could not enter the house, since Mrs. Lomer obviously was his mistress. Cold sober and visibly dismayed, James insisted that he was master in his own house, but he could not push her aside. Lola stormed, wept and laughed satirically in turn, but held her ground. The Lieutenant tried to reason with her, and then became humble and apologetic. She blistered him with scorn and he finally mounted his horse and rode off. Later that day an orderly packed his things and within twenty-four hours the entire garrison knew that Mrs. Lomer had run off to the Neilgherry Hills with Lieutenant James. The beautiful Mrs. James was an abandoned wife.

Although there were many surreptitious romances in the high command, the desertion of a bride by one of the officers was not a common state of affairs. The wives rallied around Mrs. James, whose pride was outraged. But she did not wish their pity and she kept out of sight. Years later she wrote in her autobiography: "Runaway matches, like runaway horses, are almost sure to end in a smash-up. My advice to all young girls who contemplate taking such a step, is that they had better hang or drown themselves just one hour before they start."

Her husband's defection was one of the major scars of Lola's early years. When the cantonment at Karnal broke up in 1841 she had no choice but to return to Calcutta, where her mother kept her as closely confined in their quarters as if she were a prisoner. Mrs. Craigie was furious that her daughter should have brought such scandal into their lives, after the years she had spent building up her own social image. Compromise and forgiveness would have served the purpose, she thought, since James and Mrs. Lomer had soon gone their separate ways. But Lola lost weight and spirit and became seriously ill. General Craigie was sympathetic, but he recognized the fact that the bitterness between his wife and her daughter was corrosive to both, and that the situation in army circles had become lurid. The bright garrison life of Calcutta was out of bounds now for Lola, or Eliza, as she was still often referred to by members of her family.

Genuinely concerned about her health, he arranged for her return to Britain. When he saw her off on the *Larkins* he gave her two thousand pounds ($10,000) and told her that she could return at any time to Montrose. She had jewelry valued at $6,000 that had been given to her in India by her family, and in wedding gifts, and so she was comparatively well off for her era. The General asked various friends in England and Scotland to look out for young Mrs. James on her arrival in Britain, and at sea she was entrusted to the care of Captain Charles Ingram, skipper of the *Larkins*, and his wife.

Her mother did not see her off at Calcutta, but James arrived at the last moment and tried to make peace. He had begun to feel the regimental fury he had stirred up. The General left before the ship sailed, but James traveled as far as Madras. His young wife was ill, angry and totally resistant to his pleas. But her spirits picked up after he left the ship, and she was soon spending most of her time with Captain Charles Lennox, aide-de-camp to Lord Elphinstone, Governor of Madras. There was mutual fascination almost at once between Mrs. James and Captain Lennox, who had boarded the ship at Madras. He found her seductive and a witty conversationalist. As a discarded wife she found him the perfect companion for tropical evenings at sea. He belonged to the Duke of Richmond's family, and was a thoroughly seasoned officer, for Lord Elphinstone had been Governor of Bombay and had twice refused the Governor Generalship of India.

The Ingrams, who felt responsible for Mrs. James's well-being, soon showed signs of alarm when the young pair were observed entwined in each other's arms on deck. First the Captain and then his wife Ann went to her cabin and let her know that she was causing talk on the ship. Mrs. James laughed and said that she was her own mistress. After that, Mr. Ingram would have nothing more to do with her. But Lola had other friends on board who were less censorious, and she made quite an impression on two New Englanders named Sturges, who first aroused her interest in Boston and the United States. Another American named Mrs. Stevens suggested to her that she take up dancing and try for a professional career. It was obvious to all three that she was a *rara avis*, restless, ambitious, uncannily beautiful, and uncertain which way to turn, now that she had left her husband. Mrs. Stevens was struck by the grace with which she paced the deck and her exotic way of dancing with Captain Lennox. Her low décolletage in the evenings, highly fashionable at the time, revealed the beauty of her sloping shoulders and snowy breasts.

Through her talks with Mrs. Stevens, Lola began to think of her possibilities as a dancer. Much as she resented her mother, she knew that Mrs. Craigie was almost professionally gifted in this respect. Her own ambitions soared. Why should she not be another Fanny Elssler, the Austrian ballet dancer who was then at the height of her fame? At sea Lola had endless time to think about her future, and when she landed at Portsmouth on February 20, 1841, she had decided to cut all strings with the relatives to whose care she had been assigned. James had notified his sister who had helped them get married that Lola was returning home for medical care after a fall from a horse. One of his aunts in Edinburgh invited her to go north. David Craigie, a relative of the Provost's, arrived from Perth and engaged in a furious row with Lola. She would have nothing to do with him, and her unreasonability filled him with disgust. Various retired officers of the East India Company offered to help her, but Mrs. James had decided to live her own life, on her own terms, and at the moment Captain Lennox was its central figure. At this point she did not want the embarrassment of family interference.

They arrived together at the Imperial Hotel in a hackney coach piled high with trunks, variously stamped Mrs. James and C. Lennox. They soon moved on to quarters at Covent Garden and eventually St. James's. All through the spring and summer of 1841 Lola ran a merry course in London, clinging still to some members of Sir Jasper's set, but becoming ever more involved with the sportier life of the city. The small fortune she had brought home from India melted fast. She had never learned to do without servants, or to deny herself any bauble she wished to own. Her generosity was so characteristic that she was destined to let one fortune after another slip through her fingers. When she ran out of cash she would always pawn or sell her jewels.

London in the 1840's was in a state of transition as the puritanism of the mid-Victorian era impinged on the libertinism inherited from the Georgian period. But mistresses had not gone out of fashion with the peers and other men of worldly habit. Piccadilly was infested with streetwalkers. Crockford's and Vauxhall flourished. Gambling and drinking were par for the course and there were occasional raids involving peers and statesmen. The theater was bawdy, and crime and disorder flourished, with policemen often being beaten into unconsciousness.

As her money melted Lola saw that she must not let her days slip away in social pleasures. During this transitional period of her life she had met a number of actors, and she turned instinctively to the theater. Mrs. Stevens had sent her to Fanny Kelly, an entrepreneur so noted in preparing girls for the stage that Gladstone eventually gave her a grant for her distinguished tutelage. Miss Kelly quickly decided that Lola had no dramatic talent, but she was

26

struck by her grace of movement and advised her to take up dancing. For the next four months Lola studied in London with a Spanish dancing master named Espa and then went to Spain briefly to absorb atmosphere and study the national style of dancing. Nothing was heard of her during this period, but it was characteristic of Lola to drop from sight, usually with a new suitor.

On her return James Howard Harris, third Earl of Malmesbury then on his way to becoming a well-known British diplomat and Cabinet member, found her the picture of sorrowing widowhood when the consul at Southampton asked him to take care of a Spanish lady who had just landed. He shared her railway carriage as he traveled up to London from Heron Court, his country place. She was in deep mourning and he thought her a "remarkably handsome person who appeared to be in great distress." The tale she told him between sobs was that she was the widow of Don Diego Leon, who had been taken prisoner by the Carlists and had then been shot. In strongly accented English, which he could not quite place, she added that she was on her way to London to sell some property, and that she would be giving singing lessons.

Lord Malmesbury did not doubt her story. Lola could assume a role with ease, and her fascination was apparent even in her woebegone state. He invited her to sing Spanish ballads at a concert he was giving at his home and she arrived with Spanish veils and small souvenirs to sell to his guests, who assumed that she was badly off financially. For a time Lord Malmesbury interested himself in her welfare and helped her to make theatrical connections. Years later he wrote reminiscently of this ravishing woman he had encountered in a railway train in the early 1840's, before she had become famous all over Europe for her political power in Bavaria: "This was a most remarkable woman, and may be said by her conduct at Munich to have set fire to the magazine of revolution, which was ready to burst forth all over Europe, which made the year 1848 remarkable."

But Mrs. James was in for a shock soon after her return to Lon-

27

don. News of the life she was living had reached India, and regardless of the fact that he had deserted her for Mrs. Lomer, James sued her for divorce, charging adultery with Captain Lennox. The case was heard in the Consistory Court in London in December, 1842, and all that month items about Mrs. James appeared in the papers. The charge brought against her stated simply that after their marriage Captain James and his wife had gone to India; that on account of her health Mrs. James had returned to England early in 1841; and that on her passage in the *Larkins* she had met Captain Lennox and had later cohabited with him at the Imperial Hotel, Covent Garden and in lodgings in St. James's.

There was much talk in the Anglo-Indian set in London about the case, since the Craigies and Sir Jasper Nicolls were so well known. Mrs. James's divagations at sea were detailed in court by Captain Charles Ingram and his wife, Ann. "I found it necessary to discontinue associating with her and to exclude her visiting my cabin," Mrs. Ingram testified primly. The Captain said that Captain Lennox had visited her cabin at "very unwarrantable hours" and had spent time with her when the other passengers "were attending divine service on deck." He had watched them embrace far aft and also in the bow of the ship late at night, and he had advised Mrs. James to be prudent, since she was very young. "I saw no more than violent flirting, which in a married woman I considered as very improper," the Captain added. At this point her stewardess livened up the proceedings by recalling that she had seen Captain Lennox in Mrs. James's cabin, lacing up her stays and helping her to draw on her stockings.

Mrs. Elizabeth Walters, the proprietor of the Imperial Hotel, testified that Mrs. James and Captain Lennox had occupied the same bedroom at the Imperial Hotel and although she had watched them having supper there she could not swear that she had actually seen them together in bed. Mrs. Ann Martin, who ran a lodging house on Great Rider Street, told of all callers being turned away by

Mrs. James but Captain Lennox, who visited her every day and usually stayed from nine in the morning until midnight.

Mrs. James's most influential backer at this time was Lord Brougham, the brilliant but erratic firebrand who had fought slavery, helped to push through the Reform Bill and remodeled the judicial committee of the Privy Council. At the time of the James divorce he was pushing for reform in the divorce laws, and Lola thought she was in the most knowing of hands when he advised her. But, powerful though he was behind the scenes, he could not save her from the court decree that she was guilty of infidelity. James won his case but it turned out to be merely a bed-and-board separation known as *a mensa et thoro*. Remarriage was forbidden while either one lived. Eventually this judgment would bring Lola back to court on a bigamy charge, but in the interim she seemed to believe that she was totally free. James remained with the army, serving as a captain until 1856. He lived until 1871.

When news of the decree reached India Mrs. Craigie was relentless. Her army friends agreed with her that Lola had always been a defiant daughter. Divorce was still unthinkable in her circle, however, and her Catholic ancestry made it doubly intolerable, even though she now attended a Protestant church with General Craigie. She sent out notes to her friends as if she were announcing a death in the family, and she had no further communication with her daughter until Lola was close to death. Her own social life continued at the same swift pace. General Craigie alone gave serious consideration to the effect all this might have on his stepdaughter. The recklessness he had seen in her would now have full play, but she was twenty-four and her life was her own. The rumors that reached him from London through army sources were anything but reassuring.

Captain Lennox dropped from sight when the divorce issue came up. His infatuation for Lola was overpowering for a time, but she had tired of him, and his family had persuaded him to give her up lest his own career should be irretrievably ruined. Soon after the divorce decree was granted she was running a salon in her own individualistic way, and men of political prominence as well as worldly rakes gathered at her place for evenings of music, fun and witty talk. She was preparing for a life in the theater and was weaving a network of connections to speed her course. Lola had shaken off her past completely and had assumed a new identity. From now on she would be known as Lola Montez, the Spanish dancer. Any mention of Eliza Gilbert, Marie Gilbert, Mrs. James, Betty James, Rosanna James or other names by which her friends had known her during this period would inevitably arouse a storm.

THREE

The Spanish Dancer

Lola had powerful backing as she prepared for her stage debut in London in the summer of 1843. The critics were on the alert, for they had been primed in advance that a new star was on the horizon. Some had seen her rehearse; all were aware that she was a mysterious and dazzling personality, frequently seen in the company of noted men. Lord Malmesbury, then with the Foreign Office, had introduced her to Benjamin Lumley, leading producer of the day. Lord Brougham hovered in the background as friend and guardian.

Charles G. Rosenberg, music critic of the *Morning Press*, who wrote under the byline "Q" was bewitched by Lola when he visited the quarters used by Lumley under the colonnade surrounding the theater in the Haymarket. He found her rehearsing her Spanish dances on the day before her opening, and was staggered to find that she was the beauty he had seen through a lace curtain on Upper Grafton Street, where he lived. After splitting up with Captain Lennox Lola had taken rooms by chance—or design—across the street from Rosenberg. They had never met, but he had wondered about her as she sat at her window, looking out with a melancholy air.

Now, watching her dance, he found her airy and graceful, with faultless feet and ankles. Her blue eyes flashed with excitement as she whirled round the stage "like a flower that bends with the impulse given to its stem by the changing and fitful temper of the wind." But Rosenberg's freely expressed emotions did not blind him to her real deficiencies as a dancer. She had been on trial before him and he saw at once that she needed much more training. "Good," he said to Lumley, who had asked for his opinion, "but not good enough."

The producer agreed, but both men felt that with hard work and study Lola might become an accomplished dancer, a hope that dimmed after her debut. The evening's playbill read: *Special Attraction: Mr. Benjamin Lumley begs to announce that between the acts of the Opera, Donna Lola Montez, of the Teatro Real, Seville, will have the honour to make her first appearance in England in the Original Spanish Dance, El Oleano.* The opera was *The Barber of Seville.*

A fashionable audience attended and the boxes were filled with celebrities, from jewel-laden royalty to Lord Wellington, who snoozed through the opera but came to life to watch Lola dance. The Queen Dowager, the Duchess of Kent, the Duke and Duchess of Cambridge, Baroness de Rothschild, Count Esterházy, Lord Brougham and a variety of notables had come to see the new Spanish dancer. There were murmurs of admiration as she pirouetted into view, wearing a black lace mantilla, a close-fitting black velvet bodice and a brief skirt with tinted flounces that showed her graceful legs to advantage. Her jet-black hair, gleaming eyes and scarlet lips against dead white skin created an exotic impression. One observer found her "at once inviting and challenging . . . the whole effect was sensual as she swayed and shook and stamped her way through the Spanish rhythms."

But Lola's triumph was short-lived. She was receiving her first round of applause when hissing came from the Omnibus Box, where the young bloods who could make or break a play were seated. It was led by Lord Ranelagh, a rakish young peer who swaggered around London wrapped in the Spanish cloak he had worn in the Carlist wars. He had been studying Lola carefully through his opera glasses and he suddenly exclaimed in a loud voice, "Why, it's Betty James. This is a proper swindle. That woman isn't Lola Montez."

Shouts of "fraud" and "impostor" followed and coins were tossed to the stage, to fall among the bouquets. At first Lola stood like a statue, stunned by the attack; then she blazed with anger, looking toward the box where the bearded dandy Lord Ranelagh stared back at her with contempt. She swore audibly in English, dashed the bouquet she was holding to the floor, stamped on it, then kicked it into the orchestra before running off the stage as the curtain came down. By this time chaos prevailed, with shouts and catcalls from the galleries. The shocked observers who did not share in the uproar quietly left the boxes and stalls and found their way to their waiting carriages. Lord Ranelagh had created the effect he had aimed for, and Lola later said that he was venomous because she had once repulsed him.

It was a night of defeat for Lumley, who did not let the curtain go up again. He recognized the fact that Lola's debut, so highly advertised, had been a disaster, and he feared that her dancing might be the cause as much as Ranelagh's exposure. The verdict from the Omnibus Box was decisive, since the London theater was controlled at the time by the snobs and dandies who joined forces to fill the stage boxes and hiss or applaud the actors. Lumley did not dare run counter to their verdict. In his reminiscences he said that the "whole affair was an imposture; and on the very night of her first appearance, the truth exploded. In spite even of the desire expressed in high places to witness her strange performance—I remained inflexible."

Lord Malmesbury and others begged him to let Lola continue,

but Lumley could not forget that he had been persuaded to introduce her to the public as the daughter of a celebrated Spanish patriot and martyr. He had been completely won by Lola's eloquence, if not by her dancing, and he had listened attentively to the opinions of several critics besides Q whom he had called in to observe her at a preview. None had thought her an inspired dancer, but all believed that she had the subtle qualities that might spell success.

In spite of the chaotic scene at Her Majesty's Theatre the critics rallied behind Lola and in the days that followed one newspaper after another praised her. The *Morning Herald* said that she enchanted everyone—"a bewitching lady . . . rapturously encored, and the stage strewn with bouquets." The *Era* compared her to an Elssler or a Taglioni descending from the clouds. The *Times* commented on a "certain grandeur in her performance." Although lacking buoyancy and grace she danced with such intensity that the "whole soul of the artist seems working up to a stern purpose." This critic feared that she would be underrated by ballet judges who accepted only the French and Italian standards, a taste which had much to do with Lola's early failures.

The Illustrated London News, with more time to consider the disaster, took the same stand, but admitted the débâcle that the others ignored and speculated on the reason for it, suggesting that Lola Montez might have been the victim of a jealous cabal. Everyone present knew that it was absurd to view the evening as a success, but none denied the reality of Lola Montez's beauty and her seductive quality.

She reacted defiantly to the first of many reverses that would shadow her professional career. Regardless of the noted men who knew her as Mrs. James, she wrote to the *Era* and other papers at once, denying any form of imposture and insisting that she was a native of Seville and had never set foot in England before April 14 of that year. She indignantly denied the suggestion that she was a disreputable character and said she would sue for libel. But since a number of well-known Londoners had attended her soirees, her protestations about her identity did not carry much conviction. She was now publicly recognized as being something of an adventuress and the name "Betty James" became a byword in the raciest circles.

Rosenberg, who had done his best to help her, acknowledged that she was "fast" but he considered her speed "to be that of talent." If he was not captivated by her art he was by her eloquence, and her anecdotes amused and charmed him. An hour's conversation with Lola would convince any man that he had spoken to a "sparklingly brilliant creature," said Q.

Lola disappeared from her lodgings the day after the débâcle but she reappeared briefly a month later when she danced without fee at a benefit for Edward Fitzball, a dramatist who was down on his luck, given at the Theatre Royal, Covent Garden, on July 10, 1843. Accompanied by her maid, Lola entered the theater with the air of a prima donna. Again she danced "El Oleano," and this time there was rapturous applause. Good-hearted Lola, said her backers, to dance at this benefit. She announced that it would be her last appearance in London, since she was leaving at once for St. Petersburg.

It was at this time that a tangle of errors about the ancestry of Lola Montez, the name she had assumed in 1843, led to much confusion, a state of affairs that lasted all her life, and that she sometimes promoted herself with the skill of a twentieth-century press agent. She was variously described as having been born in Spain, India, Turkey, Geneva, Havana, Montrose, or in Ireland, which happened to be the truth. One author made her the child of a Spanish gypsy, another the daughter of Lord Byron (a conceit that rather appealed to Lola), a third the offspring of a maharajah.

After assuming the name Lola Montez she usually preceded a new theatrical engagement with various embellishments about her origin. Sometimes she described herself as being the child of a famous Spanish matador named Montez, a claim that he soon denied. On different occasions she announced through the press that she was born in Seville in 1823, the daughter of a Spanish officer in the service of Don Carlos, and that she was referred to as being Irish or English because her mother's second husband happened to be Irish.

In actual fact she was born in Limerick in 1818, and her father, Edward Gilbert, was only eighteen when he married the thirteen-year-old girl who was her mother. Lola's occasional version of this event was that her mother, Elizabeth Oliver, had eloped from a convent to marry young Gilbert. In her later years she learned from her mother's embittered sister, Mary Oliver, a milliner in Dublin that, young though she was, Elizabeth had left the convent and was dancing in a music hall when she became involved with young Gilbert. He was the son of Sir Edward Gilbert, a substantial landowner in Westmeath, Ireland. Lady Gilbert treated Elizabeth with open scorn. She disapproved of her passion for dancing, her extreme youth, and the frivolity that was to characterize her all through life. The fact that a baby was on its way complicated the situation, however.

Elizabeth was not eager to marry the young soldier, for she was ambitious and did not wish to be tied down to domesticity. She hoped to go on dancing in public; the experience had been exhilarating. However, the marriage took place two months before Lola was born. It did not last long because of her husband's early death in India. When Elizabeth's social horizons widened as the wife of General Craigie, she chose to ignore her sister Mary's existence, which led to family recriminations and her aunt's scathing recital to Lola of her mother's pretensions.

The Oliver sisters had some claim to a substantial heritage, however. As the years went on and Lola's fame grew she made much of the fact that they were descended from the Montalvos, Spanish grandees with Moorish blood who had settled in Spain during the reign of Ferdinand and Isabella, acquired large estates and had then lost them in warfare. With these details, real or imaginary, Lola spread the impression at times that she was Irish, Moorish and Spanish—by her own definition a "somewhat combustible compound." Whatever else collapsed in her life, she clung proudly to her supposed Andalusian ancestry and her own identification as a Spanish dancer. It was her hallmark, and also at times her undoing, but her temperament and physical attributes were sufficient confirmation to many observers.

Filled with determination and pride she decided to leave London after the disastrous revelations that followed her first performance, and pursue her career on the Continent, where the standards were freer. Lola had no intention of giving up her dancing ambitions, but her early years had conditioned her to the advantages of being close to the seat of power and she knew that many artists flourished through their court connections. Before leaving London she studied the Almanach de Gotha with care and planned a course of action. She understood the ceremonial of courts and the rules of rank and precedence. India had done that for her, but Lola's jesting way of putting it was that she was determined "to hook a Prince."

Lord Malmesbury, Lord Brougham and other men of consequence knew her as the divorced Mrs. James. They had accepted her masquerade as a professional gesture not unknown in theatrical circles. But she now decided to shed the James name once and for all. When she left London she deliberately cut off all ties with her past life and it was as if she had never belonged to James or the Craigie family. But her isolation was not complete. On the Continent she avoided Englishmen as much as she could at first, and emphasized her Spanish inheritance.

From London she went to Brussels, a city for which she would always have special affection, although she did not fare well on this first professional visit. She was turned down for the opera, and when she failed to gain entry at the Belgian court she pawned the last of her jewels and some of her clothes. In later years she found it picturesque to recall that she had actually sung in the streets of Brussels. Her plan to insinuate herself with William II at The Hague on her arrival in Holland went awry. The King's father had fought with Wellington in Spain and had commanded the Dutch troops at Waterloo. Lola had met his son, the Prince of Orange, when he visited Lord Auckland at Simla, and she used this in a bid for recognition. Holland and India were old trading partners, with strong East Indian connections. But the Dutch court was decorous and Victorian, and Lola's reputation blocked her progress there.

Between her flight from London in the summer of 1843 and her fame in Munich four years later she moved like a glowworm across the map of Europe, occasionally appearing in the headlines as she visited Berlin, Warsaw, St. Petersburg, Constantinople, Dresden, Vienna, Prague, Leipzig, Carlsbad, Wiesbaden, Baden-Baden, Homburg, Genoa and Paris. The encompassing shadow of Lord Palmerston, Lord Brougham and Lord Malmesbury gave her entrée to the British legations in the capitals, and there was always a handsome young diplomat or officer at hand to introduce her to theatrical figures. Her army connections, when she chose to use them, opened many doors for her. Quite often she made her own arrangements simply by forcing her way into the presence of men who could help her. Occasionally she worked under professional management and at times she made large sums of money, which she quickly squandered, leaving her dependent on the bounty of her escorts. In the lean days she became a familiar figure in the little theaters across Europe, and wherever dancers and actors gathered. Her graceful use of the fan while dancing was copied by many of her associates.

Some of her appearances had royal backing, however. She was warmly received in Berlin in the autumn of 1843 and she charmed King Frederick William IV when she danced at a fete organized in honor of the visiting Czar Nicholas I. On two separate occasions the Czar had a chance to observe the dashing ways of Lola Montez. Always interested in ballet dancers, he was an amused observer when she violated court etiquette at a reception given in his honor by the King. Lola was due to dance, but being thirsty she asked for water. Court etiquette forbade a performer to eat or drink in the presence of royalty, and she was there in her professional role. With a characteristic touch of defiance she said that she would not continue her dance unless she could first quench her thirst. Grand

Duke Michael, the Czar's brother, went straight to King Frederick William, who amiably ordered a goblet of water, touched it with his own lips, then passed it to the thirsty Lola.

The King was won by her daring and the Queen treated her with courtesy and even tried to arrange a match between Lola and Prince Schulkoski. For a time they were engaged until the unpredictable dancer tired of the Prince and accused him of philandering in the South with a celebrated singer while sending her affectionate messages three times a day. On his return he received short shrift at her hands, and the Queen accepted the fact that her matchmaking had gone astray.

Lola's stay in Berlin ended abruptly after a military review staged at Potsdam for the Czar. Mounted on a hot-tempered Cordovan horse she galloped close to the royal enclosure. Whether this was deliberately planned to get attention or the guns had startled her horse remained a debatable question, but an officer riding nearby gripped her horse's bridle to head him off. Lola had her riding whip in her hand and with one of her quick rages she slashed the officer across the face and shoulders, then galloped off at high speed.

After this her whip became a symbol of her fury and from time to time she used it, but the legend spread beyond the truth until the impression prevailed that she could not walk along a street without brandishing a whip. In this instance she was served with a summons which she promptly tore to ribbons. According to her own account of the incident, the authorities later apologized for taking any action against her. But before long her zest for tearing up offensive documents and throwing them at her tormentors became something of a legend, too.

Active, impulsive, ambitious, Lola was a dynamo in all respects except where her dancing was concerned. She scorned the self-denial required of a ballet dancer, and she was the first to admit that her work lacked polish. But she always insisted that she had to earn her living, and this was the way in which she could best accomplish that end. There were times when she deluded herself into thinking

39

that she might have a future as a great artist, for she had many professional triumphs along the way and the applause that greeted her was sometimes overwhelming. But in actual fact her lovers absorbed more of her time than her work, and when deeply involved she lost all consciousness of the demands of her profession. She kept moving eastward with St. Petersburg in mind, for she said that while in Berlin the Czar had invited her to visit his court. But before reaching Russia she ran into a spectacular situation in Poland. She became involved with Count Ivan Feodorovich Paskevich, the Russian general who had suppressed the Polish rebellion of 1830–31, captured Warsaw and become Governor of Poland. The measures used had been so harsh that he was extremely unpopular, even though he was known as the Pacificator of Poland. Children were sent to the Ural Mountains, women who stood by the Catholic faith were flogged, and efforts were made to impose the Russian language on the Polish people.

The German who had accompanied Lola from Brussels, an excellent linguist who spoke Polish, managed to get her an engagement at the opera. After a few days the director told her that she could not dance at all. She talked back with such speed and skill that he laughed and said he would keep her on as an ornament. When Count Paskevich saw her dance he was bewitched. She had been angling for princely attention and now it had come her way, but when she was summoned to his palace and Madame Steinkiller, wife of the leading banker in Poland, drove her there, she recoiled from his presence and described him in devastating terms: "The poor old man was a comic sight to look upon—unusually short in stature, and every time he spoke he threw his head back and opened his mouth so wide as to expose the artificial gold roof of his palate. A death's head making love to a lady could not have been a more disgusting or horrible sight."

The Count was sixty years old, gnomelike in stature, vain in manner, cruel in practice and a bore in conversation. Although comfortably married he wasted no time, according to Lola, about offering her a place in his life, a country estate, a title, jewels and other material possessions. This was what she had laughingly told London friends that she sought, but after listening deferentially to the Count at first, not even her love for the glitter of courts or her lust for power could reconcile her to a man so misshapen and harsh. Lola tried to beat a tactful retreat but she had made a deadly enemy.

On the following day the Colonel of the gendarmes and the director of the theater called at her hotel to back up the Count's proposals. They grew threatening when Lola laughed and would not listen. Finally she ordered them from the room and when they did not move she clawed the Colonel's face. She believed him to be a spy for the Russian Government, and she knew that he was hated by the public. For the next three nights she was hissed by what she took to be a planted claque. On the third night, when the uproar grew deafening, she rushed to the front of the stage and announced that this display had been ordered by the director because she had rejected the gifts of Count Paskevich. In flouting him Lola Montez had taken her first step into the political world, and won the sympathy of the people.

She was never more effective than when she talked; if she could not dance superbly she could strike to the core of things with her fluency. The audience listened and responded with shouts that drowned out the hostile claque. They battled with the dissenters and she was escorted safely to her hotel by a crowd of outraged Poles. They were already in a mutinous state and Lola by chance had started a conflagration. Rioting followed all over town. When the police arrived to arrest her she barricaded herself behind a door and shouted that she would shoot the first man who dared to break in. They knew that she had a pistol and would not hesitate to use it. The men left, reporting to their master that Lola Montez was a tiger who clawed with her nails. The French Consul came to her rescue but she was ordered to leave Warsaw at once. Her trunks were searched on the assumption that she was acting as a spy for the enemies of the government. When a letter of introduction from the Queen of Prussia to the Czarina was found, Lola snatched it from an officer and tore it to bits. This letter and her impulsive act seemed to establish her in the searchers' eyes as a dangerous character. Relations between Poland and Russia were strained.

The suggestion of espionage and intrigue, apparent here for the first time, was to affect her later course and lead to many embarrassing situations. For years she was suspected of being a spy as she moved from country to country, and figured all too often as the focus of an inexplicable mêlée. The match had been lighted in Warsaw. More than three hundred arrests were made, and Steinkiller, the banker whose wife had entertained Lola during her stay in Warsaw, was one of them. Before the uproar died down, all Europe learned that Lola Montez had been run out of Warsaw. Quietly she made her way across the wastes to St. Petersburg, a journey that remained obscure in her memoirs, although her Polish escapade was widely publicized in the European press.

The Queens of Prussia and Saxony had paved the way for her and she was well received by the Czarina. Both Queens were sisters of King Ludwig I of Bavaria, whom she had still to meet and bewitch. "And Nicholas," Lola wrote with assurance, "as well as the ministers of his court, besides their proverbial gallantry, appeared from the first anxious to test her skill and sagacity in the routine of secret diplomacy and politics." With this encouragement she was beginning to feel that she was digging in on the political front, and particularly after she was called into counsel by the Czar and Count Benckendorff, a hero of the Napoleonic Wars then serving as director of police in Russia. The discussion, Lola recalled in her memoirs, concerned "certain vexatious matters connected with Caucasia." Top officers of the Circassian army were waiting outside for an audience with Czar Nicholas I, and she was thrust into a stuffy little chamber as they were admitted. She sweltered through the argument that followed but could hear their raised voices. Finally there was total silence and Lola realized that she had been forgotten.

After an hour the Czar arrived to release her, apologizing for his forgetfulness. According to Lola he gave her a thousand rubles ($750) for whatever service she had performed. She rated him the strongest monarch of the age and found him as "amiable and accomplished in private life as he was great, stern and inflexible as a monarch." Although discursive in her memoirs about some of her adventures at European courts, Lola did not reveal why she should have figured in the inner councils of the director of police in St. Petersburg, or whether her ouster from Poland was involved. It is a matter of record that she caught the attention of the Czar in Berlin and she was well primed on the espionage activities of Princess de Lieven, who had lived in London for more than twenty years as the wife of the Russian Ambassador there.

Born Dariya von Benkendorff, daughter of a German family from Latvia, the Princess settled in London at a time when Napoleon's march on Moscow had made Russia a valuable ally to be carefully cultivated by British statesmen. She became one of the seven patronesses who dominated Almack's, the most exclusive club in London, and one of a trio of social arbiters and sophisticates who alternately charmed and annoyed Lord Palmerston. The other two were the Countess of Jersey and Countess Cowper, who had been Emily Lamb and who became Lady Palmerston in 1839.

The Czar finally recalled Prince de Lieven when Palmerston and some of his colleagues could no longer stand the Princess's meddling in political affairs, but she would again figure powerfully on the European scene as the mistress of Prince Metternich and then of Premier François Guizot, of France. Although belonging to a younger generation Lola occasionally felt the sting of the Princess's operations as time went on but she seems also to have emulated her tendency to combine sex and politics. The Princess had been close to men who were also of prime interest to Lola for one reason or another—Metternich, Palmerston and Guizot. Some of the Princess's strategy was made clear to Lola by Sir Stratford Canning, the scholarly young statesman who was a favorite of Lord

Palmerston's but was greatly disliked by the Czar, who had refused to receive him as British Ambassador at the Russian Court when Prince de Lieven was recalled from London.

All this preceded Lola's visit to Russia by several years, but at various times she turned up in the capitals of Europe in the company of Sir Stratford and other diplomats working with Lord Palmerston to preserve the balance of power in Europe. All through the 1840's Palmerston was moving away from his rigid stand on many domestic reform issues to the liberalism that later infused his policies on continental affairs. He played a careful hand with Russia but had little faith in the friendship of other European countries. He believed in a constant show of strength abroad, with occasional compromises during radical uprisings.

Lola's visit to St. Petersburg ended without any of the uproar that had attended her departure from Poland, but in view of what had happened in Warsaw it is likely that her moves in Russia were carefully observed by the police. She was drawn to political figures as by a magnet. After her cordial reception in Berlin and the magnificence of the Russian court, with jewels outshining even those of the maharajahs, Lola began to take herself seriously as a welcome figure in the royal nimbus, but having touched the top she had to retrace her steps to lower plateaus. Germany, with all its principalities, had a wealth of minor princes. As a professional dancer she was able to move from one area to another, but it was in Dresden that she ran into one of the more publicized romances of her life. It was short-lived and intense, and was much discussed all over Europe, for her lover in this instance was Franz Liszt. He was then thirty-three years old, at the height of his fame, and he was tiring of his mistress, Comtesse d'Agoult.

Lola was dancing at the Royal Theater in Dresden, and he was creating such a furore there at the time that when he dropped his handkerchief women tore it to shreds and divided it among themselves. Lola was scornful of this trivial form of adoration as she watched them kiss his magic hands, display his portrait in their lockets, tear off his gloves, drain his teacup, or make off with the stubs of cigarettes he had smoked. This was not love as Lola understood it, but from the moment she first talked to Liszt she felt his magnetism. They gravitated to each other instinctively.

While their affair lasted it ran a tempestuous course. He found her so irresistible—as well as maddening—that he went back to her several times when their paths crossed after they had broken up. Lola, as prone to forgive as she was to quarrel, added him to her list of the elect whom she did not discuss or criticize, though she found him too diffused in his interests to be wholly hers. He had many loves but historians have bracketed Lola with George Sand and Marie Duplessis, the Lady of the Camellias, as one of the three most publicized of his romances, although none of them touched the depth of his alliance with the Comtesse.

Lola and Liszt were a remarkable pair when seen together. His long mane of hair, his aquiline good looks, his wit and intensity of manner made an instant impression on Lola. She was twenty-six and her beauty was at its peak at this time. Richard Wagner felt repelled by her when he first met her as she sat with Liszt in an opera box. He thought her a "painted and jewelled woman with bold, bad eyes" and he later described her as "demonic and heartless." However, he was momentarily struck by the dazzling power of her presence, and the spell she had cast over Liszt.

Both men were at the opera in Dresden that night to hear the new *Rienzi* that had been stirring up interest in music circles since its introduction in 1840. Liszt and Lola sat in the box of Joseph Tichatschek, the Bohemian tenor who sang for the Dresden opera for thirty years and created the roles of *Rienzi* and *Tannhäuser*. Liszt was completely won by the brilliance of the score and he discussed it briefly with Wagner, who came to the box during the entre-acte. But seeing Lola sitting impatiently in the background and knowing her to be Liszt's interest of the moment he soon moved away.

The brief combination of these two personalities was of intense interest to the music world. When news of it reached the Comtesse d'Agoult at her retreat in Switzerland, she wrote to Liszt with deep resentment. Theirs had been a tenacious affair, in which she had stoked intellectual fires, feeding his spirit with Voltairean philosophy, and reading Shakespeare and Byron to him while he improvised. She had her own writing and high ambitions, as well as deep love for the man for whom she had abandoned her family. Lola had heard of the Comtesse's rage when Liszt and George Sand had slipped away from Paris together and how on their return she had challenged her famous rival to a duel, the weapons to be fingernails. Liszt on that occasion had locked himself in a closet until both women calmed down. This was a form of jealousy that Lola understood. She, too, had been known to claw with her nails, beat with a hairbrush, and flail with a whip.

Drawn as she was to monarchs, Lola was puzzled by Liszt's ambivalent attitude to royalty. He seemed to seek their favor, to court publicity, and yet to insist on his independence. Lamennais, the philosopher condemned by the Catholic Church for his advocacy of religious freedom, happened to be one of Liszt's most treasured friends, and this made him noticeably cool to Louis Philippe, the Citizen King who was at odds with the apostate priest.

Liszt snubbed many royal figures in the course of his flamboyant career and he refused to play before Isabella II because Spanish court etiquette denied him a personal introduction to the Queen. He would not invite the Kings of Bavaria or Hanover to his concerts and during one of his performances he lifted his hands from the keyboard and waited with bowed head for the Czar to stop talking. Nicholas, who disliked Liszt's radical views, asked him why he was silent.

"Music itself should be silent when Nicholas speaks," said Liszt.

But he found his match in Lola. Always ravenous for attention she annoyed him during his working hours. And she embarrassed him publicly when she followed him to the Beethoven Festival held at Bonn in August, 1845. It was a stormy event from start to finish. Dissension had preceded the unveiling of Beethoven's statue. Lorenzo Bartelini, who had done busts of Byron, Liszt and Madame de Staël among others, had earlier threatened to throw up his commission, but Liszt had overridden the opposition and the statue was now to be unveiled. He had composed a special cantata for the occasion and celebrities from all over Europe assembled at Bonn. There were crowned heads, diplomats, music worshipers, art judges, German, Viennese, French and British reviewers, as well as the star of the occasion—Franz Liszt. Lola was denied admittance to the Hôtel de l'Étoile, where the most honored guests stayed. The impression prevailed that she had insisted on attending this event against Liszt's wishes. It was a sufficiently complicated situation without the added hazard of her unpredictability.

Both were closely observed throughout the festival by Ignaz Moscheles, the Bohemian composer and teacher who had given Mendelssohn lessons and was his lifelong friend. At Bonn, he noted, Liszt was the "absolute monarch, by virtue of his princely gifts, outshining all else." He had a "suite of ladies and gentlemen in attendance on him and Lola Montez among the former." Johann Vesque von Püttlingen, the composer of *Turandot*, was there, along with Joseph Fischhof, the Viennese composer.

Liszt was quickly in trouble when he forgot to mention the French in a speech he made at the ceremonial dinner in the Stern Hotel. The epitome of the romantic in looks and style, he tossed back his long mane and proposed a toast to Prince Albert. Then he spoke of the festival and the unveiling of Beethoven's statue. "Here all nations are met to pay honor to the master," he said. "May they live and prosper—the Dutch, the English, the Viennese—who have made a pilgrimage hither."

Hippolyte Chelard, the French composer of operas and religious music, jumped to his feet and screamed at Liszt: *"Vous avez oublié les Français."*

Instantly there was tumult and Liszt tried to make himself heard above the din. He shouted that he had lived fifteen years among

47

Frenchmen, and would not intentionally ignore them. But the excited guests pushed back their chairs, smashed glasses, and abused each other in various languages. Lola, always the exhibitionist ready to draw attention to herself, jumped up on the dinner table, aflame with anger and instantly noticeable to everyone in the room. This fed the blaze, for the French resented Liszt's desertion of the Comtesse d'Agoult, and at the moment Lola Montez was her successor.

The band played loudly to drown out the protests, and it took time to clear the dining room. The scene was well advertised all over Europe, since Queen Victoria and Prince Albert as well as other royalties had gathered in Bonn for the ceremonies. Once again Lola was in the public eye—the bold adventuress who had made a show of herself.

She and Liszt parted soon after that. Driven wild by her demands and her indifference to his work, he slipped away in a coach from the inn where they were staying but not before he had honored her with a composition. He arranged with a porter to lock her in her room and he left money for the damage that he knew she would do. When she found that she was a prisoner she smashed furniture, beat on the walls and created an uproar for hours until she was physically exhausted.

Each had found the wild strain in the other. Lola's contempt for authority, her uninhibited passions, her intelligent conversation and wit had diverted this experienced lover, but each breathed more freely when they moved on to separate interests. When their paths crossed from time to time he was always stirred by her presence but had no wish to commit himself again. They were seen together briefly in Bonn a second time, and, whether by chance or design, they were spotted in Leipzig, in Genoa and in Constantinople, during a tour made by Liszt.

But it was her old friend Sir Stratford Canning, at this time British Ambassador to Turkey, who showed Lola the beauties of the Bosporus and gave her strong social backing during her stay in Turkey. Few knew the inner workings of British diplomacy across

Europe at this time as the "Great Elchi" did and he was particularly well informed on the affairs of Russia, Turkey and Greece. In a succession of missions he had negotiated the Treaty of Bucharest between Russia and Turkey in 1812. A few years later he had helped to establish federal government in Switzerland, and he had served as Minister to the United States from 1820 to 1824. He was the cousin of George Canning, Pitt's great ally who promoted the policy of non-intervention by Britain, but fostered liberal and nationalist movements in Europe.

Lola persuaded Sir Stratford to arrange a visit for her to the Sultan's harem to see the "lights of the world," as they were then known. Except for a few of the younger girls she failed to find one beautiful woman in the "whole vast accumulation of rose-leaves and butter." The ladies of the harem were scornful of Lola's contours. To them her slimness was a "horrible deformity," and while they complimented her on her face and her feet, they were "positively disgusted at my diminutive size."

Lola made the most of her travels with Liszt, and her association with him helped to spread her fame and to get her engagements. Even when he was out of her life she never failed to show interest in his doings, and one day she asked George Sand which man she considered the greater pianist—Liszt or Sigismund Thalberg, the Swiss virtuoso who was then rivaling Liszt in popularity. "Liszt is the first," said George Sand, "but there is only one Thalberg. . . . I should say that Thalberg is like the clear, placid flow of a deep grand river—while Liszt is the same tide foaming, and bubbling, and dashing on like a cataract."

When Lola later gained ascendancy at the Bavarian court, one of her first acts was to have King Ludwig offer Liszt the highest decoration at his command. This was her way of showing him that she had forgiven him for their stormy scenes. But Liszt ignored the gesture. By 1848 he had settled at Weimar with his new love, Princess Sayn-Wittgenstein, an intellectual like the Comtesse d'Agoult, who stirred him to action and helped him with his writings. For twelve years they stayed together and worked productively, writing, composing symphonies, rhapsodies and oratorios. But it was Lola who was remembered in the American critic James G. Huneker's estimate of the women who had influenced Liszt. He wrote of the musician's love for George Sand, Marie Duplessis, and "that astounding adventuress, Lola Montez. . . ."

It was an ironic coincidence that both he and Lola, who had lived with such intensity, should toward the end seek consolation in religion at nearly the same time—Liszt in Catholicism and she in simple evangelical faith at odds with her history and previous inclinations. When Liszt joined the Franciscan Order Sacheverell Sitwell wrote: "It is difficult to think of Liszt in the Vatican without a memory of, for instance, Lola Montez. Few more peculiar characters than Liszt can ever have slept in such holy precincts."

Four years after Lola died in America, a penitent magdalen, he became Abbé Liszt, a religious zealot, neglected as the star of Wagner rose. His musical career declined until his death at Bayreuth in 1886. But in 1844 nothing could have seemed more unlikely than the fate of Lola and Liszt after they went their separate ways. Fresh from his arms, and from the well-publicized incidents in Bonn, Berlin and Warsaw, Lola the hedonist became also Lola the full-scale political rebel when exposed to the wits and savants of the period.

FOUR

The Boulevards of Paris

Though Lola's career reached its peak as the adviser and favorite of King Ludwig I of Bavaria, the most significant phase in her own development was the period she passed in Paris in the 1840's, exposed to the most advanced writers and philosophers of the era. Her reputation as an accomplished courtesan, if an indifferent dancer, gave her status in this community, and her witty conversation, added to her dramatic looks, made her a personality among them.

She had passed almost unnoticed on her first appearance in Paris in 1843 with an Englishman named Francis Leigh, who had been an officer with the 10th Hussars. This was before her affair with Liszt. They stayed at a modest hotel near the Palais Royal and Lola ran up bills for lingerie and other attire she bought on the Rue de Helder and charged to Leigh. When a lawyer's letter followed her to Munich in September, 1847, demanding the 1,371 francs due, Lola, by that time affluent and powerful, refused to pay. She pointed out that the debtor was Francis Leigh, who had ordered a riding habit and other items for her.

51

On this early visit to Paris Lola had one minor engagement at the Porte Saint Martin which ended disastrously when she was howled down by the audience. Her response was to rip off her garters and fling them defiantly at her tormentors. But her full fury was spent on young Leigh. Angered by her reception, scornful of her young lover, she brandished a pistol at him and fired a shot at random.

Her second and more formal arrival in Paris was in 1844 and it was assumed that she had come with Liszt, who showed up at about the same time, but they had already gone their separate ways. Lola soon attracted the attention of Alexandre Dumas, who had reacted to her striking looks with his customary exuberance when he had been introduced to her by an English friend. He told her that he admired her for the scene she had made at the Potsdam military review. He happened also to be a friend of Lord Brougham and he was not completely ignorant of Lola's history. Dumas was at the height of his fame, with *The Three Musketeers*, *The Count of Monte Cristo* and *The Man in the Iron Mask* being widely read and discussed. His loves were as spontaneous as his writings but much more transient in quality, so that Lola was just a passing episode in his life. But through him she was quickly involved with the press and was soon regarded with interest along the boulevards, particularly when she began to show up in the company of the learned group known as the Olympians.

Dumas continued to regard her with the keen eye of a writer but it was as the mistress of Alexandre Henri Dujarier, co-editor of *La Presse* with Émile de Girardin, that she quickly reached the inner circle. She had been taking dancing lessons from a ballet master on the Rue Pelletier in the hope of improving her technique for Léon Pillet, director of the opera. Well aware of her history, Pillet was dubious about her polish as an artist, but she had run up such support that he gave her a chance to appear at the Paris Opéra with Halévy's *Il Lazzarone* on March 30, 1844. In this stately setting Lola had one of her most crushing defeats.

Théophile Gautier, always conspicuous in his scarlet velvet waistcoat and well on his way to fame as a critic, dealt severely with her and observed that the "only thing Andalusian about Mlle. Montez is a pair of magnificent eyes." He compared her unfavorably with Dolores Serrai, a current favorite, who redeemed her imperfections as a dancer by her "voluptuous abandon and admirable fire and precision of rhythm." Lola impressed him as being more at home "in the saddle than on the boards" but he softened the blow by saying that he did not wish to be too severe with a pretty woman who had not had time to study Parisian tastes.

There was some justice in this, since Lola had offended Pillet as well as her audience by breaking one of the cardinal rules of choreography in dancing without the required maillot, or tights of the day. As hisses broke through a wave of applause she remembered the angry way in which she had tossed her garters when she played at the Porte Saint Martin, and she checked her impulse in time. With smiling charm she now threw her pink satin ballet slippers into one of the boxes, and received an ovation. Dujarier, who was present with Gautier, was dazzled by her grace. He noticed the intensity with which she reacted to the disapproval of the audience and he was less severe about her performance than the acidulous Gautier, whose critiques he ran in *La Presse*.

Pillet let Lola go. She had not come up to the standards of the Paris Opéra and the critics had had their say. But Dujarier could not forget her. He and Dumas were good friends and he knew that the obstreperous author whose books he serialized would not bear him any ill will if he took up the endless Gallic quest, where Lola was concerned. He told Gautier that he wished to meet Lola, and he soon gave her professional backing, persisting in spite of the critic's cynicism about her dancing. Although she lived in an atmosphere of the most enlightened and devastating criticism, she could never get hardened to it—a quality in her quickly recognized by Dujarier. She soon knew most of the occupants of the Loge des Lions at the Opéra, and she became a personality along the boulevards, where life was stimulating, with fresh literary history being made by the day. The arts flourished and a classic assemblage of geniuses lived between the Opéra and the Rue Drouet. Before long Lola knew Balzac, Victor Hugo, Alfred de Musset, Alphonse Lamartine, Joseph Méry, Félicité Lamennais, Alfred de Vigny, Dumas *fils* as well as Dumas *père*, George Sand, Rachel and other figures in politics and the arts. Actresses circled around these men and women, seeking publicity and attention, and women of letters were much in evidence. By finding herself on easy terms with Dumas and Dujarier she was drawn into both worlds. Her fame spread fast and she was discussed in the salons of St. Germain as well as along the boulevards and in the newspaper offices. She was an object of interest and observation to the diplomats, who were already well aware of the stir she had caused in various European capitals.

The seventeenth-century tradition of salons and royal mistresses was fading in the wave of republicanism sweeping all over Europe. But Paris was again aflame with political controversy as at the time of the Revolution. Dujarier and Dumas were close to the heart of the gathering storm, and Lola was fully exposed to the political thinking of their circle. Her worldly sense did not desert her when it came to seeking the company of aristocrats, but the rebellious spirit that had fired all her own actions from childhood was roused as she listened to Dujarier and his friends. All were rebels, revolutionaries, innovators, thinkers, from George Sand to Lamennais.

Lola felt that she was moving among the gods when she sailed into the Café de Paris at five in the afternoon to meet Dujarier. Instinctively she made a grand entrance, walking with a stately swagger, her luminous eyes sweeping the tables boldly. Balzac, Victor Hugo and de Musset did not frequent the cafés to the same extent as Dumas *père* and Dumas *fils*, but they appeared several times a week at the Café de Paris, where the critics, writers and actors gathered to discuss politics, the latest scandal, the work they were doing, the charm of their women, their debts and their honors.

All observed Dujarier's beautiful mistress. She had little in common with the other favorites at the Café de Paris. Dumas *fils* could see no one but the ethereal Marie Duplessis, the prototype of Marguerite Gauthier, the immortal Camille. His novel *La Dame aux Camélias* would come out in 1848 as Lola was fleeing from Bavaria. The two beauties, totally dissimilar in nature and looks but equally capable of mesmerizing men, often encountered each other at the Café de Paris. Lola was strong and assertive, Marie tremulous and clinging, but no less appealing to her many lovers.

Lola was aware that Liszt was visiting Marie at her home on the Rue de la Madeleine in 1844, but this bothered her less than it did the Comtesse d'Agoult, who had written to him after his affair with Lola that she had "no objection to being his mistress, but would not be *one* of his mistresses." Marie Duplessis was utterly infatuated with Liszt and begged him to take her away with him, promising to devote herself to him alone. But Liszt was wary and did not become involved with her as he had with Lola.

Unlike his quiet son, the elder Dumas was constantly in circulation, buoyant and always the exhibitionist. He felt real affection for Dujarier, who was serializing his work, and the two men met often at convivial gatherings as well as in their working hours. Lola had plenty of opportunity to observe Dumas and she described him in her autobiography as the most brilliant conversationalist among all the men she had ever met, and her list was long and distinguished. She viewed him as a "tall, fine-looking man, with intellect stamped on his brow, and sparkling in every look and motion . . . his nature is overflowing with generosity, and he is consequently always out of pocket." His impecunious ways were well known to all his friends, in spite of the large sums of money he made, and his marriage to Ida Ferrier was thought to be appeasement to her father for the fortune he owed him.

Dujarier was a key figure for the writers and actors, both as co-owner of *La Presse* and as having a financial interest in the Théâtre Français. Lola attended the theater and opera with him, and her dramatic posturings at the masked balls of the literati caused comment. But she prized most the time she spent alone with Dujarier, or Bon-Bon, as she called him. He was a brilliant, impatient and ardent young man, not given to light affairs. In Lola he seemed to have found not only an uncommon mistress but a woman to whom he could talk in the informed language of the literary revolutionaries.

As a crusading editor Dujarier was at home on all social levels, although he took scathing note of what went on at the Tuileries, and watched with disapproval the Citizen King veering away from the democratic image to the old monarchical tradition. A Bourbon was always a Bourbon, but Louis had interested the writing men because of his travels and his relatively democratic views before Thiers acclaimed him the Citizen King after the revolution of 1830. He lowered the fever point of the city as he moved about Paris in a leisurely way and encouraged business before Napoleon III transformed the French capital into a cosmopolitan center with railways bringing in fresh influences from the outside world. In Lola's time the *nouveaux riches*, barren of ancient lineage, gave elaborate suppers, dinners and receptions, employing huge staffs and using gold plate. It was an era of solid riches and expanding trade, and the revived Bourbon influence was of growing concern to Lola's republican friends.

Most of her time was passed in cafés and in endless discussion of political issues with brilliant men of radical views. She was quite at ease in the sanctums of some of the most noted editors of Paris. The sketches, pictures and feuilletons by celebrated contributors displayed on their walls gave her a lively view of contemporary satire. She absorbed impressions with ease and discussed them with understanding. Lola saw the seamy life of Paris, too—the narrow alleys with men in colored nightcaps and torn blouses described so graphically by Eugène Sue in his *Mystères de Paris* that Louis Philippe had gradually had them cleaned up. Neither the elegant cabriolets with coronets nor the little blue citadines for two that abounded in the streets of Paris found their way into these dim channels.

Equally enlightening to Lola were the reminiscences of James

Joseph Jacques Tissot, the academician who had been a well-known painter and enameler in the France that had died with the Revolution. He wandered around Paris showing where Danton, Robespierre, Marat and Mirabeau had lived, and where the events of the Reign of Terror had taken place. But these seemed only dim echoes to Lola as she later strolled happily in the Tuileries Gardens, past the glittering spray of the fountains and the parterre brilliant with flower beds above the soft green turf. When she idled in a straw-bottomed chair in the Allée de l'Orangerie, with the trees flowering above her, she felt at peace with her surroundings. She was alert to the sights and sounds of the Parisian streets, from the lemonade vendor with his barrel covered with red velvet and tinkling silver bells, to the bunches of moss roses and violets offered by wise-eyed peasant women. The violets became symbolic to Lola of her love affair with Dujarier. When she saw them in any part of the world she was conscious of his lost presence, for the gifted young editor was one of the great loves of her life—perhaps the most genuine of all on her part.

Dujarier took pride in the intelligence she showed as she sparred gaily with the bright wits in the Café de Paris, or lounged in his quarters in the Rue Laffitte. As he drilled her in French politics, he sounded her out about her own observations, shaped by her journeyings across Europe. True to her avowed intention she had found her way to courts, both major and minor, and she had listened to rulers, statesmen, peers and soldiers. Through their eyes she had picked up some understanding of the flickering political picture across Europe, and had not been dead to the rising tide of revolt. Dujarier recognized Lola's drive and ambition. He was amused to learn that she had been noticed by such divergent types as Czar Nicholas, Franz Liszt and the Duke of Wellington.

It was clear to him that she had not wholly shed her reverence for the monarchical form of government. In her earlier years she had been in the company of Anglo-Indians trained to observe the social usages, the patriotic image and the austere disciplines of army

and outpost life. She had experienced Scottish restraint and puritanism, and at the other end of the scale she had seen the carnal under-
currents of life in London and Bath during the mid-Victorian era.
Dujarier found her conversation as fascinating as it was revealing.
He passed every hour with her that he could spare from his work and
she later wrote that in this society she "rapidly ripened in politics,
and became a good and confirmed hater of tyranny and oppression,
in whatever shape it came." In fact, in her conversations with Dujarier's friends she became so enthusiastic a republican that she regretted she "had not been made a man."

Like other French journalists of the period, Dujarier knew how
to make use of a woman's wits. He kept his ears closely attuned to
passing events and understood the power of such women as Madame
de Staël, George Sand, the Duchess de Nemours and Princess de
Lieven, the Sibyl of Europe, who by this time was influencing the
decisions of François Guizot, Premier of France.

It was soon rumored that Lola Montez was some sort of secret
agent, used by Lord Palmerston and other liberal British statesmen
to help offset the Jesuitical influences flowing from Metternich in
Vienna. Church and state were inseparable in Metternich's thinking
and the issue was a live one all over Europe. After listening at
length to the eloquent Lamennais during her days in Paris, Lola
never abandoned her endless battle with the Jesuits. It became a
monomania with her and cropped up until the closing days of her
life in the United States, when a belated conversion chastened her
spirit.

Lamennais was at bitter odds with the Church, after having been
chastised officially in Munich for the fanatical stand he had taken in
advocating the ecclesiastical control of governments in Catholic
countries. He and Montalembert had founded *L'Avenir* in 1830,
and were such extremists on the subject that the hierarchy itself
threw a blanket over Lamennais's views. In bitterness of spirit he
went to the other extreme and became the proponent of total freedom in worship. Although Lola had not yet met Ludwig I of

Bavaria she had heard much about him from Lamennais, who after changing his course had tried to persuade the King that no monarch should be under the control of the clergy. He continued to fight repression wherever it sprang up in Church and government.

Lola was to ascribe most of her own troubles to religious persecution, and it was assumed by many that her amours at the European courts were deliberately promoted for political ends. Dujarier, like others, quickly saw that it seemed to be her fate to act as a bombshell wherever she settled. Was she an emissary involved in the underground revolt that was gaining momentum across Europe? Or was her goal in life simply the pursuit of passion, wherever she found it, on a high or low level? Occasionally her motives seemed to interlock. As time went on it became an accepted fact that she was just as likely to consort momentarily with a groom, with a scholar in a library alcove, with an effete prince, with a youthful athlete, with an ardent student, with a soldier, with a romantic like Liszt, with a suave man of letters like Dujarier, or with a vigorous, earthy man like Dumas, always ready for a chance encounter.

In her later years Lola was apt to laugh at allusions to her legendary affairs. Scores perhaps, she would concede, but not hundreds. She said the picture was greatly overdrawn, but she never denied that her lovers were numerous, or that passion was her special way of life. In her early years she was involved with both young and older men; later she was drawn to the young, but when she found intelligence in her lovers she struck the ideal goal. This was the case with Dujarier. After his death she insisted that he had planned to marry her, and that Dumas and Méry had promised to go with them by coach on a wedding trip through Spain.

In the company of such brilliant men and women Lola's ambitions soared, and she looked beyond a theatrical career to political power. Even Guizot was thought to have been one of her conquests. For a happy interlude she envisioned herself as the mistress of a salon in Paris. Dujarier did not underestimate her intuitive brilliance where men and events were concerned. He may well have intended to give her free rein with a salon of her own. She described her brown-haired, gray-eyed lover as a "man of uncommon genius, greatly loved and respected by all who knew him, except for those who disagreed with him in politics, and who dreaded the searching and terrible power of his pen."

Dujarier had long been under the spell of Delphine Gay, de Girardin's wife, who wrote her engaging *Lettres Parisiennes* for *La Presse*. For a time he had his own apartment in the de Girardin *hôtel* until they moved away from the Rue Laffitte and held court in an elegant Empire mansion at Chaillot. Their gatherings were literary, artistic and political. The gifted men and women who attended them spread their glow over the city, turning out novels, poems, tracts, polemics. They were as deeply involved in politics as in letters, and much of their work reflected the revolutionary spirit.

Balzac, Gautier, Méry, Lamartine, Baron Rothschild, Rachel and other celebrities passed in an endless stream through Delphine's ornately decorated reception rooms. Stage stars in particular hovered around her, since she wrote with a quiet distinction and wit of her own about the theater, fashion, the hunt, politics, the arts, and all current topics. Her husband avoided her salon as much as he could, for he disliked men of letters, although he had grown rich on them. He was essentially a political figure, lean, aloof and acid. "It would require the glance of a lion to dazzle such a man," Lola wrote regretfully when her own superlative tactics failed to move him. He and Gautier usually sat in total silence while Méry and Dumas moved about like dynamos, garrulous and exuberant.

But the guests were quiet when Delphine had her musician friends perform. Paris was as popular a center for them as for writers and artists at this time, and Rossini, Berlioz, Liszt and Chopin were much in evidence. Pierre Dupont, the lyric poet, sang *Les Boeufs* for the first time at the de Girardins'. Rachel and Dorval were the reigning stars in the theater, and Lola studied them and other actors and dramatists she met at Delphine's with particular interest. Her own frustrated ambitions made her intensely criti-

ral, and she disliked Rachel from their first encounter. It surprised her that this great star should seem such a nonentity at a party, with no talent for conversation, an art in which Lola was well aware that she shone. She decided that the star cared only for money, but she conceded that Rachel was unsurpassed in dramatic delivery and "concentrated mimicry."

Wherever she went Lola was confronted with the success of Fanny Elssler and Maria Taglioni, the Italian dancer noted for her work in *La Sylphide*. In London, in Warsaw, in Berlin they were the incomparables, and again she crossed their trails in Paris. Fanny, the raven-haired ballet dancer from Vienna, was notorious for her amours, but her professional reputation had not suffered despite the fact that she had two illegitimate children. The Bonapartists had given a demonstration in Fanny's honor when she visited Paris in 1834. It was roses, roses all the way for her. Dumas used her in *Les Mohicans de Paris* and Edmond Rostand later pictured her in *L'Aiglon* as the siren thrown by Prince Metternich into the arms of the Duc de Reichstadt to make him forget his birth, his ambitions and the hopes set on him. It was small wonder that Fanny was a disturbing image to the ambitious Lola as she moved from one capital to another.

Lola's three favorite celebrities in their circle were Dumas, Dujarier and Roger de Beauvoir, a poet and novelist with eccentric ways and flamboyant attire. Like Balzac and Dumas, he was always in flight from his creditors and had been known to throw hot coals and a tubful of water on insistent tradesmen. His gallantries, amours and absurdities amused his fellow boulevardiers. Méry, perhaps the most popular figure in their set, struck Lola as being a "charming and impossible personage." As poet, novelist, playwright and travel writer he gushed out information with endearing volubility. Sainte-Beuve, scholarly and the admirer of Madame Hugo, had no appeal for Lola, although she recognized his power as a critic. She was on friendly terms with Victor Hugo and sometimes appeared with the group of worshipers who gathered around his balcony to pay him homage. She thought that de Musset, picturesque in tall hat, blue frock coat with flaring collar, drain-pipe trousers, frilled shirts and flamboyant waistcoats, had a rakish air suggestive of his verse.

Lola often took messages to Lamartine from Dujarier, who never went out socially. She found him a "dreary, lonely man, shunning crowds, and isolating himself in a beautiful world of his own." She felt more akin to Eugène Sue, the novelist who was destined for exile in 1851 after the coup d'état of Napoleon III, but who was still in Paris while Lola was there. She considered him an "honest, sincere, truth-loving man," and admired his courage in facing threats and ostracism for his political views.

If she did not care for Rachel she was devoted to the great star's teacher, Joseph Isidore Samson, who headed the Comédie Française Company. She found him an amiable jester and a good-natured judge of men, unlike another celebrity she frequently met —Jules Gabriel Janin, the caustic critic and novelist of the *Journal des Débats*, who had helped Rachel on her way to fame. Samson called Janin the Executioner and his colleagues in the arts all feared this long-maned writer with the furious black eyes.

For once in her life Lola was overwhelmed with awe for a member of her own sex when she met George Sand, whose face seemed to be carved in ivory and whose eyes were like "living copper." At first she paid little attention to the dancer, although she must have been well aware of Lola's recent affair with Liszt. When he and the Comtesse d'Agoult lived together at the Hôtel de France in Paris, George Sand had quarters above them, and Chopin, Sainte-Beuve, Lamennais, Heinrich Heine and other men of genius came to her salon. Listening at her open window to Liszt's music George Sand said that all her instincts were exalted and her sorrows became poetry when he played. Remembering their brief elopement and the battle waged with the Comtesse d'Agoult on their return, Lola studied her mannish attire with approval, writing that it was not so much caprice as a way of dressing that enabled her to go anywhere she wished without exciting curiosity. She considered the French writer "large-brained and large-hearted, conscious of her strength, and therefore independent in her opinions."

After listening to Lola talk, George Sand studied her with attention and even copied her habit of wearing flattering black, with a lace mantilla and a bright flower for emphasis. At the same time Lola picked up George Sand's habit of smoking cigars. With some fellow feeling for the woman who had ensnared both Chopin and Liszt, and with strong feminist inclinations of her own, Lola observed that the reformers of the era, and particularly the women, were targets "to be shot at by all dark unenlightened human beings." She added with a dash of grandeur: "It is as absurd in this glorious nineteenth century to attempt to destroy freedom of thought, and the sovereignty of the individual, as it is to stop the falls of Niagara."

Lola soon learned that intellectual qualities in women went further in Paris than anywhere else in the world, as she watched the writers and actresses who flourished in Dujarier's milieu. Nowhere but in the French capital could one find so many women of wit and genius mingling with literary men, and "nowhere was literary society so refined, so brilliant, and charmingly intellectual as in Paris," said Lola with an air of authority.

Although drawn to the nobility from force of habit, Lola found the ancient families in a state of total exile from the rest of France. They refused to acknowledge Louis Philippe and considered their country in a state of anarchy. "However poor they may be," Lola wrote, "they still quietly and proudly wrap themselves in the dignity of their birth, and shut their eyes and ears to all the activities of living France." To Lola the pure old French nobility seemed "shrivelled, grim and stiff." They paid little attention to her, since her political associations rather than her history as a seductive figure, told against her.

As she swung between two worlds her knowledge of life, of the social customs of old and new France, and of the stormy political thinking of the day developed rapidly, for she was essentially a woman of acute intelligence, as well as of violent emotions. During her days in the Munich hierarchy she drew retrospective lessons from the clever Frenchwomen of this era. She was one of their kind, although she had been nurtured in the more placid British image.

FIVE

A Duel in the Bois

On a March evening in 1845 Dujarier told Lola that he was going to the Trois Frères Provençaux without her. She was annoyed because she knew that both he and Dumas liked to attend bohemian gatherings at this restaurant with the stars of the theater and the demimondaines who mingled with the writers and critics. He gallantly assured her that he did not wish her to meet some of the evening's guests, but the fact was that he had already been inveigled into escorting Mademoiselle Anaïs Lhévienne, an opulent vaudeville star.

The restaurant, one of the three liveliest in Paris, was under the arcades of the Palais Royal, and it had small private *cabinets* screened by gilded trellis work, where diners could see without being seen, and talk without being heard. Louis Philippe was in process of cleaning up the galleries of the Palais Royal, which had long been regarded as the showcase of sin in the French capital. The girls from the Rue Montmartre and the Place de la Victoire flowed in to parade with considerable dash, or to sit on the stone benches around the garden where fountains splashed and flowers bloomed in season. The elite of the half world had made this their gathering ground, bringing gamblers, roués and adventurers of all kinds in their wake.

The luxurious boutiques, glittering with light, stayed open most of the night, displaying jewels, bonnets and parasols, pomades, swords, miniature clocks and bibelots of all kinds. The restaurateurs fared well in this atmosphere of free spending and careless living, and their small marble tables and freshly painted chairs ringed the garden area. The Trois Frères Provençaux matched Véry's and Véfour's for popularity but was considered the gayest of the three.

Before the evening was over a storm blew up that led to a duel and one of the most sensational trials in French jurisprudence, with Dumas and Lola both appearing as star witnesses, and Gustave Flaubert, as yet unknown, looking on and commenting on Lola's beauty. Not only was Dujarier reluctant to have Lola meet the women who were coming to the party but he was determined to keep her away from Rosemond de Beauvallon, a handsome young Creole of twenty-six from Guadeloupe who had offended him with his frank comments on Lola's charms. Her susceptibility was well known and she had expressed interest in de Beauvallon, whose path seemed to cross Dujarier's with a certain inevitability. The editor's most intimate companion when Lola came into his life was a Madame Albert, who testified later at the trial that Dujarier had ceased visiting her when de Beauvallon became her friend, lest they run into each other. But by that time Dujarier was wholly committed to Lola, and he was doubly determined that she should not meet this young Don Juan.

A score of guests showed up to dine, dance and play lansquenet, which was becoming more popular at the time than écarté. All paid their own way—fifty-five francs—except Mademoiselle Lhévienne, who was Dujarier's special guest. The first hint of trouble flashed out at the supper table. Dujarier, warmed by wine, rattled the coins in his pocket and in a toast to Anaïs said that within a matter of months she would be his mistress. Tears came into her eyes and she seemed to be offended. Roger de Beauvoir and several of the other men showed resentment. Dujarier apologized. He kissed her hand and they were friends again. Much was made of his hostile attitude that night when the proceedings were later detailed in court, but in this bohemian company the offense could not have seemed cataclysmic.

Shortly afterward de Beauvoir, always an amusing figure with his huge coiffure, multicolored waistcoat and extravagant postures, approached Dujarier and asked about a novella he had written that had not yet appeared in *La Presse.* Serials were immensely popular at the time and young writers plagued their editor friends, hoping to have their work accepted. The women writers who haunted the boulevards were even more insidious than the men in their approach. A sophisticated and pleasure-loving man, Dujarier was annoyed by this direct challenge from de Beauvoir, since he preferred to keep his professional life separate from the recreations of the evening, although it was customary for the leading politicians, artists and members of the *beau monde* to mingle with the princes of the press after working hours.

Always plagued by his creditors, de Beauvoir urged Dujarier to use his novella without delay, but Dujarier told him tartly that he thought first of the public taste, and who could question the fact that Dumas must take precedence? The exchange was laughed off at first, but the Beau Brummell of the boulevards was piqued and persisted. The two men argued until Dujarier finally asked impatiently: "Are you looking for trouble with me—a duel?"

"I don't look for affairs, but sometimes I find them," de Beauvoir whipped back, a point that he made to some effect at the trial as an indication of Dujarier's manner that night.

This was one of the disagreements revealed when the case came to trial, but the argument that brought things to a head occurred over the gaming table. This time Dujarier's antagonist was de Beauvallon and more was involved than the feeling over Lola. As on many of these occasions, enemies from the press glossed over their hatred with civilities. It happened that Dujarier and de Beauvallon were at deadly odds professionally, for de Beauvallon was the brother-in-law of the vindictive Adolphe Granier de Cassagnac, an ardent Bonapartist then editing *Le Globe*. He had been with *La Presse* and had left in a feud with Dujarier over a debt he owed the paper. Dujarier had won a judgment against him and the two men were antagonistic, both on professional and personal levels. Granier de Cassagnac's wife felt that they had been socially damaged, and her brother was eager to settle this score.

Their feud was at its height when young de Beauvallon, working as literary and dramatic critic for his brother-in-law's paper, came to grips with Dujarier at the Trois Frères Provençaux. Both papers were sounding boards for their owners. One was republican, the other royalist in its sympathies. This was a traditional battleground in France. Dujarier championed the people, and made enemies as well as friends with his irony and crusading fervor. *La Presse* was nine years old and highly successful, with Dumas's sparkling fiction helping to build up its prestige. Émile de Girardin had founded it as the first cheap paper in Paris, and at times it was so vitriolic that he was called out for duels. But after killing Nicolas Armand Carrel in one of these encounters he sheathed his rapier forever. Carrel had founded *Le National* with Louis Thiers and François Mignet, statesmen and historians. He had a substantial reputation and de Girardin came under heavy fire when he killed this fellow journalist.

Dujarier had never fought a duel. His special talent was for administration. Crystal clear in making decisions, his dry wit was chilling to some, but his friends, Dumas among them, thought him generous, brilliant and sympathetic. He had built up a large fortune, but he did not like to be reminded of the speed and drive with which he had risen to power. It was no secret that he disliked de Beauvallon, but political passions burned high among all these men. It was mere chance that the party Lola did not attend was the one at which they exploded around Dujarier, to her eternal regret. By early morning Dujarier and de Beauvallon were locked in an insoluble argument at the gambling table. They played until five o'clock and when they parted both men were furiously angry and mutually insulted.

The trouble started when Dujarier complained about the low limit imposed by the banker. He and de Beauvallon offered to share the risks and the winnings, with Dujarier putting up the larger sum. Dujarier lost heavily and the two men argued about the manner of paying off the debt. Neither one trusted the other and the editor did not wish to be beholden to de Beauvallon when the youth suggested deferring payment. After an argument in which each seemed to impugn the honesty of the other, Dujarier borrowed on the spot from friends who had heard part of the altercation. He was 2,500 francs out of pocket when he headed for home with a confused memory of de Beauvallon having said that more would be heard of the matter.

His head had cleared by the time he reached 39 Rue Laffitte, where Lola awaited him as usual. But she saw at once that something was wrong. He was flushed and distraught, and he brushed off all her inquiries. The cool morning air had sobered him on his walk home and he left for his office at an early hour. It did not occur to Lola or to any of his friends that a duel was in the making until de Beauvallon initiated proceedings by sending the Comte de Flore and Vicomte d'Ecquevillez to Dujarier with a challenge.

Furious and bewildered, Dujarier referred them to two of his friends, Charles de Boignes and Arthur Bertrand. He had neither the skill nor the inclination for an adventure of this kind. Moreover, the motive was far from clear to him. When Bertrand arrived next day to discuss the situation he ordered Lola out of the room, saying that they were going to talk of something that was not a woman's business. But as they lingered over the breakfast table she heard snatches of conversation that made her uneasy. Dujarier was talking heatedly of a pamphlet duplicating *La Presse* that Granier de Cassagnac had distributed in the French colonies. She also gathered that her lover was deeply resentful of the scurrilous articles later written about him by Granier de Cassagnac.

When Bertrand left, Dujarier was in deep gloom. Although he told her nothing she knew that some crisis had arisen. She had no immediate clue to the challenge made by de Beauvallon's seconds, but the three complaints cited seemed absurd to Dujarier, and to Dumas, who had moved in as adviser with all the power and imagination of his forceful personality—a past master in the strategy of dueling and intrigue.

Dujarier was accused of showing discourtesy while playing cards; of insisting on discharging his debt to de Beauvallon at once even though this entailed borrowing from others; and of going out of his way to avoid meeting de Beauvallon at Madame Albert's. De Boignes brushed off the involvement of Madame Albert as wholly irrelevant, but de Beauvallon's seconds held firm and said that he demanded satisfaction.

The duel was set for the Bois at 11 A.M. on March 11, 1845, only three days after the disastrous evening at the Trois Frères Provençaux. Dujarier chose pistols, although de Beauvallon was equally expert with rapier and gun, and he was totally inexperienced with both. His seconds urged him to avoid pistols, and Dumas spent hours trying to swing him away from the weapon that he knew might be fatal to his friend. He visited Dujarier on the afternoon before the duel and watched him pick up a rapier and try to fence with it. Dumas could see from the way he handled it that he was completely unfamiliar with its use. Studying his awkward lunges he asked Dujarier if he knew how to serve with the other arm, but he was at a loss either way.

Knowing de Beauvallon's reputation Dumas thought he had better warn his friend that his adversary was a master in the art of dueling. Dumas fils had shared a course in fencing with him and had told his father that the youth was unbeatable, but he added that he did not think de Beauvallon would kill Dujarier when he saw how inexpertly he wielded the rapier. Dumas had his son join them for dinner and asked him to take Dujarier to a shooting gallery, where he hit the mark only twice in twenty-four attempts. But Dujarier still insisted that pistols were his choice. With the sword he would surely be killed. Dumas decided that he was fully aware of the danger he ran, but that nothing could stop him from going ahead. One of his adversary's seconds had told Dujarier that if he did not accept this challenge he would be forced to fight for another reason. "He will force you," the editor was warned, "for he doesn't like your face."

Dumas offered him his own new pistols and said: "Take care, my dear friend. You have been happy too long for things to endure." But he could see that his insistence was upsetting to Dujarier, who finally exclaimed impatiently: "No, no. De Beauvallon is brave, his reputation is made. When I have fought with him, I will have no more quarrels; that will end the lesser quarreling. It's my first duel. It's an experience to which I must submit."

From this point on Dumas was sure that it was primarily a war between *Le Globe* and *La Presse,* and not between Dujarier and de Beauvallon. Realizing that there was no more to be said he went on to the theater at nine o'clock but he felt so tormented and uneasy that he returned at midnight, only to find Dujarier making his will. He owed Dumas a thousand crowns at the time, which he insisted on paying at once. Not having enough money at hand, he gave Dumas a bank voucher, and told him to draw the money before eleven in the morning, adding: "I don't know what may happen, and later perhaps my credit will be dead." As Dumas left he passed Lola coming in. They exchanged glances but neither spoke. Lola recalled later that he looked pale and moved; for once in his life he had nothing to say.

Dujarier had let her go alone to the Porte Saint-Martin that evening, the first time he had done this since her current engagement had begun. She found him at his secretary, writing with concentration. He looked up and handed her a "very gracious article" that M. de Boignes had written about her dancing. But she could see that he was preoccupied and not in the mood for dalliance. He soon told her to go home, because he had too much to do to spend time with her. Lola protested. She did not wish to leave him, feeling that something was deeply wrong. When he raised the curtain slightly and told her that perhaps she should leave Paris and look up some of her old friends, she asked him if he was about to fight a duel. He did not deny it, but brushed it off as an inconsequential affair, a mere trifle. Finally he insisted that she go home and come back to see him at nine in the morning.

Dujarier was up at seven and was having soup when a message came from Lola, urging him to hurry to her place as soon as he was dressed. He told her maid that he would be over soon. Instead, he sent Lola a note by his own servant Gabriel, telling him not to deliver it until after nine o'clock. Then he went to de Boignes's rooms for the final arrangements before leaving for the Bois.

After a sleepless night Dumas arrived at his friend's apartment a few minutes after seven, but found that Dujarier had already left. Gabriel, looking sorrowful, had nothing to say. Dumas returned home and told his secretary to mount guard and bring him news if anything developed. "I was preoccupied," Dumas later testified, "for I was convinced that Dujarier was wounded or dead."

When Lola opened her lover's note soon after nine o'clock she read what seemed like a farewell message:

My dear Lola:
   I am going out to fight with pistols. That is why I did not come to see you this morning. I have need of all my calmness. At two o'clock all will be over. A thousand embraces, my good little Lola, the good little woman whom I love so much, and the thought of whom will never leave me.
                                                                              D.

This sounded like a death knell to Lola. She dressed hurriedly and rushed to his quarters. The only sign of disturbance was the glimpse she had of Dumas's pistols lying on Dujarier's bed. Gabriel told her that he had started out without any expectation of returning alive. Lola choked back a scream and took a carriage to Dumas's dwelling. For the first time she learned from him that the antagonist was de Beauvallon. "Ah, my God, he is an *homme perdu*," she cried.

Later Lola testified that had she known what was involved she would have gone to the police with a warning, or else she would have sped in person to the site of the duel and used the pistol herself, something that she was well equipped to do. She had ceased to worry when Bertrand's brother told her that Roger de Beauvoir was the aggressor. Knowing him for the dilettante he was, she felt sure that there would not be bloodshed.

She went back to the Rue Laffitte to wait for news. Dumas stayed where he was. Meanwhile, Dujarier's life was at stake in the Bois. He had driven as far as the Rue de Pinon with his two seconds and M. de Guise, a doctor. They arrived at the Madrid Restaurant, the place of rendezvous, at ten o'clock. Snow had fallen and lightly crusted the ground. The sky was overcast and mottled with drifting clouds. De Beauvallon kept them waiting for an hour and a half while Dujarier shivered from the cold and showed such signs of nervous excitement that his seconds urged him to leave. De Guise insisted that he must go home but Dujarier stood his ground.

When de Beauvallon and his seconds finally drove up in a fiacre the ground was chosen and the pistols were produced. By the toss of a coin it was settled that de Beauvallon should fire first. Bertrand noticed that his finger was blackened when he poked into the barrel of the challenger's pistol, but the seconds assured him that de Beauvallon knew nothing of the arms he would use and that the powder was due to caps fired to make sure that the weapon was in working order. D'Ecquevillez swore on his honor that the pistol had never been in de Beauvallon's hands.

De Boignes made a last-minute plea for a settlement but de Beauvallon stood his ground. Thirty feet apart they advanced six paces and Dujarier, shivering with cold, fired wildly and out of turn. He threw his pistol to the ground and turned full face to his opponent. De Beauvallon took aim with deliberation and was so slow about firing, a breach of duel etiquette, that de Boignes shouted, "Shoot!"

For a moment it seemed as if Dujarier had not been hit; then he fell to the ground like a log. M. de Guise and the seconds rushed to his side, and the doctor saw at once that his wound was fatal. Although on the brink of death Dujarier was still conscious. De Guise held him and spoke lightly of the wound, as if it were a minor injury. Just before he died in the doctor's arms Dujarier murmured that he did not know why he had fought.

He was borne to his carriage, which was driven slowly back to the Rue Laffitte. Lola heard the lumbering wheels on the cobbles as it drew up at the entrance. She rushed downstairs and pushed her way through the group of men surrounding the carriage. When the door was opened Dujarier literally fell into her arms. He was already dead, shot through the face, with blood oozing through bandages. Lola shrieked and would not let go of her lover as he was carried upstairs. She knelt in floods of tears by the bed where he was placed.

At half past eleven word reached Dumas that Dujarier had been brought home dead. He raced through the streets, coat tails flying, his bristling hair on end, and found his friend lying on his bed, alone. Lola had been led away in a state of collapse. Dumas took charge until the editor's brother-in-law arrived. He showed him where Dujarier's money and papers were and then he went to Veron to get the details of the duel from Bertrand and de Boignes.

Dujarier's bloodstained will had fallen out of his coat pocket as he was being borne into the house. It started significantly with the words: "On the eve of my fight for an absurd cause, on a frivolous pretext, and because it was impossible for my friends Arthur Bertrand and Charles de Boignes to avoid an encounter . . ." He left the bulk of his fortune to his mother, who lived at Châlons-sur-Marne. His farewell note to her, written the night before his death along with his last message to Lola, read:

If this letter reaches you, it will be because I am dead or dangerously wounded. I fight tomorrow with pistols; it's a necessity of my position, and I accept as a man of heart . . . honor is imperative, and if you must shed tears, my good mother, you might better weep for a dignified son of yours than for a poltroon. One thought should at least sweeten your chagrin; that my last thought will have been of you. I will go to combat a calm man and sure of himself. . . . I embrace you, my good mother, from an overflowing heart.

Dujarier had not forgotten Lola in his will. He left her eighteen shares in the Palais Royal Theater, valued at 20,000 francs. It was difficult for her to accept the fact that this young lover, who had established her in his charmed circle, was dead. Not until she watched Dumas, Méry and de Girardin holding the corners of the French flag at his bier in Nôtre Dame de Lorette did she realize that this phase of her life was over.

The most distinguished literary Frenchmen of the day attended the funeral. Large crowds identified with the theater and the other arts were present. Lola's dramatic beauty was screened with a heavy veil, but all of the writers took note of her presence. A storm was in the making as murmurs spread even on the day of the funeral that Dujarier had been murdered by his adversary. Dumas, in particular, was suspicious because of what Dujarier had told him, and he would not let the matter rest. Bertrand kept insisting that he had found powder on his finger after testing the barrel. Both men were convinced that the challenger had made sure that his adversary would die by practicing beforehand with the pistol he would use, and that he had deliberately forced the duel for vengeful purposes. Why had he been so late in getting to their rendezvous while Dujarier suffered agonies from the biting cold and his own uncertainty? Why had they fought on such trivial grounds, and particularly when they were so unevenly matched?

In later years Lola was sometimes accused of having caused the duel that had all France talking, and that the trouble had begun with comments de Beauvallon had made on her bodily charms. But this was far from being the truth. She happened to be Dujarier's mistress at the moment, much cherished, but not a *casus belli*. However, it was after this that Dumas viewed Lola as a symbol of ill luck. The mere sight of her reminded him of his lost friend.

Because of the pressure brought by Dumas and his influential friends an investigation was begun, and the lower court in Paris failed to find grounds for prosecution. Within three weeks de Beauvallon, who had slipped across the border into Spain with d'Ecquevillez, had returned voluntarily, feeling that he was safe. During his absence, however, further digging had produced fresh evidence that led the Cour de Cassation to overrule the lower court and order de Beauvallon to stand trial for murder in the Assize Court at Rouen.

More than a year elapsed from the time of the duel until the trial finally began on March 26, 1846; it lasted for four days. In popular interest it was outranked only by the Dreyfus trial. The courtroom in the Palais de Justice was packed each day with persons bearing famous names; the most fashionable and clever women sat spellbound through hours of testimony, eager to watch Dumas in action, and to view the notorious Lola Montez. The best legal talent in France had been drawn into the case. Letendre de Tourville presided in scarlet robes. Pierre Antoine Berryer, the most acclaimed pleader of his day, represented the defense. He had helped his father, Pierre Nicolas Berryer, defend General Ney, who was condemned for treason after Waterloo. Lawyers everywhere followed this trial with interest. Berryer was regarded as being second only to Mirabeau in the power of his oratory. Léon Duval represented the civil interests of Madame Dujarier, who claimed damages.

Lola had not testified at the earlier hearing because of her distraught state immediately after Dujarier's death, but she volunteered to appear in Rouen as the "person most interested in avenging the dead man." For nearly a year she had kept out of sight, ill and depressed, except for seeing some of Dujarier's friends. She had shocked them by continuing right after his death the engagement he had arranged for her at the Porte Saint-Martin until she was hissed off the stage once more, and for the last time in Paris.

But now she caught the international spotlight at Rouen. Subdued, melancholy and uncannily beautiful, she played an authentic role this time and did it with style. When her name was called she moved forward gracefully and was immediately the star of the proceedings. As she lifted her veil and drew off her gloves a murmur of admiration ran through the courtroom. Her answers were quick and revealing. She convinced listeners that she had been deeply in love with Dujarier, and that he had intended to marry her.

Her black satin gown, softened with lace, clinging to her figure above the waist and billowing below, was the simplest in the courtroom. The entire effect was one of subtle appeal, and the women watching appraised her as bold and dangerous—more deadly to their interests than the demimondaines in flashy clothes who were also called as witnesses. She was of a breed well understood by the French—the ambitious and intelligent courtesan.

Lola recalled the night of the party and testified that Dujarier had not wished her to meet the guests who would be there, and particularly de Beauvallon. "I reproached Dujarier for going thus to play in society when he could not take me," said Lola. " 'It's the last time that I will go,' he assured me. 'I have promised a woman that I will take her tonight.' "

"Did Dujarier know how to shoot?" she was asked.

"No, but I shoot sometimes for pleasure. I know how to use a pistol. Dujarier thought it a singular amusement for a woman."

"Do you remember saying to Dujarier: 'You are going to fight. Take care with whom, for there are duels and duels, and choose well your seconds.' "

"Yes," said Lola. "I would have preferred older seconds."

"Didn't you say: 'You know, of course, that I am a woman but if the duel is just, I will not prevent it'?"

"Yes. I thought he was going to fight Roger de Beauvoir. If I had known his antagonist was de Beauvallon I would have been greatly agitated, for that quarrel with M. Granier de Cassagnac had moved me greatly when I learned of it from Bertrand. Had I known who the antagonist was I would have gone to the police, or to the Bois."

When asked if Dujarier had said to her: "This duel is nothing," Lola's great blue eyes were melancholy as she murmured: "Yes, but his smile was very sad."

She burst into floods of tears when his last letter to her was read. The men in the court were moved, if not all the women. A tall figure at the back of the courtroom moved restlessly as Lola's performance ended and he asked a man he had seen talking to Dumas and Berryer for information about her. She seemed like the heroine of a novel, a third bystander commented, but the tall youth, who looked like a farmer, replied: "Yes, but the heroines of the novels of everyday life do not usually look like that."

This was Gustave Flaubert, son of a local physician, who fourteen years later would be prosecuted for the immorality of his novel *Madame Bovary*, and then be acquitted of the charge. He was as obscure at the trial in Rouen as Dumas, who had driven to Rouen from Paris with Méry in a four-horse carriage, was famous. The arrival of these two celebrities had caused a stir in the court. Ruddy-faced, hair standing on end, the forty-three-year-old novelist and playwright amused the spectators with his witty answers and boisterous manner. Introduced by the court as an "auteur dramatique" he quickly pointed out that this might have been true were he not in the country of Corneille. His listeners warmed to this pointed observation, since Rouen was the birthplace of Pierre and Thomas Corneille.

"There are degrees in everything," the Judge conceded, but no one questioned Dumas as being the final authority on the subject of dueling; he had been criticized by some for not having prevented the duel. He spoke with warmth of Dujarier as a man of dual nature— "full of grace and abandon with his friends, but tight and dry with strangers. He was charming with us; we loved him with all our hearts."

When asked why he had not acted as an intermediary Dumas replied: "He told me that I was too busy, that he did not wish to waste my time. Then he said: 'It's my first duel. It's an astonishing thing that I haven't had one before now. It's a baptism to which I must submit.' "

"Did he tell you the cause of the duel?" Dumas was asked.

"He told me that it was futile and that he did not know why he was fighting. But underneath, it was the war of *Le Globe* with *La Presse*, and not of Dujarier with de Beauvallon."

The ease and flow of Dumas's testimony delighted the spectators and they settled down for some rich entertainment when he began to discuss the fine points of dueling. "In a duel," he commented, "the questions of generosity and delicacy matter less than the great question of existence."

The Advocate-General protested that this was not a moral viewpoint, and the Judge checked Dumas's entertaining discourse by reminding him that *Le Code du Duel* had no place in his library. This caused some merriment in the court and drew a somber smile from Lola. Dumas was a more entertaining witness than his son, not yet a popular idol, but busy with his collection of verse *Péchés de Jeunesse* and the early draft of *La Dame aux Camélias*. He was less concerned than his father about public appearances, and he was in a hurry to get back to Paris and his work, but he testified briefly on the knowledge he had of the accused as an excellent shot. He swore that, like all Creoles, de Beauvallon knew every aspect of the art.

When Roger de Beauvoir was called Lola thought of him as a "cupid taken out of a band-box." He was then thirty-six, a well-known man of letters, and his eccentricities amused the spectators at Rouen as they did his fellow Parisians. He preened himself in court and annoyed Lola by saying that Dujarier was an aggressive man. Recalling events at the famous supper party he described

Dujarier's toast to Mademoiselle Lhévienne as: "Anaïs, I will sleep with you within a month."

The spectators roared with laughter when de Beauvoir was reminded that earlier he had said five months.

"Oh, I don't calculate by distance; the time doesn't matter," he quipped.

M. de Guise gave a touching picture of Dujarier's last moments and of his dying murmur that he did not know why he had fought. De Guise knew instantly when he reached his side that he was lost. He recalled Bertrand showing him his blackened finger and saying that the pistol must have been fired in advance. And de Boignes, a man of letters, had told him that Dujarier had insisted it was strictly a shop quarrel.

The assembled ladies in the courtroom looked with some curiosity at the three demimondaines who tripped into view as participants in the evening's revels at the Trois Frères Provençaux. They made a flamboyant group, although they had little to say. Mademoiselle Lhévienne, twenty-one, wore a blue velvet costume with a bright red Indian cashmere shawl and a pearl-gray satin bonnet smothered in lace. She denied all memory of the party, because of the jumble of people who were present. She admitted that Dujarier had offended her momentarily but that they were quickly reconciled when she took his hand in a friendly way. Although unconscious of the argument over the game, she had learned from later talk, she said, that the quarrel was based on journalistic rivalry.

Victorine Capone, twenty-one, and Cécile-Julie John, twenty-three, all describing themselves as artists, were even more forgetful than Mademoiselle Lhévienne about the night's events. Lola studied them thoughtfully as they sat huddled in a corner, well away from the ladies of Rouen and the fashionables from Paris. Madame Albert testified that the editor stayed away from her place after she began seeing de Beauvallon. She was certain that there was bad blood between them, and that she herself figured in it to some degree.

The diverse personalities aroused so much interest in the court that de Beauvallon was almost unnoticed until called on to testify. Handsome, young and wholly at ease, he was closely watched by Lola, who had long been curious about him. She had never seen him until their courtroom encounter. She noticed that he was faultlessly dressed, in contrast to the peacock attire of Roger de Beauvoir. As he began to talk she leaned forward with breathless attention.

De Beauvallon told a smooth story of the events leading up to the duel. He insisted that he had been on excellent terms with Dujarier and had no animosity toward him, but he had felt hurt that after a hard night's play at the gaming table Dujarier seemed to suggest that he was claiming something not due him. After talking to Dujarier his seconds had deemed an encounter necessary. De Beauvallon swore that he had proposed rapiers to lessen the danger for his adversary. "I had a certain skill," he admitted modestly, "but I gave my word that I sought only to disarm, not to wound Dujarier. But he declared for the pistols."

Since his own pistols were in poor condition de Beauvallon borrowed others from his brother-in-law. They were brought to him late the evening before the encounter, he said.

"Did you know these pistols?" he was asked.

"I had never fired them," he answered firmly.

He blamed the delay in getting to the Madrid on a long wait he had for a carriage, and then on the necessity of going round for his seconds some distance from Chaillot. But de Beauvallon went to pieces when the prosecutor changed the course of the testimony and asked him about a watch he had once stolen from an aunt and had taken to a pawnbroker. For the first time he lost his nerve as this minor charge was introduced. Its irrelevancy puzzled the spectators until de Beauvallon linked it up with a threat he had received after Dujarier's death: "I shall kill M. de Beauvallon by calumny as he has killed Dujarier with a shot."

The witness was weeping as he retired, after announcing to the court: "I have told you the truth, and if I have committed this

81

fault, I have paid cruelly." He and Lola alone shed tears during the trial.

Half a dozen lawyers on both sides gave pyrotechnic displays for the benefit of the knowledgeable audience. Everything from the ethics of dueling to the night life of Paris came in for discussion. Lawyers all over France studied the evidence given in this trial, to sharpen their own technique. They were surprised by the verdict. Berryer's defense of de Beauvallon was so persuasive that he was acquitted of the charge of voluntary homicide with premeditation. Dujarier's mother and sister were awarded damages of 20,000 francs in the civil suit they brought at the same time as the major charge.

But this was not the end of the case. Dujarier's friends, conscious that Berryer's brillance, and not the facts in the case, had defeated them, decided to pursue the matter to a finish. Charles de Maynard, a spectator at the trial, stood silently in the background until it was all over. Then he told Dumas a strange story at the Jockey Club, and Dumas quickly spread it through St. Germain. De Maynard had known both Granier de Cassagnac and de Beauvallon for a long time, and had once been a second in a duel fought by the young Creole. The tale he now told was that he had been in de Beauvallon's garden at Chaillot on the morning of the duel and had seen him fire a number of shots against a wall which had a target marked with a stone. De Beauvallon had used dueling pistols belonging to d'Ecquevillez, said de Maynard, and the bullets were of the same caliber as the one that killed Dujarier.

As a result of this fresh evidence d'Ecquevillez was tried for perjury in August, 1847, and his operations with card sharps and swindlers was proved. Passing as the Vicomte d'Ecquevillez he turned out to be plain Victor Vincent, a militia captain in the Spanish service. He was sentenced to ten years' imprisonment. De Beauvallon, who had been in hiding since he could not meet the damages due Madame Dujarier, appeared to testify on his friend's behalf. But he too was caught in the net and was charged with perjury. He went on trial in Paris in October, 1847, and repeated his earlier testimony on the duel. This time he did not have Berryer to plead his case. And he did have de Maynard facing him in court with an eye-witness account of the shots he had fired in the garden at Chaillot before killing Dujarier in the Bois. He too was found guilty, but with extenuating circumstances, and he was sentenced to eight years' imprisonment. This time he did not weep but looked tranquil and relieved when he heard the verdict.

Both men were serving time in the Conciergerie when the doors were thrown open during the revolution of February, 1848. D'Ecquevillez disappeared, but de Beauvallon returned to his family plantations in Guadeloupe, where his liberation received official sanction. When the Second Empire was established he appealed for reversal of his sentence so that he could return to France, but this was denied by the Cour de Cassation in 1855.

While both men were in prison Lola was fulfilling Dumas's grim prediction made after Dujarier's death. He had found something hypnotic about her himself, a sudden violence that came to the surface, an overwhelming passion. Her eyes were at once "soft and terrible, the orbs that are either veiled with tears, or launching lightning and poignards." He went further than that: "She has the evil eye, and is sure to bring bad luck to anyone who closely links his destiny with hers, for however short a time. . . . If ever she is heard of again, it will be in connection with some terrible calamity that has befallen a lover of hers."

This time the stakes involved the overthrow of one of the most stable monarchies in Europe, as Lola turned her eyes on Bavaria. But before she reached Munich and ensnared King Ludwig I her life continued at the fashionable spas. She had become an embarrassment to Dujarier's friends and she felt that she must leave Paris. Since she knew that the rich and wordly, the princelings of Europe and the gamblers sought recreation at the spas, she went from one to another, but avoided Weimar, where Liszt had settled with his new love. She also stayed out of Prussia, where her encounter with the police might be recalled.

Before long she was seen at Wiesbaden, Homburg and Baden-Baden, where she made a particular impression in the summer of 1846, dramatically gowned in black, and easily recognizable as the recent star of a *cause célèbre*. The money left her by Dujarier enabled her to live in high style for a time, and her clothes and jewels were noted wherever she went. With Germany's thirty-six principalities it seemed likely that she might find the prince she had sought since consulting the Almanach de Gotha when she left England. And she did—in Baden-Baden. He was not a major prince, but he was rich and reasonably good-looking and lived in a small castle modeled after Versailles. When Prince Henry of Reuss-Lobenstein-Ebersdorf, head of a principality later amalgamated with Thuringia, saw Lola ride at Baden-Baden he was impressed with her dazzling looks and expert horsemanship. He invited her to visit his kingdom and for a brief space of time she held sway at his miniature court at Ebersdorf.

She was of great interest to Prince Henry's subjects as she drove past their windows, the Spanish dancer who had come to life among them. But the Prince was parsimonious and Lola's extravagance appalled him. The palace functionaries resented her arrogant interference, and things were going awry in the government of the principality when the Prince called a halt and from ardent wooing turned a chilly eye on Lola. She was bored with the Biedermann influences in any event, and the rigid formality of a petty court. But the final explosion came when she slashed her way through the Prince's orderly flower beds in riding boots and heavy skirt, taking a short cut across the palace grounds.

The gardeners ran around in consternation, and Lola mischievously repeated this act on horseback, riding through the flower beds and breaking up their inviolable symmetry. The Prince was furious and called her a devil. She answered in kind and was ordered out of his kingdom. This was the final clash and Lola left hurriedly by coach for Homburg, after billing the Prince heavily for her "services" and leaving a pile of debts behind her.

Baron Maltitz, a Bavarian who had admired her in Baden-Baden, turned up again in Homburg, and persuaded Lola that she should try her luck in Munich. She had now had a taste of court life after a succession of statesmen, musicians, writers, soldiers and adventurers as lovers. In their long talks in the gambling casinos at the spas and during their walks in the English garden at Baden-Baden, the Baron had given her provocative information on Ludwig I of Bavaria. His passion for beautiful women, his political troubles and his interest in arts and letters were already well known to Lola when she drove toward Munich in a coach that broke down with her luggage along the way.

When she finally arrived at the Goldenen Hirschen Inn outside the city she made a scene at once when she found that her rooms were not ready. The local tradesmen, hearing that Lola Montez was about to arrive, crowded around her coach as she stepped into view in riding costume and carrying her whip. She demanded instant service and soon had porters flying in all directions.

The best suite in the inn had been assigned to her. She looked it over with scorn and ordered her maid to unpack the brocade bedspread, the porcelain, crystal and mirrors with which she traveled, to give her surroundings the air of the great world. Lola traveled with the style of a theatrical star and she was now prepared to conquer a kingdom.

SIX

Adviser to the King

Lola Montez moved into the life of King Ludwig like a whirlwind, stirring this gifted monarch to an infatuation that shook up his kingdom and cost him his crown. No royal favorite ever worked with such speed and cataclysmic effect, a process apparent almost at once to the Bavarians, and soon to all of Europe. The repercussions rippled across a continent deeply stirred with the unrest that culminated in the revolutions of 1848.

Bavaria was already involved to some extent in the blaze of revolutionary spirit that Lola had learned to understand in Paris as she listened to Lamennais and his fellow philosophers. In Munich she found herself in the eye of the gathering storm, and if she did not actually initiate the revolt there, she lit the match with her high-handed domination of the King. By chance she had found in Bavaria the time, the place and the ruler responsive to her influence. Her wanderings across Europe in search of some elusive goal of her own had brought her into the sphere of the Wittelsbachs, who had been warriors, poets and artists for forty generations. They had fought in the Crusades; they had presided at Mannheim and Munich after the fashion of Versailles. They were a royal line endowed with talent and charm, but plagued by intermittent madness. More than twenty Wittelsbachs were insane, and although it was Ludwig I's grandson, Ludwig II, who was known as the "Mad King of Bavaria," eccentricity along with a touch of genius was evident in Lola's Ludwig.

He had made Munich a city of classical magnificence, and had brought treasures from all parts of the world to enrich it. A thousand years of power lay behind the Wittelsbachs when the line came to an end in 1918. And with the close of World War II Munich was in chaos, many of Ludwig's buildings were in ruins, and the gas ovens of the region remained as a scar for all time.

Lola's appearance on the scene in 1846 marked a new phase in Bavarian history, and she became a crucial figure in the fight for freedom. With indomitable faith in her own power to charm, she found her way directly to the King, ignoring obstacles and formal court procedure. She knew that her best weapon was her own physical presence. The King was a poet, a romantic, a worshiper of beauty in all its forms, from architecture to the human body. He was a complex man, an intellectual interested in the theater and all the arts, but simple in his habits and bohemian in his dress as he wandered through the streets and stayed close to the people.

Baron von Maltitz had introduced Lola at Baden-Baden to Count von Reichberg, the court chamberlain, who proved to be her ultimate link with the King, for she always made her associations count. With complete assurance she sought the director of the Court Theater, Herr Frays, but was brushed off by an attendant who told her to write a letter stating her qualifications as a dancer. She pushed him aside and forced her way into Frays's presence. He already knew something of her history in the theater—a dancer who had been hissed off the stage in London, Paris and Warsaw, whose love affairs were notorious across Europe. However, momentarily influenced by her hypnotic gaze and compelling arguments he agreed to a demonstration of her art. His doubts about her professional capacity were quickly confirmed. She was weak in the fundamentals of her art and Frays pinpointed every fault. She lacked the polish, training and precision needed for the Court Theater, which was exacting in its demands and reflected the King's discriminating taste. Lola's training had been haphazard and she did not keep in form.

To Frays's amazement she danced without a maillot, an effect that he knew would never pass muster with Karl von Abel, the most powerful member of Ludwig's Cabinet and the censor of the arts. Moreover, Fräulein Frenzal, the *première danseuse*, disliked Lola on sight and condemned her *pas seul*. Lola's rejection was inevitable but she promptly turned her attention to Count von Reichberg, believing that if he led her to the King the director of the Court Theater might be overruled. The Count urged the King to give her an audience but, busy with other matters, Ludwig replied: "Do I need to see every strolling Spanish dancer?"

"But this one is worth your while," the Count assured him.

Lola, waiting in an antechamber while the King studied the adverse report that Frays had made on her, took matters into her own hands. Once again she pushed her way past a guard to get what she wanted, without waiting for the royal permission sought by the Count. Looking slightly disheveled from this brief encounter she glided through the door of the red-and-black Pompeian chamber of the Residenz, past the inscription *Quis amare vetat: quis custodit amantes.*

The King was busy at his desk. When he looked up inquiringly he was struck by his visitor's boldness as she moved closer and took the initiative with a quick flow of words. He saw at once that this was no itinerant dancer but a beauty with fire and magnetism. The atmosphere between them grew electric as she told him of her ambition to dance at the Court Theater, and of the obstacles she had met. Her quick wit and overwhelming drive impressed him, along with her physical bearing. Finally she drew up her silken skirts and danced for him. His interest grew as he watched her, his glance flickering over the black gown that emphasized the grace of her body. Her huge blue eyes never left his face. Shiny black hair fell loosely to her snowy shoulders, framing delicately chiseled features.

Within a matter of days the story ran through the beer halls as well as the court circles of Munich that Lola Montez had snatched up a pair of scissors from the King's desk and ripped open her skin-tight bodice when Ludwig asked her if her curves were nature's work alone. At many times in her life the impulse to disrobe was strong in Lola, but on this occasion it had international implications. "Lola's beauty," said Eduard Fuchs, one of her German biographers, "particularly the splendour of her breasts, made madmen everywhere."

"I know not how—I am bewitched," the King told his Council a few days later, and he formally presented her at the court as his "best friend." Almost overnight she was established as a royal favorite and her place at the Court Theater was assured. Arrangements were made for her to appear during the entre-actes, wearing Spanish costume and performing Andalusian dances.

The King was in the royal box and all the court dignitaries were present when Lola Montez made her debut in Munich on an October day in 1846. She bowed to the King before her dance began. Her silk-and-lace costume sparkled with brilliants but, as always, something was lacking in her performance. Through the applause came the familiar hissing sound of disapproval that had now become familiar to Lola. Was it contempt for her dancing, or was it the Jesuit influence that she thought pursued her everywhere? Luise von Dobell, a young Bavarian aristocrat who had been transfixed by Lola's beauty when she met her on the street a day earlier, wearing a mantilla draped over her hair, recalled in her memoirs half a century later that her parents had told her the hissing was because Lola was an adventuress and was "the enemy of the Jesuits."

But her own impression of Lola that night was of fire darting from wonderful blue eyes and "everybody's eye following her sinuous movements, now indicative of glowing passion, now of frolic-someness . . . the audience went mad with rapture and the entire dance had to be repeated over and over again." On her second appearance she danced the cachucha in the entre-acte of the comedy *Der Weiberfeind von Benedix* and did a fandango in *Müller and Miller.* Furious that there had been hissing at Lola's first performance the King had ordered special protection for her. An organized claque of guards and theater attendants had been assigned to drown out any adverse demonstration. This was a night of triumph for Lola and the applause was deafening.

But soon there was no need for her to appear in the theater. Lola had moved into the royal circle and the King had ordered his favorite architect to build a bijou palace for her. He showered favors on Lola. She appeared in the theater, not as a performer but as a spectator, ravishingly gowned, with deep décolletage and sparkling with jewels the King had given her. Lola's box was next to the royal box, and Ludwig and she exchanged understanding glances.

Although royal mistresses were no novelty in Bavaria, or elsewhere in Europe, Ludwig, building up Munich in the image of Rome and Athens, was not romantically obsessed when Lola Montez came into his life as he reached the age of sixty. But he found something wholly irresistible in her combination of seductive arts and bright wit. The clever women he had known had often offended his aesthetic sense. He was so much the hedonist, the art collector, that women did not play an overwhelming role in his life. He had been married for a quarter of a century to Theresa of Saxe-Hildburg-hausen, who had borne him seven children and was a tolerant and unobtrusive wife.

Known as the best-looking princess in Europe when Ludwig married her, she had aged gracefully, and had never shown alarm over her husband's occasional mistresses. They were usually actresses, and she was too sure of her own place in the King's life, and of the needs of his strange nature, to let her emotions get out of hand. She accepted the fact that queens were expected to survive this embarrassment. Deeply religious, devoted to her family, never acrimonious with the King, she was much loved by the courtiers and the Bavarian people. She knew that Ludwig sought an intelligent understanding of his own wide scholarship and assorted interests in the women with whom he spent his time.

In Rome he had had a platonic romance with the Marchesa Florenzi, no beauty, but a student of metaphysics and a worshiper of Hegel and Schelling. The Marchesa had translated Hegel's *Die Phänomenologie des Geistes,* and she engaged in long metaphysical discussions with Ludwig. He had had more earthbound affairs with Charlotte von Hagn, the comedienne, and with Sophie Schroeder, wife of the tragedian Friedrich Schroeder, to whom he composed a series of poems. The women who interested him invariably stirred up his poetic impulse, usually expressed in faulty Greek meter. But an earlier romance with Lady Ellenborough, one of England's most reckless and beautiful women, had come closest to his passion for Lola. It was not until Lola came into his life, however, that Ludwig figured as one of the great romantics. Many thought that a touch of the family madness was in operation during her regime, for his other romances had never embarrassed him politically. In spite of his many loves, he was more a worshiper of beauty and brains than a man of passion, and few were deep-rooted affairs. Twenty years after his abdication he was still insisting that Lola Montez had never been his mistress in actual fact, but merely a friend and political adviser. And to the day she died Lola swore time and again, in public and in private, that their mutual devotion had been misunderstood and that he had merely found her a comforting friend who had supported him in putting through his own liberal views and plans.

Neither the Queen nor close members of the royal entourage seemed to question this interpretation while the King still reigned, although the aura of romance was overwhelming during the hectic year and a half that Lola held sway in Bavaria. "Shameless and impudent," said Heinrich von Treitschke, German historian, "and as insatiable in her voluptuous desires as Sempronia. She could converse with charm among friends; manage mettlesome horses; sing in thrilling fashion; and recite amorous poems in Spanish. The King, an admirer of feminine beauty, yielded to her magic. It was as if she had given him a love philtre. For her he forgot himself; he forgot the world; and he even forgot his royal dignity."

There was no doubt that the King's dignity suffered considerably when Lola took it into her head to kick a champagne bucket through the air because a waiter annoyed her in a restaurant. But her husky voice, singing a ballad with the intonations of a Marlene Dietrich; her warm response to the verses he read to her as they strolled in the Nymphenburg woods or in the English Garden close to the Residenz; her spirited conversation and fund of racy anecdotes kept him in a state of bewitchment.

The English Garden, where they spent much time, had been laid out by Benjamin Thompson, an American physicist and adventurer from Massachusetts who fled as a loyalist at the time of the American Revolution. He went first to Britain, then to Munich, where he organized the Bavarian Academy of Arts and Sciences and was known as Count Rumford.

The Queen must have been the first to realize how deeply Ludwig was under Lola's spell, but she did not hesitate to receive her at court, and to give her full acceptance in the public eye. Their daughters received her in the same friendly spirit, and no member of the royal family showed open animosity, although agents for Count Metternich, the master diplomat of Austria for nearly forty years, watched for every nuance in their behavior and reported their findings to Vienna, to be relayed to the Dowager Empress Caroline Augusta, who bluntly said that her brother Ludwig had always had fire in his flanks. The diplomats, the Cabinet, the clergy, the army and the large student body in Munich were well aware that the King was under the spell of a formidable siren.

George Henry Francis, an English diplomat who lived in Munich when Lola did and later became editor of the *Morning Post* in London, wrote in *Fraser's Magazine* of January, 1848: "Her manners are distinguished; she is a graceful and hospitable hostess, and she understands the art of dressing to perfection. . . . She is merciless in her man-killing propensities. . . . She loves power for its own sake; she is too hasty and too steadfast in her dislikes; she has not sufficiently learned to curb the passion which seems natural to her Spanish blood . . ."

If the courtiers and burghers viewed her with fear she had solid standing and a court of her own with the men of wit, scholarship and achievement who moved in Ludwig's circle. With the passion of a Renaissance patron, he had surrounded himself with architects, sculptors, artists, writers and musicians, and Lola bloomed in company of this kind. These men reminded her of the brilliant days in Paris, except that in Munich the royal milieu gave added sparkle to her ascendancy.

The King told Lola, as they moved among his treasures, that he had first dreamed of Munich as the modern Florence when visiting Italy in his late teens. He was only eighteen and enjoying Rome when he was called home to head the Bavarian Army, but in the years that followed he returned more than fifty times. On his third trip he bought the Villa Malta on the Pincio, with a view of the campagna. Orange trees grew in his garden. Water cascaded on his terraces and bright-plumaged birds flashed through his trees. He seemed a true Prince of Bohemia as artists and sculptors surrounded him and he bought paintings, bronzes, vases, cameos and all manner of treasures to take back to Bavaria.

The young Prince, idealistic, a good soldier but hating war and his father's alliance with Napoleon, felt the Italian mystique that was then drawing artists to Rome from many countries, including young American sculptors, writers and painters. He lounged in the smoky interior of the Caffè Greco in Rome, gossiping with Canova, Thorwaldsen and Goethe, who wrote in 1809 to his friend Bettina Brentano: "The Prince Royal of Bavaria is a spring day carefree and luminous. He is perfumed with youth, of exquisite freshness. It's a florescence of spirit . . . his best gifts are still in him without having received the disenchantment of the outside world."

Ludwig had now accomplished what he had set out to do with Munich. His worn, clever face, almost Mephistophelian at times, with piercing eyes and cleft chin, bore the stamp of his history as he continued to function like Lorenzo the Magnificent, patron of the arts. Lola played up to this vanity in him when he discussed with her the art treasures of the world. He chose to talk sometimes of his travels, his cherished years in Italy, his philosophy, his mystical approach to life, or to read the verses he composed with such ease, and frequently dedicated to her.

Long before the King met Lola he had poured out verse about other loves, about nature, political events, his monumental buildings, the life of the people in the streets, his travels and his love of country. He had started writing it in his youth when the sensitive young, tired of the Napoleonic Wars, were leaning strongly toward the mystical and metaphysical. As a student he had been exposed to three scholars who had influenced him profoundly. One was Johannes von Müller, the Swiss historian who roused in him a deep love for the Germanic states, and made him an articulate patriot. Another was Friedrich Rückert, an expert in the Oriental classics and the occult who was identified with Erlangen, and Göttingen. And the third who helped to shape the course of his life was Andreas Justinus Kerner, the lyric poet and physician who started the Swabian school of poetry at Weinsberg, where he lived from 1819 to 1851.

Kerner, whom he also met at Göttingen, was profoundly versed in the occult. Ludwig helped him establish his school of poetry and many strange experiments were conducted in this environment. The King's interest in cults was well known to his people, and it came to the surface intermittently in affairs of state. His family, well used to the Wittelsbach eccentricity, had tolerant understanding of these characteristics in the gifted and kindly Ludwig. In actual fact, he and Lola shared an interest in the mystical that ran like a thread through their strange love affair. She had been having visions ever since the death of Dujarier, and she said that a clairvoyant had told her to come to Munich.

The public openly called her the sorceress, but to many she was the new Du Barry as she rode triumphantly along the Ludwigstrasse in a gilded carriage lined with ermine. Her behavior in public soon aroused comment and resentment. She made scenes and was rude to tradespeople. It was noted that she swaggered about in riding costume, superbly tailored, and in the evenings she blazed with jewels at the opera. Stories spread that she beat her servants and even tore at their faces with her nails. According to Francis, again writing in *Fraser's Magazine*, she had been known to spit in the face of a bishop, thrash a coalheaver, smash shopwindows, crack her whip or break her parasol over the head of a courtier who had defied her. Francis was careful to add that most of these stories, which he considered "monstrous and ridiculous imputations," were sent to the French and English papers from Munich, and he felt that they might be inspired by Lola's enemies.

However, there was no doubt that she stirred up scenes as she descended like an empress on the Munich shops, buying clothes or bibelots and wrangling over trifles. "My Louis will pay," she would say when presented with a bill. But the King put a stop to this when it came to his attention through tradesmen and state officials, and Lola soon learned to modify her use of his name in public.

The hours she passed alone with him were an education in themselves. They read Cervantes together and each helped the other with German and Spanish. Ludwig was charmed by Lola's accent. The mélange of languages that she knew contributed to an impression of illiteracy that was misleading. Her ghosted autobiography and the letters she left do little to correct the feeling that Lola was not a scholar; but the fact remains that she was brilliantly responsive and informed. Although English was her mother language, she spoke it with a pronounced accent, and she felt most at home in French. Her

German was limited but she learned much from the King. She knew just enough Spanish to persuade the knowing that she was not Spanish born, the fiction that she spread from time to time. She could rattle off snatches of Hindustani, remembered from her childhood days, and with a little Italian and Polish it was her boast that she could speak seven languages.

Lola soon moved from dalliance and poetry to politics. Astonished to find herself in so significant a role, she quickly seized the reins and made a play for power, something she had always longed for but never achieved. Unlike the famous French courtesans who were subtle in spreading confusion between monarch and courtiers, she showed the tough drive and violent exhibitionism more characteristic of the 1970's. Lola made no attempt to hide her power; she gloried in it.

Her fame as a courtesan had obscured to some extent her intellectual gifts. Men like Dumas, Dujarier, Balzac and Méry had acknowledged her skill in expressing herself and her special gift for influencing men. Until she became the King's favorite in Bavaria her chief preoccupation had been her own social climb, but her literary friends in Paris had given her a broader view of mankind. Ludwig was impressed with her political prescience, her liberal ideas, and the association she had had with great men of letters. She had come into his life at the crucial moment when the liberals were locked in combat with the establishment that he represented but did not inwardly approve. As he grappled each day with the mounting problems of incipient revolt, Lola forced him to act with firmness and decision. The old order was resisting change and the students were intent on running the university as they saw fit.

In Munich, as in Paris, it was soon observed that she was not the illiterate wanton she had been assumed to be. Men listened with attention when exposed to her power of persuasion. She was by no means gauche or untutored in social usages. By the time she attached herself to the Bavarian court she had seen most of the capitals of Europe and had learned how to bend powerful men to her will, but when charm failed she did not hesitate to assert herself, often to her own undoing. In moments of stress she was apt to lash out with maniacal violence. The people of Munich soon viewed her as a Jezebel and she was hissed and booed when she appeared in public.

But the men close to the King recognized her power and in spite of their deep resentment they found it advisable to defer to her at first. They visited her in the house that the King had rented for her on the Theresienstrasse while her own mansion was being built. She was known to have discretion in keeping state secrets and she listened attentively to the experts in different fields, but there was no limit to her lust for power and homage. From her earliest years she had observed women influencing men with their minds as well as with their charms, and she had learned her lessons at unusual sources. If she lacked the subtlety of the more famous courtesans she had a magnetic approach that served her well until her violent temper exploded and repeatedly wrecked her plans.

The women of Munich thought that Lola dressed deliberately to ensnare men, as they studied her suggestive attire, usually fitted to her naked body and skin tight in its emphasis on her curves. Her portrait circulated all over Munich and was used on stickpins and tobacco boxes. The students serenaded her until she became their enemy. But her whip, her dogs and her explosive temper intimidated many. Page boys cringed when she boxed their ears. Messengers could never speed fast enough to satisfy her. A fumble by her maid in dressing her threw her into a passion. When she took her ailing bulldog to a veterinarian and he did not improve, she slapped the man, picked up the dog in her arms and took him home, where she nursed him back to health. Lola had a passion for animals of all kinds, dating back to her early days in India, and she often said that she preferred them to human beings. When she was annoyed she thought nothing of letting loose her dogs in a group of people, and chaotic scenes were apt to follow.

The King's infatuation for Lola was ridiculed in stinging cartoons.

His well-known eccentricities were played up, and he was constantly pictured as the troubadour with the guitar. The fact that this time his mistress was an outsider, an unfathomable character with a tarnished history, outraged the people, who were sympathetic to the Queen. The situation lent itself to ridicule, and in one of the cartoons Ludwig was drawn as a crowned satyr with a flute sporting with a naked nymph and a dog. Another by the well-known artist Wilhelm von Kaulbach, who became director of the Munich Academy after Ludwig's abdication, roused his fury. When he heard that von Kaulbach had drawn Lola with a snake twined around her naked body, and a cup of poison in her hand, he went to the artist's studio, studied the cartoon and lost his temper, although his disposition in general was equable. "Lola will pay you out for this," he said. And Lola did. Within an hour the King was back, this time with Lola and one of her most formidable dogs. Von Kaulbach, knowing what to expect, was waiting for her with a whip of his own and his Newfoundland dog. He cracked his whip as Lola freed her mastiff. The Newfoundland met him head on and chaos ensued, with both dogs fighting their way into the courtyard. The King, Lola and von Kaulbach followed, creating another one of the ridiculous scenes that had all Munich talking.

This artist was never forgiven by the King, who was surrounded by painters of all kinds whom he commissioned to do portraits of Lola, clad and half-clad. His most prized was one by Joseph Stieler, now in the Nymphenburg Palace at Munich, and in the days of Ludwig a treasured entry in his famous gallery of beauties at the royal residence. It shows Lola in black velvet with a red carnation tucked into a drift of lace on her shining black hair. No sooner was it added to the King's collection than Count Arco-Valley insisted that Stieler's handsome portrait of his wife in blue velvet be removed from this collection, no longer composed entirely of angels.

Ludwig's beauties were selected regardless of rank or importance. If he saw an uncommonly attractive face in the street its owner was a candidate for immortality. The wife of a chicken merchant and the daughter of the butcher who supplied the royal residence with meat were included because they were types. So was the shoemaker's daughter. But most of the thirty-six paintings were of court beauties, elaborately costumed in velvets, ribbons and laces, in contrast to the simpler peasant attire. Ludwig's daughters were included, as well as the cold-faced Lady Ellenborough and Lady Spencer, an Englishwoman much admired by the King. The pictures of the Marchesa Florenzi and Charlotte von Hagn were testimony to the fact that in looks they were no match for the gorgeous Lola, whom the King so blithely described in one of his countless verses about her:

> Eyes as blue as vaults of heaven,
> Sunlit as the summer air!
> Like the plumage of the raven
> Is thy soft and shining hair.
>
> Form divine and every feature
> Framed to set the heart awhirl,
> Like some wild and woodland creature
> Is my Andulasian girl.

It was Ludwig's custom to retreat at times from affairs of state to spend dreamy hours in this gallery of beauties, and it was here that he composed most of his verse. From the moment Lola walked into his life he saw her as the ideal subject for his collection. M. Lesniowski, a Warsaw editor who fell in love with her when she visited Poland and eventually was dismissed from his paper, described her rhapsodically in the Warsaw *Courier* as possessing in perfect proportion the twenty-seven requisites for beauty defined by a well-known Spanish poet. Her eyes alone differed from the specifications, suggesting sixteen different shades of forget-me-not and her Irish heritage. In all else she was the Andalusian type. "Hair soft as silk, rivalling the shining plumage of a raven, falls luxuriantly down her back; on her slender, delicate neck, whose gleaming whiteness puts swansdown to shame, is poised her lovely face," wrote this observer after he had seen her dance in Warsaw in 1845.

After Lola's portrait was hung in his gallery the King spent hours gazing at it when he could not be with her in the flesh. He saw nothing but charm and tenderness in her, if one is to accept the evidence of this rambling verse:

> Never thou grievest thy lover with heartlessness and idle caprices
> Never with him dost thou play a wantoning game,
> Self-seeking knowest thou not; generous and kind is thy nature,
> Bounteous thou art, my beloved, and ever the same.
> Happy is he who commands thy heart for his eager possessing! . . .
> "Happiness, happiness," still I cried with insatiable longing,
> And such I discovered in thee, thou woman of Spain.

When Lola moved into her own establishment at 19 Barerstrasse everything possible had been done to perfect her miniature palace, which stood until 1914 and was occupied years after her time by the British Legation. She and the King together supervised the work, and his best designers and craftsmen collaborated in harmonizing the period details. Francis, who lived nearby and often called on Lola, thought it strange that "such a tigress should choose so beautiful a den" and described it as one of the "most bijou homes in Munich." Its murals were done by artists from designs found in Herculaneum and Pompeii. A Raphael hung on the walls of the reception room, along with works by the best of the modern German painters. A good portrait of Ludwig had the place of honor, next to an indifferent one of Lola.

The house was two stories high, with bronze balconies at the upper windows and delicately tinted curtains screening the rooms where history was being made. In course of time iron grilles were needed to protect Lola from the people who jeered at her from the street. Visitors were impressed with the simplicity and airiness of the dwelling as compared with the heavy furnishings of the Munich mansions of the period. Although the drawing room was English in feeling, the house as a whole was Italianate, with gleaming marble floors, costly tapestries and huge mirrors reflecting statuary in alcoves. The gilded paneling of the public rooms, the crystal staircase down which Lola descended with the air of a ruler, a Sèvres porcelain mantelpiece, the silver chandelier above that shed its beams on her jewels, made a handsome setting for her receptions.

Books from the royal collection were scattered about, and her embroidery frame suggested that she practiced the traditional feminine arts, even through a cloud of her own cigar smoke. A spinet and guitar, both of which she played, were in evidence, close to the fauteuil where she relaxed when the King was with her. Music was an essential part of all her receptions, and the guest list was diverse and at times bohemian. There were poetry readings and topical conversation, with Lola moving from group to group, stirring up talk on politics, the theater and the ways of the people. There was always a tenor to sing, a poet to read his verse. Things might get boisterous around her generous buffet as the night wore on, but Lola kept her head with moderate sips of Tokay, even while she topped one ribald story with another. Sometimes she was all in black, with a circlet of diamonds resting on her hair; again she would come down her crystal staircase in scarlet velvet, her lips as brilliant as the rubies round her snowy neck. Uniformed sentries stood on guard outside the house on party nights; her indoor staff were decked with braid and insignia. A flag flew over the semi-royal residence.

The King and Lola sometimes held their political consultations in the large flower garden behind the house. The coach house and stables were comparatively modest. The King usually arrived on foot and was ushered in by servants more ceremoniously uniformed than those at his own court. Lola often kept him waiting while she completed her grooming. Her costume, her hair, her complexion were always in perfect order and in high style before she would show herself. On the one birthday he spent with her the King gave her 40,000 gulden and a silver service valued at 6,000 gulden. She was insistent on having her way in all respects, and when Ludwig thought it extravagant to pay 500 gulden to have one of her ceilings

101

repainted in the tint she wished, she said she would pay for it herself since he was such an old miser. The upshot was that the King footed the bill.

Lola laughed over his small personal economies, viewing him actually as Lorenzo the Magnificent, the title he had earned for himself in Munich for his great contribution to its development, its possessions and its style. The city was variously known as the "Second Athens" and "Modern Florence," and he was still enjoying the worldwide attention the Walhalla at Ratisbon was attracting. This was his Hall of Fame, paid for by himself and dedicated in 1842. Franz von Klenze, an architect and landscape painter who specialized in Greek design, had worked on it for twelve years. It was a replica of the Parthenon, overlooking the Danube, and in Lola's day it had busts of Gluck and Kant, of Blücher and Holbein, among others.

Munich was a city of meandering streets and its chief ornament was the Nymphenburg Palace when Ludwig first knew it, but by the time Lola came into his life its buildings and art possessions were known the world over. For years the King had been rounding up choice possessions for his dream city. Archaeological diggings had been fostered in Italy for the young Prince, who had been made a citizen of Rome in 1820. He was known as Il Miracolo when he toured Sicily with von Klenze, who had designed his Walhalla and also the royal residence, with its maze of galleries, grottoes and baroque decoration. Von Klenze worked in the Italian Renaissance and neo-Greek traditions. The classical chambers in the palace had rows of figures larger than life, done by Ludwig von Schwanthaler, who sculptured the colossal statue *Bavaria* for the King. He was responsible for most of the statuary housed in the Old Pinakothek, which contained the paintings that the Wittelsbach Electors had been buying from the sixteenth century on. The Glyptothek, also designed by von Klenze, housed the archaeological treasures.

The two men worked together under the eye of the King, planning the museums, monuments, arches and churches that surrounded the Ludwigstrasse and the Odeonsplatz, once these had been laid out to Ludwig's satisfaction. The Arch of Triumph, reminiscent of those in Paris and Berlin, stood at one end of the stately thoroughfare. Statues of Homer and Aristotle guarded the State Library. The Ludwigskirche was Romanesque and the King violently disliked the fresco of the Last Judgment and banished the muralist, Peter von Cornelius, who had worked with him in Rome.

It had taken time to accustom the people to the magnificence Ludwig had given Munich. The burghers sometimes marveled but more often they sneered at the huge marble buildings going up, the art treasures that filled them, the wide avenues with lordly vistas. Ludwig had spent thirty million marks of his own money on art treasures he had picked up all over Europe, and twenty million on scientific and other institutions. "Only the very best is good enough for me," he told the archaeologists, architects and sculptors who did his bidding.

In many respects he emerged as one of the most learned and progressive monarchs of the nineteenth century. Lola, in her autobiography, chose to describe him with extravagance as the Father of his Country. She never failed to point out, and with truth, that Munich had advanced from being a third-class to a first-class European capital. "No monarch of a whole century did so much for the cause of religion and human liberty as he," she added, but there had been some serious variations of this theme along the way.

In making Munich one of the well-designed cities of the world Ludwig practiced parsimony at the court and with his family, if not with Lola. Expenses were cut to a minimum, black bread was served at the royal table, and uniforms were simplified, although it was still the era of rococo furnishings and elaborate costumes. Ludwig, tall and spare, leaning forward like a reed bent in the wind, hurried through the streets in threadbare clothes, wearing narrow trousers with gaiters, a long, tightly buttoned coat, and a nondescript hat or, more often, none at all. He frequently carried an umbrella at a time when this accessory was a curiosity, and Lola told of a dressing

103

gown he had, green with age, that he had worn for ten years and would not give up.

Although he observed full court decorum he seemed to be happiest wandering about unnoticed by night or by day, enjoying his majestic buildings and the ways of the people. His nomadic tastes and his impatience with formality did not alter the fact that he maintained a regal air, and reacted sharply when people took liberties with him. He nodded friendly greetings to those who lined up and doffed their hats to him according to Lola, and, he liked to be called "Mr. Wittelsbach" instead of Der König. Yet there were times when he ignored his people completely and dashed along without a glimpse or a word, depending on his mood. He had been known to knock the hat off a bystander who had failed to bare his head as he passed, but he was more likely to throw his arm around the shoulders of a burgher sitting in a beer hall reading his paper.

When Prince Ludwig became King in 1825, after the death of his father, King Maximilian Joseph, he was already forty, a highly cultivated, traveled and experienced man but with the mild touch of eccentricity that characterized him all through life. He never failed to interest the knowledgeable and throughout his life he preferred the company of scholars and artists to that of politicans and soldiers. The impression prevailed when he ascended the throne that this wandering Prince, this lover of the arts, this footloose poet who joined wandering groups in pastoral revels, was too much the Haroun-al-Raschid to fill his father's shoes. Maximilian had ruled with such power that Bavaria had become the most influential kingdom in South Germany. Its links with Prussia and Austria were close through the marriage of two of his daughters to the rulers of these kingdoms.

But Count Metternich and the other diplomats of Europe had chosen to make fun of the young Prince at the Congress of Vienna in 1814, when he represented his country in discussion of the problems that had developed from the Napoleonic Wars. His passion for art came to the fore at that time, when Metternich played host in Vienna to Talleyrand and Lord Castlereagh, to Czar Alexander of Russia, King Frederick William of Prussia and young Prince Ludwig of Bavaria.

The Prince startled them all with his emotional plea for the restitution of the treasures that Napoleon had confiscated in his drive across Europe. He argued that the Elgin marbles and paintings should be turned over to Lord Wellington. Gesticulating wildly and blazing with anger when he got no response, Ludwig saw that he was being laughed at by the imperious Count Metternich, who would try again to curb him when Lola Montez came into his life. There had been much interference and animosity in the intervening years between the lordly Metternich and the bohemian King.

But elsewhere in Europe Ludwig was soon recognized as a liberal king, learned, progressive, humane. The fact that he wrote deplorable poetry was much commented on, but it was widely read for its novelty as the work of a picturesque monarch. Moreover, it often reflected his political outlook. The *Illustrated London News* of April 3, 1847, described his poems as being "curious rather than excellent," the work of a "man of more taste than talent, more sensibility and feeling for the beautiful in art than true knowledge of its principles."

For the first decade of his rule King Ludwig tried to liberalize the prevailing laws, and surround himself with broad-minded men. He modernized the courts and swept away old feudal customs and privileges. He simplified royal procedure, and minimized ceremonial fuss. Every department of state was reorganized and he insisted on economy, except where his own plans for a stately city were involved. Press censorship was abolished and Protestant representation became part of the academic and church life of Bavaria. Things were going smoothly along these lines when the tide turned with the revolution of 1830 in France. The German princes who had been breaking away moved back into the Catholic fold, Ludwig among them. He realized that what had happened to his godparents Louis XVI and Marie Antoinette in 1793 could also happen to him. He had lived for six months at the Tuileries and he knew Paris well. His early memories included revolutionary horrors and the flight of his father with his family from Strasbourg when Maximilian finally decided to desert the Napoleonic legions in 1813.

As the Ultramontane party, representing the most conservative policies, assumed full power in Bavaria the King moved with the tide and was subject to its influence. Its followers represented a revival of the Gallicans, who had sworn by full papal authority in France before the Revolution. Ultramontane meant "beyond the mountains" and its fundamental philosophy was that the Roman Catholic Church should exercise control in state issues, and particularly in education, the arts and sciences. Its chief protagonist in Munich was Karl von Abel, who had held the post of Minister of Education for years until Lola crossed his path and destroyed his power. Most of his appointees were Jesuits, so that the entire field of education in Bavaria was subject to church edict at this time.

With the Ultramontane party crowding him on all sides Ludwig restored the press censorship he had once abandoned. Monasteries and church schools were everywhere and the black robes of the religious orders were seen all over Bavaria. New laws involving crimes of sacrilege and lèse-majesté went into effect and Protestant as well as Catholic soldiers were ordered to kneel when the Host was borne past. Lutherans and Calvinists felt oppressed under this regime, and when the King appointed von Abel to enforce these measures, this Ultramontane minister symbolized to Protestant Bavarians the ultimate in religious tyranny.

This was the situation in Munich when Lola arrived on the scene and created another major problem for the King. He was already bitterly embroiled with his ministers and was tired of intrigue and repression. He knew that the people in the beer halls were ready for trouble, and in many ways he sympathized with them. His more liberal friends at the university were restless under the Jesuit regime and a tribunal had been set up at Landshut to study adverse opinion. The feeling prevailed that the law-abiding Bavarians were in the grip of another Inquisition. Opinions hardened and they began to scoff at the King's magnificent buildings and to agitate for freedom and better living conditions for the poor.

This was all too clear to Lola. But things happened fast after her appearance on the scene. Nothing the King did met with the approval of the people. His Ultramontane ministers and clerical advisers were all too ready to find incriminating evidence in the fact that the pair shut themselves up for extended talks and then came out with drastic edicts, such as the royal decree shifting von Abel from his post as Minister of Education to the much less significant portfolio of Minister of the Interior. This in effect was designed to curb the Jesuitical influence in the colleges and schools, and it was Lola's idea. Von Abel had been exercising complete control over education and the arts.

Von Abel's fall from total power was clearly a defeat for the Jesuits, and the Catholic clergy promptly denounced Lola Montez all over Bavaria. The papers ridiculed the devotion of the sixty-year-old King to his twenty-nine-year-old inamorata. But the more the public bedeviled Lola, the more the King loved her, he said in one of his poems. Through her his life had been ennobled, he told her in rhyme, adding that he gave her his affection, his confidence and his esteem.

The people of Munich were slow moving and entrenched in their ways. They lived on the beer they brewed and shortly before Lola appeared there had been a revolt over a rise in the price of beer. The King prided himself on being a man of the people, and he wished them to enjoy the magnificent city he had built for them. He favored music in the streets, good food in every home, superior schools and a renaissance of the arts but, as William Bolitho has put it: "He had settled for a heavenly second-best . . . to put up with priests instead of troubadours, bells instead of fairs, clericalism instead of universal good-will."

This was an aspect of life in Bavaria that impressed Lola as she studied the white churches gleaming through dense forests alive with deer. All her prejudices were aroused by the sight of so many monasteries close to the picturesque Bavarian houses. She knew that the King had been under the influence of the Ultramontane ministry for a decade, and that his conservative Cabinet could no longer cope with the rising tide of hatred and discontent among the people. However, Lola herself proved to be the fuse that set off the bombshell.

The King listened attentively to her comments on the men she had met across Europe, and to the liberal views that had swung her from the imperialistic outlook of her Anglo-Indian days to the iconoclasm of the French philosophers, and particularly the anticlerical outlook of Lamennais. First by insidious indirection, then by an open show of power, she strengthened in him a revival of his own early liberalism. Lola had her own sources of information, for she corresponded with army officers, young diplomats and political dissenters in various parts of Europe. She was always ready to convey news to the King on his visits and she listened attentively to his recital of his arguments with his ministers. Occasionally he invited her to the Residenz to consult directly with him or with his advisers.

Count Metternich's allies in Munich had much to report about the courtiers who alternately fawned over Lola and snubbed her. The clergy and the courtiers had always deplored Ludwig's bohemian habits and his disregard for form, but nothing had ever equaled their resentment when they realized that they were being ruled by Lola Montez. The ladies of the nobility avoided her as much as they could, but took stock of the jewels and favors the King bestowed on her. Finally Metternich persuaded the Empress that the King must be freed from the spell that the Spanish dancer exercised over him. The courtiers were upset, the townspeople and students were in revolt, and the peasants believed that she was practicing black magic and must be banished from Bavaria.

SEVEN

A Woman Rules

Lola was in trouble within two months after establishing herself in the King's counsels. Just as she was beginning to influence his decisions, Baron von Pechmann, the Munich chief of police, pronounced her a "mere adventuress" who should be ousted from the Kingdom. The fearless Baron had his ears boxed by Lola for daring to question the demotion of von Abel. The King turned on him, too, and banished him from Munich, telling him that he might find the air purer in Landshut. Private appeals from the men around him, such as von Pechmann's devastating report on Lola's history before reaching Munich, made no impression on the stubborn sovereign.

But a major crisis followed when Ludwig decided to have his beautiful counselor naturalized. By giving her official status, with a title and property, he hoped to strengthen her position and allay public anxiety about her status. When the decree for her naturalization was submitted to the ministers for signature they met in angry conclave and drew up a remonstrance on February 11, 1847, unique in the annals of kings, except on the brink of abdication.

Von Abel sent the document to the royal residence by messenger although the text had leaked out in the *Augsburg Zeitung* and was already in circulation across Europe. Ludwig read that the naturalization of Señora Lola Montez would be the greatest calamity that could be inflicted on Bavaria, and that the Bavarian people in "the cabin of the poor and the palace of the rich believed themselves to be governed by a foreign woman whose reputation is branded in public opinion."

Lola's sins were listed in sequence. Because of her, the King read, respect for his sovereignty had declined. National feeling was impaired. The European press daily printed scandalous anecdotes and made degrading attacks upon him. "It is not alone the glory and well-being of Your Majesty's Government that is compromised, but the very existence of royalty itself," the remonstrance read.

Each signer of the document was ready "to sacrifice his fortune and his life for the King" but this assurance did not alter the fact that they were giving him an ultimatum. All would resign unless he changed his course. Von Abel called with a personal plea after the King had had time to study the remonstrance, but he left the Residenz disheartened. The King had already consulted Lola and he gave the ministers twenty-four hours in which to reconsider their decision. That night he was heard to remark at a reception given at Lola's house: "I will not give up Lola. I will never give her up. My kingdom for Lola!"

The Cabinet was dismissed and with von Abel completely out of the picture, another, known as "Lolitto's Cabinet," was appointed, headed by Baron von Schrenk. It soon fell from grace with Lola, too, and in a moment of crisis she approved the King's choice of Baron von Maurer, a scholarly liberal, to serve as Minister of Justice; Baron Zu-Rhein, a Viennese gourmet versed in arts and letters, to take von Abel's place as Minister of the Interior; Councillor Zenetti to be Minister of Finance; and Major General von Hohenhausen, an ambitious kingmaker, to serve as Minister of War.

All were lawyers, liberal in their outlook, and von Maurer was the first Protestant to hold office in the Bavarian Cabinet.

But von Maurer was a man of independence. He refused to kowtow to Lola and he showed resistance to her naturalization as a Bavarian. He resented both her seductive tactics and her overbearing manner, and he refused to go to her house for political consultation; nor did he think that his colleagues should surrender their pride and status in this way. But only von Hohenhausen did. However, unrest and mutiny continued among the King's closest advisers. The aides who accompanied him on his expeditions changed constantly, and the courtiers preserved a cool but wary attitude where Lola was concerned.

A further reshuffling of the Cabinet by the King brought von Berks into prominence as Minister of the Interior. Wholly committed to Lola's desires, he was also in love with her. But his influence was counterbalanced by that of Prince Wallerstein, whom the King had brought back from his embassy post in Paris to serve as Minister of Foreign Affairs. The Prince not only was immune to Lola's charm, but was frankly antagonistic. Although a foe of the Jesuits, his anticlerical views did not make him her ally, and he openly disapproved of her naturalization as a Bavarian.

Nevertheless the naturalization of Lola by the King gave her official status and a fresh access of power that could not be denied. She was created Baroness of Rosenthal and Countess of Landsfeld, and received patents of special naturalization. At the same time she was granted an annuity of 20,000 florins ($25,000) a year and the Landsfeld estates, with feudal rights over more than two thousand people. The Queen made her a Canoness of the Order of St. Theresa, which she had personally founded, and the King, in announcing her honors, spoke of her "artistic services rendered to the Crown." Her Montalvo ancestry was used to back her right to a coronet, and her title was devised from the first syllables of Landshut and Feldberg, her new domain. Her coat of arms, surmounted by the coronet of a countess, displayed an upright sword with gold hilt, a lion rampant, a silver dolphin and a red rose.

Zu-Rhein, contradicting other ministers who had dealt with her, insisted that she had not interfered in Cabinet affairs or influenced the King in these councils. Ludwig talked openly of the help Lola was giving him, and expressed his gratitude in public and in the floods of verse he poured out while the crisis was acute.

Few details were lost on the Austrian Empress as Metternich and she watched this rising tide of power. When it was clear to them that Lola's hold on the King could not be broken by reason or persuasion, a decision was made to use the age-old technique of buying her off. But they made a serious miscalculation in Lola's case, for it was power rather than riches that she valued. With the King at her command it seemed no sacrifice to reject an offer of $250,000 drawn on the Banque Rothschild to leave Bavaria and promise never to return. She had no fear for her future, and her sense of power was in full play.

Working with the Archbishop of Munich, Count Metternich sent an emissary to plead with her at the house on the Barerstrasse. As the most experienced diplomat in Europe the Count had subdued statesmen, churchmen and famous women in his time, but he had picked up the wrong cue in Lola's case. She listened attentively to what his intermediary had to say, and watched him with curiosity as he opened a portfolio and flourished notes, suggesting that she leave "this drunken town." She asked from whom the offer had come and was told that it was from the Imperial Government at Vienna. He added that her life was in danger and that the people of Munich were in the mood to rise against her. Lola reacted violently. She clutched the notes that lay before her and flung them in all directions. This seemed to her to be the ultimate insult, although other measures had been tried to remove her. She had already haughtily rejected the suggestion that she marry a nobleman who had been carefully selected for this role. The King deeply resented his sister's interference and Metternich's assumption that "Lola was for sale."

A fresh storm blew up when she demanded a Spanish chaplain of assured discretion for her private chapel. None of the Bavarian clergy wished to have anything to do with Lola, knowing the up- roar it would entail. One of the jokes current in the Munich beer halls was that not even a priest could maintain the image of moral- ity in Lola's presence. The Archbishop of Munich was called in at this point and he remonstrated personally with the King and urged him to set a good example for his people. When he found he was being wholly ineffectual he turned the matter over to the Cardinal of Breslau, Primate of Poland, who traveled to Munich to confer with the King. This time Ludwig was warned that he would lose not only his country but also his own soul.

The King tried to persuade the Primate that his relations with Lola were platonic. "This love inspires an ardent friendship, the most high that one could imagine," he said. "If you drive me to extremes you will have my death on your conscience." The Cardinal left, persuaded that the King was possessed. This opinion was shared by dignitaries all over Europe. The London *Times* of March 2, 1847, noted that a ministry that had directed the Bavarian councils for ten years had been "shattered to pieces" and the King had been carried by storm. Nor did Lola show any sign of giving up her prize. "She reigns supreme at Munich, dispenses all dignities, and bestows all favors," the editorial continued. "She has just bespoken a Countess's title and fine domain, and is clearly not at all inclined to appreciate or reward herself illiberally . . . if the only political consequences of the disreputable connexion were the naturalization of a French and Spanish dancer, there would be little occasion for the Bishop of Augsburg's daily tears and the Bavarian Ministry's public remonstrance."

Lola's experiences in London were recalled and her subsequent trip to Warsaw, where she clawed at the eyes of an officer who tried to arrest her. Now, however, she "had made a bargain of her boleros and had bounded *per saltum* from the precarious shelter of provincial patronage into a Royal palace and a King's favour." And if she had not physically attacked Ludwig's ministers she had managed to oust them. But the *Times* expressed the view that it would be treating the King harshly to deprive him of his throne for a folly in which many sovereigns had afforded him a precedent.

Immediately after this attack Lola replied to the *Times* on March 11, 1847, that the change in the Ministry was a spontaneous act of the King's and that it was paying her too great a compliment to suppose that she was a party to such a measure. "From what I have seen and heard of His Majesty," she wrote, "I should think he had very just grounds for taking the step which he did."

For more than a year Lola was in full command, while all Europe took note of the King's infatuation and her growing power. She met each issue head on, thereby intensifying an already dangerous situation. Ludwig would hear no ill of her from any source. In the end the courtiers found it politic to fawn, the clergy were outwitted, and many of the scholars and artists openly admired her. Even her enemies acknowledged her charm and her intelligence. The free thinkers and Protestants of Germany as a whole viewed her for a time as something of a Joan of Arc, an articulate idealist fighting the powers of reaction. She had persuaded the King to introduce the Code Napoleon, a process that was under way when revolution broke out.

After acquiring her title she tempered her rages at first and functioned with more decorum and restraint in public, until a tide of resistance swept her back into her instinctive way of meeting frustration with fury. When attacked she championed herself in the press, and responded sharply to a *Times* inference that she was a fraud with a crisp explanation of her life history that she used with variations on many occasions. Londoners read with interest on April 9, 1847, Lola Montez's own version of her ancestry:

114

I was born in Seville in the year 1823 [sic], my father was a Spanish officer in the service of Don Carlos; my mother, a lady of Irish extraction, born at the Havannah, and married for the second time to an Irish gentleman, which I suppose is the cause of my being called Irish and sometimes English, 'Betsy Watson,' 'Mrs. James,' etc. I beg leave to say that my name is Maria Dolores Porris Montez, and I never have changed that name.

In a curious way Lola was always inclined to be modest—or perhaps realistic—about her art, and on this occasion she added that she had never had the presumption to think she had any theatrical qualifications. Circumstances had obliged her to adopt the stage as a profession, which she had now renounced forever, "having become a naturalized Bavarian, and intending in future making Munich my residence."

But her reign was short. With von Abel out of the way serious trouble developed at the university. Munich had a large student body, much of it conservative and Catholic. When Professor Ernst von Lasaulx, a popular Jesuit professor of philosophy, gave an address on von Abel, deploring his retirement and praising his loyalty to Ultramontane principles, the Countess interpreted this as an attack on the King's authority. He was removed from his chair, and the students gave him a tremendous ovation. They gathered outside the professor's house on the Theresienstrasse but the police would not let them hold a torchlight procession. From there they moved on to Lola's little palace and shouted and jeered beneath her windows. The strong young Bavarians threw heavy chunks of ice at the house and shouted to her in German and Latin. She was lunching at the time and she came to the window with a glass of champagne in her hand. At first she toasted them gaily, but this did not win the angry students, and a stone fell at her feet. She drained her glass and threw chocolates down at them, again with a laugh on her lips, but not until she had tossed back the stone over the heads of the students. She was angry and unafraid.

The King arrived around five o'clock with an armed guard, and when he saw how ugly the mood of the students was he called in

115

mounted police, who cleared the street. He was heard to say: "If she were called Loyola Montez I suppose they would cheer her."

At nightfall he went home on foot with his guard but again found himself surrounded by a hostile crowd. The students had moved to the Residenz and were tossing stones and ice in the direction of the palace windows. He could not push his way through until a military escort cleared a path for him. By this time it was much more than a student demonstration; some of the most extreme elements in the city had gathered. Many had come straight from the beer halls and by ten o'clock that night they were rampaging through the city streets, smashing windows and shouting abuse.

The King played lotto calmly in the Residenz through the uproar, for he lapsed readily into moods of abstraction when storms blew around him. But Lola, keenly alive to the growing menace, goaded him when he visited her into bearing down more heavily than ever on the rebellious elements at the university. The most conservative professors were urged to find other positions and liberal thinkers were appointed to their chairs. The rigid censorship of books that had been imposed by the clergy was withdrawn, and other rules were relaxed. Things calmed down temporarily but the student body split into factions and a savage cartoon of the King, linked to Lola by handcuffs, was widely circulated.

Bismarck, Bernstorff and other German diplomats observed the power play with interest, and gave Lola credit for reforming zeal. The King's more progressive policies were welcomed, particularly in Franconia, which was largely Protestant, and while the *Augsburg Zeitung* was the mouthpiece of the Jesuits, the *Münchner Zeitung* welcomed the new liberal ministers in the Cabinet. All recognized the fact that to get at the King one had to work through the Countess of Landsfeld. But the reaction in Vienna to the new alignment in Munich was severe. The all-powerful Metternich, with his history of three wives, fourteen children and innumerable loves, had been a thorn in Ludwig's flesh for many years, fighting him through the King's own sister. Ludwig's democratic habits and at

116

the end his conflict with the Ultramontane party were abhorrent to both.

When revolt flared up in Munich the Ultramontane were fighting for their lives all over Europe. The French Legitimists, the Polish Catholics, the Swiss Jesuits all were involved. When the Sonderbund, or Catholic League in Switzerland, was crushed its members had fled to Bavaria. The Swiss Confederation had been backed by Britain against the Sonderbund, and neither Austria nor France was disposed to help them because of Lord Palmerston's influence. Bavaria seemed to be their natural refuge and they crossed the border in droves until the tide of revolt in 1848 destroyed their influence.

The stories that had followed Lola all over Europe caught fire again, and many viewed her as an agent worming her way into councils of state and spreading propaganda for political ends. But in spite of the mysterious power she wielded it was never established that she was linked to any organized movement. Her history suggests that she was merely pursuing her ambitious drive for power. It had always been her habit to attach herself to the top men in any field, a policy she had pursued in Britain. Her knowledge of languages, of court procedure, of the political figures in different countries, and of the trouble she stirred up, made her a natural target for speculation as to her true role. The British diplomats in all the capitals treated her with kid gloves, in spite of the confusion she caused from time to time. Now and again Lola was inclined to boast of her influence, and she acknowledged in Paris that she had been approached by agents who had asked her to influence a powerful Russian nobleman. She had reported this to M. Guizot, then Premier of France, who had already observed that a number of Russian noblemen in Paris were Ultramontane in their sympathies.

The story that had true substance in Lola's life was her often acknowledged enmity to the Jesuits. In her autobiography she made no attempt to conceal this feeling, tracing it back to the early days of her life. In Ireland she had been exposed to Catholic teaching. In Montrose this influence had worn thin in Calvinist surroundings.

117

In Paris she had shared in the agnosticism of the French savants and had absorbed the philosophy of Lamennais. All this was an essential part of her nature and her history. The London papers kept pounding at the Catholic issue, and in her letter to the *Times* of March 11, 1847, she wrote: "I had not been here a week before I discovered that there was a plot hatching in the town to get me out of it, and that the party was the Jesuit party. . . . Bavaria has long been their stronghold, and Munich their headquarters. This naturally to a person brought up and instructed from her earliest youth to detest this party (I think you will say justly) irritated me not a little."

Her presence on the scene tended to unite all the influential elements in Bavarian society in sweeping condemnation of the King. His hand was forced on many issues, as he swung between Lola's insistent advice and that of the statesmen on whom he had always leaned. The political unrest that stirred his people was common to most German states at the time, but Lola was a complicating factor that none of the other rulers of principalities in the south of Germany had to face.

Occasionally there were public scenes that caused talk at the court. At a royal ball the King disappeared and went to his private apartment, where Lola and von Berks, one of her favorite ministers, waited for him. They settled down for tea and talk. Although inclined to be abstemious where food and drink were concerned Lola encouraged the King in his addiction to the English custom of drinking tea. Finally the Queen sent for her consort, and her emissary reported back that he was sound asleep. In the end the guests went ahead with supper and Ludwig did not reappear.

With thrones in peril all over Europe Lola's "idyllic carelessness made an almost tragical farce of the serious situation," Count Metternich commented when this episode was reported to him. He was convinced that the Countess was trying to isolate the Queen at this time, and to create dissension between her and Ludwig's sister, who disapproved of Lola. The favorite was widely quoted as having said that "only two eyes stood between her and the throne—the Queen's." The philandering went on—part power play, part dalliance, and the King poured out his heart to Lola in the following vein:

> Two rocks are we, against which constantly are breaking
> The adversaries' craft, the enemies' open rage;
> But scorpion-like, themselves, they pierce with deadly sting.
> The sanctuary is guarded by trust and faith:
> Thy enemies' cruelty will be avenged on themselves—
> Love will compensate for all that we have suffered.

As the picture darkened he whipped off another that he called "Sonnet to Lolitto," one of her many pet names:

> If, for my sake, thou hast renounced all ties,
> I, too, for thee, have broken with them all;
> Life of my life, I am thine—I am thy thrall—
> I hold no compact with thine enemies.
> Their blandishments are powerless on me,
> No arts will serve to seduce me from thee;
> The power of love raises me above them.
> With thee my earthly pilgrimage will end. . . .
> So, until death, with thee my being is blended.
> In thee I have found what I ne'er yet found in any—
> The sight of thee gave new life to my being.
> All feeling for any other has died away. . . .

The Queen remained philosophical throughout, and when Ludwig was indisposed for a time she made arrangements for Lola to visit him twice a week in his private apartments. On two occasions she and the Queen encountered each other at the palace gateway, and once Theresa returned unexpectedly and found Ludwig showing Lola her own personal domain. This may have ruffled the courtiers, but it did not seem to distress the Queen.

However, their second son, Otto, who had been King of Greece since 1832, disliked the waves of scandal and ridicule that were smearing his father all over Europe. He was not sorry to see von Abel out of the picture, for he had always felt that this particular minister had helped to separate his father and himself. But he found

119

it difficult to accept the fact that his mother was being subjected to such affront. Ludwig had helped to make Greece fashionable with the worldly when he made a triumphal tour there at the time of Otto's ascension to the throne. The young Prince brought strong German influences to the Hellespont, but his wife, Princess Amalia of Oldenburg, was unpopular beyond belief, and at one point an attempt was made to assassinate her.

Hoping to temper the political unrest and reassure the people of Bavaria, King Ludwig traveled through southern Germany in the summer of 1847. Lola joined him at certain points along the way and at Bamberg a demonstration of sympathy was staged for the Queen. At Würzburg the commandant of the garrison tried to keep Lola from finishing her journey. But the monarch's popularity was still intact in other regions and notably at Brückenau in the Fulda Forest. Here the Countess entertained herself at the castle with handsome members of Ludwig's crack corps of cuirassiers. In strongly Protestant Franconia, where his new policies were approved, she acquired some local prestige as his adviser. Altogether Ludwig was well pleased with his summer tour. "I was agreeably surprised by my joyful reception in the Palatinate," he reported on August 31.

At this point Metternich noted that the King's romance was being discussed in every farmhouse in Bavaria, as well as in the mansions and beer halls of Munich. His agents also informed him that as her power increased Lola was tempering her rages and being more agreeable to people she had formerly snubbed.

When Parliament reconvened in the autumn of 1847 peace seemed to loom on the horizon as various progressive measures were put through. Lola was credited by some with having led the King along this thorny road. He was a sincere Catholic and, according to the London *Times* of March 12, 1847: "The authority of the Roman Catholic party had possessed itself of the King, with an absolute sway of his conscience, his tastes and even his vices." Only in Austria, under the direction of Metternich, had the Jesuits and the Ultramontane Party the power they showed in Bavaria.

But the King's ingrained Catholicism did not extend to his relations with Lola, who was helping him to break down prevailing church forms. She watched with satisfaction the abandonment of many of the clerical practices, noting the decline in the emphasis on the miracles of the Middle Ages, and in the school of art closely tied to monastic images. None doubted that the omnipotent Countess had dictated the Protestant additions to the Cabinet and to university chairs. She saw to it that a bust of Luther was added to the other great names of Germany enshrined at Walhalla, and she thought it valiant of Ludwig that soon after being crowned King he had taken off his diamond collar and swung it around the neck of the aging Goethe. This had been shocking to the more conservative Bavarians, to whom Goethe seemed another Voltaire.

The *Times* of London turned the spotlight on Lola's role in Bavarian politics with such persistence that she grew angry and tried to propitiate this powerful newspaper. It irked her to have old stories about her escapades in London and Paris dug up and reprinted in detail. She knew that these dispatches would be read by Dumas and other friends in Paris and London. In fact, all Europe from St. Petersburg to Madrid was well primed on the royal romance in Bavaria. Stung by this notoriety she spoke for herself and wrote to her critics:

Since my residence here I can safely say that I have in no way interfered in any affairs not concerning myself, and as I intend making it my future abode, it is particularly annoying to me, hearing so many scandalous and unfounded reports which are daily propagated, and in justice to myself and my future prospects in life, I trust that you will not be unwilling to insert this letter in your widely circulated journal, and show my friends and the public how unjustly and cruelly I have been treated by the Jesuit party in Munich.

The *Times* relented and thanked her for choosing its columns to convey a candid avowal of her political principles, "and while we

121

disclaim the function of a censor of the morals of Munich, or a critic of the professional merits of the saltatory Pompadour, we see great reason to applaud the spirit and the direction of her political influence." Had it been customary in England for ministers to moan and weep over the private immoralities of their royal masters, showers of tears would have fallen constantly during the reign of certain monarchs, this editorial conceded. But should she not abandon "acts of insolence, indecorum and absurdity and use the strange accidents of her life to higher ends"? Since King Ludwig was only then "emerging from the darkness of the Middle Ages" he should be allowed to pass through the license of the intermediate stage before arriving at the "decorous constitutional regime of a King in the nineteenth century." Whatever his faults, the writer added patronizingly, they were those of a "genial and impetuous nature, rather than of the frigid fanaticism of his spiritual directors." And, however ridiculous the events in Munich, "the change likely to result from them may prove a matter of great importance to Germany, and of some interest to Europe at large."

Punch published a cartoon of Lola Montez holding a banner inscribed "Freedom and the Cachucha." Ridicule again, but her war with the students had taken on the deeper implications of the political uprisings of 1848 as Bavaria was swept into the tide of revolt that flooded all Europe.

EIGHT

Student Revolt

Lola Montez sealed her own doom when she persuaded the King to close down the University of Munich, and thereby stirred up the entire student body and all the townspeople. The smoldering discontent that already infused the academic world burst into flame and rioting broke out. The city rang with shouts and oaths. Pistols and knives came into play. There were fires and looting. Chunks of ice and stones were again thrown through windows. Mobs defied the police and were charged by military cavalry.

The royal residence was surrounded, the city fathers led a march to reason in person with the King, and Lola's life was in danger as she met each assault on her house with defiance and bravado. Liberals and conservatives were sharply aligned in factions. Friend turned against friend, and students jeered professors they had been taught to respect. The most learned of scholars left the Munich they had loved. One died, crushed in spirit, in the midst of the scrimmaging. It was a revolt of major proportions and it was also the end of Lola's rule.

All Europe had followed events in Bavaria as the student body played its role in the overthrow of a King and the exile of his favorite, who by this time was publicly called "the concubine." The townspeople liked the bright and exciting student body of two thousand. They brought youth, dash, romance and sophistication to the city. Their learning, their songs, their beer-house revels, and their patronage were a valued part of daily life, an economic asset as well as a mark of distinction. Ludwig had transferred the old and honored university from Landshut to be incorporated in the classical setting he had created in Munich. The scholars of many countries gathered in its precincts and it represented the intellectual life dear to the native German.

There were five student clubs, brightly uniformed and named after the provinces Franconia, Istria, Palatinate, Swabia and Bavaria. The Palatinate was largely Protestant, and when some of its members attended one of Lola's bountiful receptions they were thrown out of their club by their fellows, since she had become the focus of their demonstrations. With the King's approval she created her own club, whose members were known as the Alemannians. Their motto was "Lola and Liberty" and they swaggered about in white silk culottes with black velvet vests and yellow sashes. Their jaunty red caps with gold embroidery and the uniforms were provided by Lola, who had designed the ensemble. She had converted a building close to her own house for their use, and she attended their festivals, wearing their uniform to good effect. Von Berks gave a banquet for them at the Nymphenburg Palace and spoke of their zeal in the cause of enlightenment and progress.

But when the Alemannians showed up in lecture halls there were hisses, arguments and fights, until finally the King asked the rector, Dr. Friedrich Thiersch, to put an end to this friction. He did his best but the hostile students continued to demonstrate, both in and out of their lecture halls. "Down with the sorceress!" they cried. "Death to the Spaniard!" Meanwhile, the Alemannia guarded her, deferred to her, ran her errands, serenaded her, escorted her carriage and fought off interference. On Christmas Day they planted a tree in her garden and they called her their honorary sister. Count von Hirschberg, whom she had won completely so that he refused to join in demonstrations against her, headed the corps, and three young men—Peissner, Hertheim and Laibinger—trotted beside her carriage and were known to Lola as Athos, Porthos and Aramis, an echo of her Dumas days. But to the people of Munich they were Beelzebub, Astoroth and Samuel. Her personal bodyguards were two brothers, C. and L. Nüssbaum.

Dr. Joseph Ignaz Döllinger, a well-known Catholic prelate and friend of Gladstone's, called them Lola's male harem, a state of affairs that he believed existed with the King's approval. This outraged observer had been dismissed from his chair when von Abel's ministry fell, and he wrote feelingly of the "anxiety and embarrassment of the professors when left alone in lecture halls with one or two members of Lola's corps, the other students having all walked out in protest over their presence."

Dr. Döllinger's letter, sent from Munich on February 25, 1848, was addressed to a prominent Catholic known as Elise Marie, who later married Arthur James, tenth Earl of Fingall. She had been in Munich while Lola was gaining ascendancy and Dr. Döllinger was reporting to her what had happened after she left. In it he wrote bitterly of the King: "Evidently he is acting not only under a thirst for vengeance, but also under the fatal influence of an irresistible and sinister passion for that woman." This letter was not made public until the *Irish Ecclesiastical Record* used it in 1914 but it summed up the clerical feeling of the period.

In addition to communications of this kind Count Metternich received detailed reports of all-night revels in the hall used by Lola's corps, with the King tipsily taking part in the merriment. He was pictured with Lola seated on his knees, his saber in his right hand, the red cap of the Alemannia perched on his head, singing their traditional songs with the students. And again the element of caricature entered into this picture of the King. The fact remained that the student body was wholly divided, and the rector sternly insisted that the Alemannia must be allowed to attend lectures, like the other students. But this had little effect on the angry students. The King asked Prince Wallerstein to intercede. He immediately addressed the students, pointing out that academic freedom could not prevail without order, and concluded with cheers for the King.

This half-hearted truce was shattered with events following the death of Joseph von Görres on January 29, 1848. He was an aged mystic who had turned Ultramontane in his later years, and although a close personal friend of the King's, he had been ousted from favor by Lola. He and Ludwig had often discussed the occult forces in which both believed, and after his death the story took wing in Munich that in his last moments he had stretched out his arms in the general direction of Lola's little palace and murmured: "I die because I cannot live under the rule of a harlot."

Von Görres was one of the most popular of the professors and all the students corps but the Alemannia turned out for his funeral. The King ignored it, which shocked and angered them. Although the police forbade speechmaking at the ceremony, they could not stop the later pilgrimage to the grave, to demonstrate with banners draped in crepe. The red-and-gold insignia of Lola's corps was missing, and this was considered an insult to the memory of von Görres, who the students insisted had died of a broken heart. Later they paraded in the general direction of Lola's house and the nearby hall used by the Alemannia.

Lola heard the shouts and commotion in the street and with one of her bold and fearless impulses she walked out and faced the hostile students. They shook their fists and yelled at her. She stood in the icy wind, blue eyes blazing, black hair swinging around her pale face, and in imperious tones harangued them for several minutes. Inflamed with anger and beer they stood their ground and cried in chorus, "*Pereat Lola!*"

As so often in her life she lost her self-control and shouted: "I will have the university closed."

Immediately there were shouts of outrage and the students closed in on her. Count von Hirschberg and two or three other members of her corps rushed to her defense. The Count drew a dagger and in a tussle with a guard he stabbed himself, but his heavy coat saved him from serious injury. The hostile students demanded the Count's arrest, but were told that carrying a dagger was only a disciplinary offense. The law dared not move against one of Lola's followers.

But she saw that she was trapped and hurriedly sought refuge, with the mob at her heels and her protectors pushing them back. No door would open to her and the Swiss Guard stationed at the Austrian Embassy pointedly ignored her appeal. Meanwhile, a member of her corps had conveyed word of her plight to the King. He arrived in person with a small guard, but his appearance did not quiet the mob. Lola had finally taken refuge in the Theatinerkirche, knowing that the students would not pursue her there, although one had raised his hands as if to strangle her as she reached the church door. The King had ordered out the military guard, and emboldened by this knowledge she walked from the church with a defiant smile on her face, waving a pistol that she had snatched from a guard. Lola fired it negligently into the air, and the students roared and shouted until the cuirassiers galloped up and dispersed them.

Her house on the Barerstrasse was guarded all that night, and as the rain came pelting down she sent a servant to ask the soldiers if they would like some beer, wine and food. They coldly rejected her offer. The students roamed the city in little groups and gathered in the beer halls. Lola's threat to close the university had further inflamed them. The storm had broken and would not die down.

Next day the King called the rector of the university into consultation. Lola had issued her ultimatum and she now stood in the background, determined to have her way. Ludwig loved his university, the young students, the whole world of scholarship. It went deeply against his instincts to take this drastic step. He knew that feeling was mounting among the townspeople, too, and that any move he made might lead to chaos.

But Lola won. On February 9 he issued a decree that the university would close for a year. The students who did not live in Munich were ordered to leave the city within twenty-four hours. Under pressure from his other advisers the King wavered for the next week, with a series of orders which, summarized, first decreed a total shutdown, then the temporary suspension of classes and ultimately the reopening of the university with conditions that were forced on him. Meanwhile, the student demonstrations had triggered insurrection by various dissident groups in the city. People stayed indoors as threats of total revolution swept over Munich. The students went to the rector's residence and he appeared on his balcony and urged them to remain calm and to comply with the royal edict. Finally the city fathers moved into the picture and for two tumultuous days it seemed as if all Munich might go up in flames.

In a handwritten document now in the state archives of Munich, entitled *City Chronicle. The part which the Magistrate and the population of the community and citizenship in Munich played on February 10 and 11, 1848,* the hour-by-hour events are recorded with all the immediacy of topical news. The prologue crystallized the issue by pointing out that everyone should realize that "these street incidents had been caused by the Comtesse Landsfeld (Lola Montez) called Lola by the people, and also by the members of the student corps Alemannia, the so-called Lola students, and in the public opinion the whole thing was the result of the hurt feelings for law and decency."

The Magistrate first asked Ludwig's ministers for precise information on the decree affecting the university. When this was settled the City Council sent a deputation to the King protesting this act, but not going into the "deeper reasons." In other words, Lola would not figure in the discussion. But before this meeting had ended more than a thousand citizens had jammed their way into the concourse of Town Hall. Their spokesman demanded that the university be opened again, that a complaint be filed over the "excessive actions of the royal gendarmerie against the students," that Captain

Bauer, its leader and a friend of Lola's, be removed, and that the student corps Alemannia be dissolved.

In firm tones the Mayor assured them that the first point had already been debated by the council and the second would be considered. He urged the deputation to have the crowd dispersed, since neither the city authorities nor the army could approve such an unorthodox gathering. But the murmurs from outside were insistent. Nearly all were tradesmen, professional men or businessmen who lived by the income the students brought them. When it became clear that they had no intention of leaving, the two municipal corporations involved decided that it would be dangerous to order them out of Town Hall. Inside, they were petitioners to the legal authorities. Outside, they would be removed from the jurisdiction of the municipal authorities and would inevitably come into conflict with the police. Barricades were already up all over the city.

At this point a deputation of students arrived and described to the Magistrate "in gripping words the disadvantages resulting from the interruption of their studies." With the university closed they could no longer be represented by their Dean and the Senate, and they asked for the protection of the municipality to represent their interests. Mayor von Stein assured them that their case would be laid before the King. He urged the youthful deputation to wait patiently for the results, to accept the censure whatever it might be, and not to overstep the limits of the law.

The students proved to be more amenable than the waiting crowd, who insisted on accompanying a civic deputation to the Residenz. Some of the councilors argued that this would be regarded as a demonstration and might prejudice the King against them. The Mayor thought that Ludwig should be warned of the coming invasion, so an apothecary, a baker, a confectioner and a merchant, all members of the municipal council and all directly involved in loss of trade with the university closed, were sent to the palace with a written request for the reopening of the university, the dismissal of von Bauer for the rough handling of the students by the gen-

129

darmerie he headed, and the dissolution of the Alemannia Club as a student body.

The King was out walking but the petition was left for his return. Prince Wallerstein was notified to prepare Ludwig for the arrival of a thousand citizens at the gates of the Residenz. The Prince haughtily told them there was nothing he could do because he had just resigned his office. Actually, he had been notified by Lola to get out by March 1, and he was furiously resentful of her mandate.

While the Mayor and his small group were away from Town Hall the waiting citizens drafted their own address to the King, setting forth their grievances and demands, but not mentioning Lola. They were angry when the Mayor returned with the news that he had not been received by the King but had left a warning of their coming. He proposed that they now send the civic deputation to the palace. This did not mollify the crowd. They began to shout and stamp, exclaiming, "We will all go there."

The Magistrate and municipal authorities tried to talk them out of it, but the citizens promised to be calm, orderly and silent. However, the city fathers were well aware that they were being squeezed in a consolidation of separate factions, and that anything might happen. It was finally settled that they should go separately, and the Mayor drove off by coach a second time with other members of a small civic deputation.

Ten minutes later the citizens proceeded to the Residenz in close formation. They lined up outside the gates. A detachment of cuirassiers and a company of infantry stood guard between them and the East Gate. They were unarmed, and they were soon joined by onlookers until the street held a restless wave of humanity. Old and young, fashionable and rustic, in town attire or peasant blouses, feathered hats and mountain boots the mixed crowd moved restlessly in a flowing mass. It was easy to spot the apothecary, the wine merchants and Munich's most famous brewer, who was a member of the deputation. He had made a rich living on the student body.

They soon learned that the King had returned from his walk but could not be disturbed. The answer that finally came was brief and to the point. He would not see them. A second appeal brought into view Freiheiten von Seefried, an aide who had recently been in Lola's entourage. He announced that the King would not receive them with two thousand people standing in front of the palace. He was told that the municipal authorities had not come with this crowd and had done their best to dissuade them from leaving Town Hall and surrounding the Residenz.

The self-evident danger of not giving some assurance to this angry crowd was emphasized, but again von Seefried came out with a negative answer and this time a supercilious smile, or so it seemed to the suppliants. Then the King went to dinner, without giving any assurance that he could be reached afterward. Frustrated and angry, the Mayor appealed to popular Prince Luitpold, who was with the King. He was a favorite with everyone in Munich and a message to him brought an instant response. The Mayor in black frock coat and small round hat, with his symbolic gold chain clanking around his neck, was led with his anxious deputation to an antechamber close to the King's quarters. Luitpold told them amiably that he would present their case to Ludwig and after dinner they saw the Prince and his popular Austrian wife Augusta traversing the long corridors after the King.

Soon strange sounds were heard from the antechamber. Angry voices and a woman's sobs came from the King's audience chamber. Princess Augusta was pleading with Ludwig to relent, and he was shouting at her in angry tones. The clang of his saber on the marble floor as he marched up and down was audible to the quaking listeners.

Finally the doors swung open and the Luitpolds came out. Both had tears in their eyes and Princess Augusta was swaying as she walked. She had knelt before the King to beg for his people, and now she told the waiting group: "The King is going to see you but do not expect a friendly reception."

The Luitpolds went to their own apartment in the palace, and

131

the royal head marshal led the deputation into the King's presence.
His son Prince Adelbert, dressed in the uniform of his cavalry regiment, was with him, leaning on his saber at the window and watching the crowd outside. The King's hair was ruffled. His color was
high. There was no sign of his customary amiability as he said impatiently:

Does a deputation that wants to file a plea come backed by 2000 men? My
edict upon your written request has been issued and you will be informed
about it by my minister. . . . I have refused the request and this decision
stands and will not be changed. I have carefully thought about the decree
to close the university and no one can defy me in changing it.

The King added petulantly that the people who lived in Landshut
had not complained when he moved their university to Munich, but
the people of Munich acted as if their lives depended on keeping
the students "because they lose some hundred thousand gulden income." Then, in a burst of bitterness, Ludwig added: "The citizens
of Munich are ungrateful. They forget what I have done for this
city for twenty-three years, but I can move my residence somewhere
else. Nothing can prevent me from doing so."

His visitors tried to assure the King that their gratitude for what
he had done had not diminished in any way, but his feelings were
not assuaged. He walked back and forth, violently pounding the
floor with his saber and shouting: "My decision stands. I'm not
afraid. They can take my life from me but not my will."

In silence the deputation drove away from the Residenz and returned to Town Hall. The citizens who had surrounded the palace
marched quietly back to the town square and took up their vigil
there again. But bottled-up feelings were beginning to explode, and
all over town there were reports of rioting and bloodshed. The trouble in the Barerstrasse which had driven Lola to take refuge was
blown up to major proportions. The crowd at Town Hall seethed
with anger when stories reached them that the cuirassiers had
charged the students, that guns had been used, that citizens, students
and police had been killed. According to Lola's exaggerated account

of this in her autobiography: "They came with cannon, and guns, and swords, with the voice of ten thousand devils." She saw "a thousand guns" pointed at her and heard a "hundred fat and apoplectic voices" fiercely demanding that she persuade the King to repeal the university mandate.

But this time, with the crowd swarming at Town Hall, Lola was barricaded in her house under heavy guard. She smoked furiously and vented her wrath on her needlepoint, as she stabbed angrily with her needle. For once she was out of touch with the King, but she knew that events were developing fast. There was no magic she could conjure up at this point to check their course. Her Alemannians were fleeing; only three or four stayed with her through the chaotic finale. When von Berks arrived at Town Hall with the King's ruling, the auditorium was dark and two lanterns were held beside him as he read: "Now that the citizens have quietly retreated it is my intention to reopen the university with the summer semester, instead of the winter semester, if up to then the people of Munich behave to my satisfaction. The welfare of the citizens is close to my heart and I have proved that for more than twenty-three years."

Pale and agitated, von Berks hurried off to the Residenz again while the Magistrate and his colleagues read the King's decree to the crowd of waiting citizens, which kept growing larger as people flowed in from surrounding streets. They learned that the university would not be closed down permanently. The Alemannia would go. Von Bauer would go. But the King still had to withdraw his order that the students should leave the city by noon next day. The time for compromise had passed, however, and the real issue flashed into view with cries of: "Down with the concubine! Set fire to the house on the Barerstrasse."

They scattered in an angry mood, to roam through the streets, throwing stones; to argue in beer halls; to shout at passersby; or to seek shelter in their own barricaded homes. It had been a night of terror at the Residenz, too, with the King facing his consort, his

133

courtiers, his ministers and his closest advisers, in a desperate attempt to uphold Lola and keep her in Munich. Word had been brought to him from Town Hall of the ugly mood of the people. The Minister of the Interior had made plain to him that the real issue now was the Countess of Landsfeld. For fifteen months she had kept the city in turmoil, and even on the previous Sunday had appeared at the theater loaded with jewels given her by the King and had behaved in a conspicuous and provocative way. All the civic bodies were determined that she should go. All classes were against her. All condemned the King for his association with this dangerous adviser, and here the extreme elements had won the solid support of the more moderate burghers.

Ludwig, who in his youth had defied Napoleon, did not altogether confuse the rebellion at the university with the moral indignation of the Bavarian people about Lola. He knew them too well for that; no one knew them better. But when he heard cries from the street of "Long live the republic," and saw the menacing crowd that would not move away from the palace gates, he knew that his own Bavaria was on the brink of revolution. All Europe was heading in the same direction at that time, but for the moment he was lost in agony and consumed with the urgency of his own problem and the witchery of Lola. He was a stubborn man, benign in his instincts, but mulish when driven. This quality blocked his ability to reason when his ministers came to him in a body, convinced after listening to the municipal authorities that nothing would quiet the town but the banishment of the Countess.

Many saw in the crisis the hard-core efforts of revolutionaries at work in every country, seizing on regional issues to create chaos in the community. To Prince Wallerstein, a smooth diplomat in the Metternich tradition, the political and religious implications of Lola's hold on the King were infinitely more important than his besotted admiration for her person. But the one interest interlocked with the other, and rendered her doubly dangerous.

It took hours of pleading to make the King break down. He defended Lola and met argument with argument. He stormed. He grew hysterical and again shouted: "I will never abandon Lola. She is the most noble of creatures. My crown for Lola." Time and again when the Queen urged him to accept the will of the people he rejected her plea with violence such as she had never seen her amiable Ludwig display. Finally she sank to her knees and prayed through the night, but on the morning of the 11th the King was as determined in his stand as he had been on the night of the 10th.

Again the Luitpolds besought him to reject Lola, and soon after seven in the morning the King's sister the Duchess of Leuchtenberg knelt before him and with tears streaming down her cheeks told him what it would mean to Bavaria if he did not act at once. They all had bitter memories of revolution when they had fled with their father Maximilian from Strasbourg. But Ludwig, knowing that the citizens were back at Town Hall again, waiting for his final message, held his ground until the Minister of the Interior bluntly told him that if he did not sign the decree banishing the Countess she would be killed by the mob.

At last the King had been reached. Weary, beaten, he seized a pen and signed the order ousting Lola. Looking up into the chilly, scornful face of Prince Wallerstein he said: "I am but the shadow of a King."

The Countess was to leave Munich within an hour and the Royal Police Director was ordered to go to her house at once and see to it that she responded immediately. When this news was conveyed to the crowd at Town Hall cheers rang through the concourse. But the King's signed decree had still to be seen to be believed. They had already had ample proof of Lola's witchery.

At half past ten a cry went up that the ministers were coming. Prince Wallerstein walked in with his colleagues. The crowd waited in grim silence while he made one of the notable announcements in Bavarian history. He held up the signed decree for all to see. The university would stay open. The current lectures would be resumed at once for all students. The Alemannia would be dissolved.

135

The Prince's listeners waited attentively for his final announcement, which landed like a bomb among them in spite of its ambivalent assurance that "further proof of the good intentions of the King was seen in the free decision of the monarch" to banish the Countess of Landsfeld. The ultimate had been achieved. Now nothing stood between the King and the people, or so it seemed at the moment. A roar came from the crowd and questions were hurled at the diplomat. Had Lola really left? Was she being banished from the city or from the country?

"Without doubt from the country," Prince Wallerstein told them icily.

"Where to?" they asked, and were quietly told that she was then on her way to Nuremberg by train.

The crowd scattered, some to take up their stand at the Residenz and cheer the King, who had capitulated; others to head for the Barerstrasse, where many of the students had already gathered.

"We thank God for the peaceful solution of these many confusions which have gone into the depths," the *City Chronicle* finished piously. "May God grant that such events will never recur and will not be lost for the lessons in history."

NINE

Flight and Abdication

When the police, backed by Prince Wallerstein, arrived with the King's decree at the little palace where Lola had reigned, she refused to believe that Ludwig had deserted her. Only when she saw the familiar signature was she convinced that she was not being trapped. Not for a moment had she believed that he would banish her from his kingdom or let ill befall her. All night long she had stayed on the alert, knowing that Munich was in turmoil and her own life in danger, but her faith in the King's power had not faltered.

Her immediate impulse was to get to the Residenz as fast as she could and have the order countermanded. Impulsively she appeared at her own front door—cool, defiant and determined. But when cries of *"Pereat Lola"* came from the angry mob outside she was dragged out of sight by her attendants. Words were still cascading from her lips she disappeared from view. One of the Nüssbaum brothers jumped from an upper window and brandished his sword for her protection. She had locked him and three other Alemannia upstairs, knowing that their lives were in greater peril than hers, but Nüssbaum's sword was seized as he landed and he was rolled in the gutter.

The windows blazed with light. Men shook their fists and cursed or chanted the refrain *"Pereat Lola"* as they watched to see how she would make connections with the carriage that waited for her at a distance. The murmuring rose to a spontaneous roar when she finally came out, deathly pale, with a huge fur hat perched at an angle on her black hair, and swinging a muff with one hand. She was Lola the actress, making an entrance. Even though a small squadron of cavalry now mounted guard, she saw at once that the waiting carriage could not be driven to her door through the jammed crowd that pressed against her railings.

The mob quieted and seemed mesmerized as she walked proudly and alone to the carriage. In spite of their hatred no one attempted to touch her. They froze into silence, hypnotized by her solo performance. Count Louis Arco waited in the carriage to receive her. They followed a twisting course on their way to the station, and once away from the Barerstrasse maledictions followed Lola as if she were Marie Antoinette on her way to the guillotine. She asked the driver to stop for a moment at the royal church. Before the Count could stop her she gathered up her skirts and jumped out of the carriage, heading for the Residenz, but she found the East Gate closed. All the gates were now barred to the Countess, and she sank back resignedly as they left the old town and drove to the station where Fritz Peissner, Hertheim and Laibinger, three of her faithful Alemannia, awaited her. Nüssbaum had been arrested on the Barerstrasse, but he and his brother would turn up again in Switzerland. Count Arco saw her placed on the Augsburg train. She was supposed to be heading for Lindau on Lake Constance, but she and her escorts got off at a wayside station and drove back to Blutenburg, a village close to Munich. Arrangements had been made secretly for her to stay at the royal hunting lodge and, if need be, to find sanctuary in its historic chapel.

No sooner had she left the Barerstrasse than the mob took over. They burned and looted, shouted and danced in the street because the sorceress was no longer among them. Bewildered and shattered, the King appeared suddenly, alone and on foot. With a wild-eyed and blighted look, shivering in his old blue redingote, he leaned against a building watching. The rioters closest to him stopped yelling and stared. Had he come to watch the funeral pyre? Did he think that Lola might still be inside the house? He helped one of the Alemannia who had been thrown into the gutter. Then he tried to reason with the crowd and to urge them to spare the house. Some paused; others made menacing moves.

"Vandals!" the King exclaimed with sudden fury, a few minutes before one of Lola's treasured mirrors came crashing down on his head. By accident or design he had been hit. Dazed and bleeding, he reeled through the crowd with the help of a small guard. Some bared their heads, made way for him, and the shouting died down. He was still their King and the mood of compassion tempered their lust for vengeance.

Back at the Residenz, a more friendly crowd waited to acclaim him for having banished the Countess and ordered the reopening of the university. The more moderate who had besieged Town Hall wished to show their appreciation. So did many of the students. They sang the national anthem and shouted *"Vivat der König."* As he came out and bowed three times the roar grew tumultuous. A glimpse of the Queen at the window was the signal for another outburst, but the King was visibly exhausted from his experience on the Barerstrasse, his injuries and the crucial events of the night. He did not appear again and the crowd scattered. The streets were jammed with carts of grain for market when the Mayor tried to arrange a procession of jubilation. He addressed the students in front of a church and urged them to remember the privileges accorded them at the university and to abandon the violation of law and order that had stirred up the city.

They were in good spirits and there were cheers, songs and

friendly embraces as the younger generation headed for their lecture halls or the beer cellars. The name of Lola Montez flashed from one group to another, and the students speculated as to whether Munich had seen the last of her. They tossed around the medal that had been struck bearing the inscription LOLA CASTIGIT LOYOLA. They brandished the cartoon of Lola with a birch in her hand and a Jesuit priest in pursuit. As the evening advanced they chanted Lola's private version of the Lord's Prayer. It had been flaunted at many of her parties but never with more gusto than on the night of her banishment:

Our Father, in whom through my life I have never yet had much belief, all's well with me. Hallowed be thy name—so far as I am concerned thy kingdom come, that is, my bags of gold, my polished diamonds, and my unpolished Alemannia. Thy will be done, if thou wilt destroy my enemies. Give me this day champagne, and truffles and pheasant, and all else that is delectable, for I have a very good appetite. . . .

But the following night, disguised in a boy's riding clothes, she was back in Munich after a bumpy trip in a gamekeeper's cart over fields and rough roads. They entered the city by stealth and she was driven to the home of von Berks. He was to have followed her with her passport, money and clothes, but was at a loss when he found that her destination had been changed. Although she knew that the rioting had terrified him, she believed that he was the one person she could depend on to take a secret message to the King. She felt sure that Ludwig would see her and in later years she always insisted that he did and that she found him sunk in despair. Lola's story, as told in her autobiography and to many friends, was that they had had one last meeting, and that she had then obtained a promise from him that he would abdicate. She pointed out to him "the impossibility of holding his throne, unless he went down into the disgraceful humility of recanting the great deeds which he had proclaimed he had done under a sense of immediate justice." And then, according to Lola's romantic account, she went out in her boy's disguise "under the stars of a midnight sky, to look upon the turrets and spires of Munich for the last time." She knew that if she were recognized she might be shot, but she did not "think or care much about that. Her thoughts were on the past."

Others on the scene at the time insisted that Lola had not seen the King, rather, that two police officers arrived at von Berks's house and flashed her expulsion order into view. She tore it from them and threw it in their faces, but when they brandished their pistols she went with them quietly. This time, on the advice of the King's confessor, she was sent to the establishment of Andreas Justinus Kerner, the poet-physician who practiced in Weinsberg and had long been Ludwig's friend. The King, knowing more than most about her interest in the supernatural, now thought her truly possessed, and both he and Lola had dabbled enough in mysticism for this to have meaning. But his act seemed to add to the long list of absurdities that surrounded their relationship.

Kerner was by no means pleased to have the most controversial figure in Bavaria on his hands. He had known enough about Lola and her influence on the King to dread her presence at this time. She arrived on February 17, 1848, less than a week after her expulsion from Munich. "Lola Montez arrived here the day before yesterday, accompanied by three Alemannen," he wrote to his married daughter, Emma Niendorf. "It is vexatious that the King should have sent her to me, but they have told him she is possessed. Before treating her with magic and magnetism, I am trying the hunger cure. I allow her only thirteen drops of raspberry water and the quarter of a wafer." With this treatment Lola's generous curves diminished so rapidly that he wrote again that she had grown astonishingly thin. His son Theodore had mesmerized her and he had let her drink asses' milk.

For Lola, who loved truffles, pheasant and champagne, all this was too much, and she and her three students left Weinsberg and the custody of the King's devil exorciser. The Aeolian harps at each window that sent Ariel-like voices floating through the air held no conviction for her, although she shared Ludwig's interest in

141

the spirit world. Many tales of witchery were attached to her spell-binding power over men. One of the favorite Bavarian legends about Lola was that a great black bird hovered around her. Some of the stories suggested erotica that the home-loving Bavarians abhorred. According to her autobiography: "The priests used to preach that there was no longer a Virgin Mary in Munich, but that Venus had taken her place."

With her passport, her clothes and the promise of an income from the King, Lola decided to find a haven in Switzerland. She could no longer linger on the German side of the border. "I came to Munich with one hundred thousand francs," she later wrote, "but I left with nothing." Whatever she may have thought of Ludwig's act she was a realist and highly intelligent. As long as she lived she never said or wrote anything derogatory about him, but described him as the most gallant, accomplished and honorable of men.

Ludwig and Dujarier were the only two men in her life to whom she gave unstinted praise, and they may well have been the only ones she respected. Dujarier did not live long enough for their romance to end in marriage or to die away. And her idyll with the King was quickly over, although it changed her life for all time and left resounding echoes on the European scene. She knew perhaps better than most that the King's troubles would not end with her departure. And she was right.

"Munich has had its three glorious days and Lola is out of Bavaria but by no means out of the heart of the King," Prince Metternich noted in his diary on February 14, 1848. "He gave in at the last moment out of fear of the citizens and the Reichscounsel and in anxiety for her life and his love for her, for at this price alone was she to be saved. Everyone wanted to be rid of that hated slut." Metternich added that without the pleas of Augusta Luitpold of Austria the King would never have received the municipal deputation and a "bloody catastrophe would have been inevitable."

His wife, Princess Mélanie Metternich, had predicted that the "shocking conduct of Lola Montez would finish by plunging the country into revolution."

Deeper forces were at work in Bavaria than a King's love, although the presence of Lola had sharpened the issues and brought about the crisis, which one faction promptly blamed on the Ultramontane. Reports reached Dr. Döllinger that the King was finding this explanation a godsend for "he has now something tangible to vent his anger upon and to wreak his vengeance." But this was far from being Ludwig's mood. He stayed out of sight, deeply depressed and writing fatuous verse to his "Absent Lolotte."

Although he tried to calm himself by reading from Herodotus, the historian exiled from Athens, and Tacitus, who wrote of the oppression of kings, he had moments of excitement bordering on frenzy. His scholarly instincts, so totally lacking in his verse, prevailed even in this moment of crisis, but neither reason nor mysticism could help him at this point. Without Lola he had lost his bearings and he vacillated in meeting the demands of the people. He was slow to convene the Reichscounsel and he refused to get rid of von Berks, who was scoffed at as being the keeper of Lola's dogs. Prince Wallerstein had played such an ambivalent role that he was safe for the moment, but a courtier that the King had seen consorting with the rioters was banished from the royal circle. The Luitpolds stayed with him to the finish.

News of the abdication of Louis Philippe and fresh revolution in Paris reverberated throughout Europe and the tremors weakened the already shaky throne in Bavaria. The crisis of 1848 had reached its height and the people of Munich were reflecting the general image. The radical elements stirring simultaneously all over Europe had a deep focus among them, and after a few days of calm the dissidents were up in arms for a new cause—the overthrow of their once-beloved King. The "Marseillaise" was sung ominously in the streets; there were shouts for revolution. Prince Charles, the

King's brother, went down to the palace gates and told the mob that Ludwig would meet their wishes. But he stubbornly refused to convene the Reichscounsel before the end of May.

In the meantime the story spread that the Countess of Landsfeld had returned to Munich and was secretly in command again. This caused the King to issue a decree withdrawing all rights of citizenship from Lola, and forbidding her to return to Bavaria. But the people were not appeased, and the King had been badly shaken by correspondence laid before him that suggested Lola's role as a secret agent. Prince Wallerstein had had her house searched after she left and had found what he considered incriminating evidence. Letters arrived from Rome, Berlin and London when she was already out of the country, and one of the King's sculptors named Loeb confessed that he had transmitted the secret correspondence seized by the police. He happened to be married to the daughter of an Italian Carbonarist. Abject before the King, he acknowledged his own complicity. The most significant letters were from Giuseppe Mazzini, who was masterminding the revolutionary outbreaks in Italy and other countries. The mystery surrounding these letters produced by Prince Wallerstein was never cleared up, but if authentic they would tend to fortify some of the charges brought against Lola that she worked with enemies of the Ultramontane in other countries. They also served further to inflame the mob.

The ministers watched this drama going on in the palace while day after day the crowd roared outside. On March 2 the arsenal was seized and the mob brandished pikes, swords, halberds and muskets. Barricades were set up, but the soldiers, ordered to fire on the insurgents in the market place, refused to move against them. On March 16 the rioters threw bombs in the Commissariat and at the National Guard. They pillaged police headquarters. The city was in insurrection.

Ludwig was cornered by his ministers, who arrived with papers for perfunctory signature by the King. The decisions had already

The Countess of Landsfeld at the age of twenty-nine. Portrait painted in 1847 by Joseph Stieler for King Ludwig's collection now hangs in the Nymphenburg Palace.

Lord Auckland, Governor-General of India who, with his sister, Miss Emily Eden, befriended Lola when she came to India as an army bride in the 1830's.

Picture Collection, New York Public Library

Ranjit Singh, "The Lion of the Punjab," India's most powerful maharajah, who lavished admiration and jewels on Lola.

Engraving by Rebel from a painting by Dedreux. Supplément a Galéries Historiques, compiled by Charles Gavard, Versailles

Holly House, an ancient mansion in Montrose, Scotland, where Lola lived in the late 1820's as the ward of Sir Patrick Edmonstone Craigie.

Photograph by Ian Murray, Montrose

Lord Brougham and Vaux, Scottish jurist, political reformer and Cabinet member, an admirer who backed Lola in political circles in England.

Painting by Sir Thomas Lawrence. Courtesy the National Portrait Gallery, London

Benjamin Disraeli, who disapproved of Lola's influence on some British statesmen in the 1830's.

After the painting by Sir Francis Grant. Picture Collection, New York Public Library

PASKEWITCH

Count Ivan Feodorovich Paskevich, Russian field marshal who became governor of Poland. Lola was banished hurriedly after she defied this admirer and stirred up mutiny in Warsaw.

Library of Congress

Prince Metternich, Viennese diplomat, who was Lola's implacable enemy and helped oust her from Bavaria.

Lord Palmerston, British statesman, for whom Lola was believed to have worked in her fight with Prince Metternich and the Jesuit forces in Bavaria and Switzerland.

George Sand, admired and copied
by Lola Montez after the dancer
was introduced to her salon.

Painting by Eugène Leygue. Picture
Collection, New York Public Library

Franz Liszt, whose romance with
Lola Montez in the early 1840's
was one of her more publicized
adventures.

Brown Brothers

Félicité Lamennais, French priest and philosopher, who influenced Lola Montez's political outlook.

Alexandre Dumas, père. He introduced Lola to the wits and savants of Paris in the early 1840's, but predicted disaster for the men who crossed her path.

Lola at the bedside of Alexandre Henri Dujarier after his fatal duel in the Bois de Boulogne in 1845.

King Ludwig I of Bavaria, who was sixty when Lola Montez came into his life.

Portrait by Wilhelm von Kaulbach in the New Pinakothek, Munich

Lola in the late 1840's in Munich, a period of power and arrogance.

Stadtarchiv. Munich

The "bijou palace" built for Lola Montez on the Barerstrasse in Munich by Ludwig I.
Here, before her exile, she received his political advisors and gave lavish parties.

The Residenz, the palace of King Ludwig I of Bavaria, in Munich. Here Lola Montez
was received as advisor and favorite.

Lola Montez caricatured as she
danced in Germany in 1847.

By W. Stek from Eduart Fuchs, Ein Vormärzliches Tänz-Idyll: Lola Montez in der Karikatur

Berrymead Priory at Acton near London, England. Here in 1849 Lola spent a brief
honeymoon with George Trafford Heald, her second husband, before being charged
with bigamy and fleeing to the continent.

From Lola Montez, Die Spanische Tänzerin by Erich Pottendorf

Lola Montez, a defiant feminist, shocked Americans in the 1850's by smoking in public.

Marie Comtesse de Landsfeld Heald when she was touring the United States posing as an intellectual and social reformer.

Engraved from a daguerreotype by Meade Brothers, New York. Courtesy Harvard Theatrical Collection

Lola Montez presented as author and lecturer.

Cover illustration for a book by Charles C. Burr, 1958. Picture Collection, New York Public Library

Lola Montez and Patrick Hull at Grass Valley, California, in 1854.

Courtesy, Bancroft Library, University of California, Berkeley

Lola Montez in her late thirties, when she was turning from spiritualism to religion.

Daguerreotype by Richards, engraved by H. Davidson. Century Magazine, May, 1904

been made. When he understood that his hand was being forced he looked up at Prince Wallerstein, appraised the icy glance leveled at the papers, and signed them thoughtfully.

"What have you done?" Ludwig demanded.

"It was with forethought," the Minister replied. "You had no other choice. Otherwise all is already expedited."

"Then you have no further need of me," the tired King responded with a mixture of surprise and anger.

"It would be chivalrous, sire, to abdicate," another of his ministers pointed out blandly.

A deputation from the Palatinate, eager to help the King, was denied admission. "Tell them that I am no longer free," he said. "I can no more agree to anything or make promises. All that I am made to sign is against my wish."

Ludwig showed no fear. He was saddened, disillusioned, but he realized that to save the crown for his son Maximilian he must abdicate. Otherwise the monarchy would come to an end in Bavaria. As the roar outside the Residenz became more threatening the sound of the tumbrel echoed down the years for Ludwig. The undertones of total revolution were not new to him.

On March 21, 1848, five weeks after Lola left Munich, he signed his abdication papers, after his ministers and members of his family had persuaded him that he must bow out. He may even have felt relieved to lay down the burden that had become overwhelming, and to escape from the hate and disorder that shadowed the magnificent city he had fashioned over the years. He was already under the heel of the nobles, and he had passed the night in consultation with his family before issuing his farewell:

A new state of feeling has begun—a state which differs essentially from that embodied in the Constitution according to which I have governed the country for twenty-three years. I abdicate my crown in favor of my beloved son, the crown Prince Maximilian. My government has been in strict accordance with the Constitution; my life has been dedicated to the welfare of my people. I have administered the public money and property as if I had been a republican officer, and I can boldly encounter the severest scrutiny. I offer my heart-

felt thanks to all who have adhered to me faithfully, and though I descend
from the throne, my heart still glows with affection for Bavaria and for
Germany.

The King's speech was delivered with quiet dignity at the Residenz, and immediately silence fell over Munich. He decided to tra-
verse the entire city as a farewell gesture, and the crowds responded
according to their political feeling. "What a day for the people to
see me for the last time as a King!" Ludwig remarked without a
trace of reproach.

He drove along the handsome streets, surveying the marble monuments that had been his life interest. Crowds followed him from
point to point as he bowed to passing burghers, to soldiers, to artists,
to the people with whom he had long conversed. A strain of
sympathy flowed to him from some; others vented their hate for
the King. It was the official end of a picturesque ruler, and the older
residents realized that they would no longer encounter Ludwig
rambling through the streets, his hair blowing in the wind, his long
redingote flapping against his gaitered legs.

The students showed mixed reactions, according to their Ultramontane or Protestant sympathies, when officially informed that
Ludwig had abdicated. They were the younger generation, caught
in a tide of reforming zeal, but they were also imaginative enough
to see the drama of Ludwig's eclipse. The artists of Munich united
in an address to him, lauding his genius and regretting that they
had lost the patronage of the throne. Maximilian was a hard-
headed and strict ruler who carefully husbanded the public funds.
But it took time for the Bavarians to forget Lola Montez.

She was in Switzerland when she heard of the King's abdication.
The news was no surprise to her, and she chose to think that it was
she who had persuaded him to give up his throne, and live in peace
as a private citizen. The Swiss received her with enthusiasm, made
her their guest, and offered her sanctuary for life. She later regretted having refused a permanent residence in Switzerland, for
had she remained there she might have wielded further power

"among those scheming nations." Lord Palmerston, sympathetic to the Swiss liberals, thought that the Countess had been badly treated in Bavaria. He followed each move she made with close attention.

Before long she reached Lindau on Lake Constance, her original goal, and there she was joined by Fritz Peissner, Count Hirschberg and young Nüssbaum. As her ambition revived she leased the Château de l'Impératrice on Lake Geneva, where the Empress Josephine had once lived, and she did some yachting on the lake in the summer of 1848. For a time she stayed at Prégny, two miles from Geneva. She clung tenaciously to the thought that Ludwig would join her in course of time, and that the château and the yacht would be part of the picture.

Her horizon soon narrowed down to the boredom and monotony of a static existence in Berne, the spotless capital of Switzerland. She missed the feeling of power and excitement that had colored her days in Munich. She had persuaded the King to change his ministries three times in one year, and had used her influence frankly and despotically on public issues. It had been a period of tension and high excitement, which was the very breath of life to Lola Montez. But now the misty skies, the encircling mountains, the unfathomable scrutiny of the Swiss women, the feeling of reaction that followed her fantastic days in Munich, the knowledge that the King had moved out of her orbit made her restless and moody.

She was studied with the greatest interest as she strolled through the winding streets and squares of Berne. Viscount Robert Peel, the youthful and handsome chargé d'affaires at the British Legation, took Lola under his protection, and they were soon seen riding, dining and sauntering together. The Viscount was the son of Sir Robert Peel, whose name made "peelers" of the Irish constabulary. Lola was well aware that the elder Peel had supported the Whigs in the emancipation of Jews, and had removed penal laws against Roman Catholics. He opposed Lord Palmerston's policy of interference in Greece, where Ludwig's son Otto reigned unhappily.

147

Young Peel had played an active role for Palmerston in the battle between the Swiss liberals and the Sonderbund. His infatuation for the Countess was manifest to all who watched them. Each day there were fresh political developments across Europe and Lola talked brilliantly and knowingly of the changing scene.

For thirty years the Great Powers—Great Britain, Russia, Prussia and Austria—had sustained the principle of hereditary government with Metternich the key figure. France was admitted to the Grand Alliance in 1818, after Napoleon had shaken the balance of power in Europe, and the Treaty of Vienna had made fresh disposition of territory. Russia annexed Finland and enlarged the grand duchy of Warsaw. Norway was transferred to Denmark and then to Sweden. Prussia was enlarged at the expense of Saxony. Austria took over northern Italy in exchange for Belgium, which was united with Holland until 1830. The states of Germany were organized into the German Confederation, replacing the rule of the Holy Roman Empire.

But the pressure exerted by the Great Powers in this reshuffling of people with common racial and territorial attachments could not block out the rising tide of political and industrial revolution. Hereditary government was challenged by strong industrial forces opposed to a privileged nobility, and the landed gentry of the agricultural age. The invention of the steam engine had hastened the development of factories and railways, and had changed the social pattern for all time.

Anticlericalism flourished and the distrust of absolute monarchs developed in France by the Revolution spread rapidly throughout Europe. It was particularly strong in Catholic countries, where there were more restraints. France had replaced its absolutist Bourbon monarch with Louis Philippe, who fostered business and the arts until he too fell victim to the uprisings of 1848. The situation had come to a head that year, when small fires across Europe exploded into a general conflagration.

Each move that Lola observed from her haven in Switzerland was understandable to her as the logical sequence of events she had been following for years. She felt that she had had her own small part in it with her stiff fight against the Ultramontane. In the spring of 1847, while she had been dominating the scene in Bavaria, there had been revolutionary demonstrations in Modena, Parma, Florence and various cities in northern Italy. Soon there was insurrection in Vienna, protest in Spain, and bloodshed in Paris and Ireland. Prince Louis Bonaparte was elected President of the French Republic by plebiscite. The French entered Rome on the July day that Garibaldi left the city with his corps. By December the Emperor of Austria had abdicated in favor of his nephew, the Archduke Franz Josef. The term *communism* came into use as the insurrectionists toppled monarchies and tried to set up republics. They were also responsible for the exile of Europe's most spectacular diplomat.

Lord Palmerston was not sorry to see the downfall of Metternich or of Guizot, his leading foes on the Continent, although he had preserved diplomatic amenities with both men. Guizot had schemed to establish an anti-British alliance of the great European powers, and Palmerston had played a variety of roles, backing the revolutionaries in Spain and giving some degree of countenance to those in France and Italy but preserving neutrality in Hungary and opposing revolutionaries when an abortive revolution developed in Berlin in March. The republican cause was lost in both Spain and Italy but by 1849 Palmerston had reached a new peak of popularity in Britain as the champion of liberalism—a long step from his earlier reputation as an unbending Tory.

Germany for a time was in chaos and the Grand Duke of Baden had been driven from his dominion, a matter of great concern to Queen Victoria. But with Ludwig and Lola both out of the way Bavaria settled down by degrees. Maximilian ruled solemnly and prudently. Ludwig had compromised with the inevitable and was following his natural bent—as the scholar, the poet, the artist, the traveler, the dreamer, free of political shackles. He was not unhappy or wholly regretful. Years later he wrote about the Countess

149

to a friend, the Baronne von der Tann: "They were blissful days. How elevated, how gay her presence, and so the future did smile at me. If we feel happy we *are* happy and now . . . what a change has taken place!"

Lola, too, thought of these days with tenderness. "He was the greatest and best King that Bavaria has ever had," she wrote after Ludwig's abdication. "It would take half a million like his son . . . to make one like the old King himself. Louis had really little admiration for that bauble, a crown. It was the last thing he took pride in. His manners and his social habits were rather those of a plain and honest gentleman, than of a King."

In the final analysis Lola described him as "great in the arts, a friend of peace, abhorrent of war, and adverse to the tricks and stratagems of diplomacy." She thought it characteristic of him that he should say after his abdication: "It took me about an hour's consideration to resign the crown, but it required two days to separate me from the idea of being protector of the fine arts."

When the anger that had driven him from office died down, many of the critics who scorned his Pantheon and Renaissance buildings gave Ludwig credit for the practical things he had done to modernize his medieval kingdom. He had lavished the same care on blueprints for canals and waterways that he had on those involving classical architecture. He was responsible for the canal uniting the Maine and the Danube that gave an uninterrupted line of water communication from Rotterdam to the Black Sea, and he had helped plan the national railways of Bavaria, beginning with a short line from Nuremberg to Fürth in 1833. One of his pet projects assured state aid for the farmer, and he revolutionized the tax system of Bavaria.

But from the day Lola came into his life he ceased to be his own master. In the early days of his overthrow both were plagued by the blackmailing operations of the Marquis Auguste Papon, a Frenchman who had accompanied Lola to Munich and later served as her secretary and household manager during her days of power in Bavaria. At the time of her flight Papon was entrusted with the financial arrangements that the King made for her future. At an early stage in their negotiations Ludwig wrote to him that he was being blamed for giving the Countess too much. "Still, I want my dearly beloved Countess to be satisfied," he wrote. "The whole world cannot part me from her."

Papon, who eventually was imprisoned for swindling and for impersonating a priest, belonged to one of the oldest families in Provence and his father had a high post in the Treasury of France. Lola had taken the Marquis from his family stronghold in Nyon and established him at the court and in the good graces of the King. She assured him that Ludwig would compensate him well for his services, and he brought his mother to stay at the house on the Barerstrasse for a time. But Papon's subsequent operations did more to smear Lola's reputation, particularly in America, than almost any of her other associations. After the flight from Munich he saw a chance to line his nest with gold and he worked rancorously toward this end after she dismissed him as her secretary in Geneva when she realized that he was intent on blackmailing both her and the King.

Before they separated Papon discussed with the Countess the preparation of a book about her experiences, but she had no intention of making use of her dramatic history in this way, or of embarrassing the King. However, Papon quietly took notes on all her adventures in Switzerland, including transient affairs with a baron, an artist and a sailor. He later used his findings to deadly effect, but seeing where things were heading Lola abandoned him and moved on to Berne.

When Papon found that she would not support him in his efforts to extort money from Ludwig he turned all his batteries on the former monarch. A succession of guileful letters threatening full revelations in a book he was writing were addressed to the King. At first they were fawning, then accusatory, and finally openly threatening. Ten million francs was the price he asked for the suppres-

151

sion of Ludwig's letters to Lola, and he added that the Countess "would support this reparation." All along he gave the impression that she was behind his demand for money, but this was altogether false. Efforts to head him off by Joel Cherbuliez, a Geneva bookseller and wine merchant, were futile and Papon's threats continued. Frustrated by the fact that the King ignored all his letters he volunteered fresh information on Lola's life in Geneva to stir up his interest. He wrote of conduct "so scandalous" that one of the Countess's lovers had had to flee from Geneva and the police had ordered her to leave town. A letter from Papon to the King dated December 1, 1848, suggested that she was involved in spying operations with this young man, a prominent German count, and that they were linked with the Ultramontane controversy.

By that time Ludwig was staying at the villa he had taken in Nice. He wandered about among his orange trees, wrote poetry and dreamed of Lola, even while he noticed passing beauties. Papon's threats were dim rumblings that failed to tarnish his idyllic memories of Lola, but his family and friends were concerned about the promised revelations. In spite of efforts made to suppress its publication the book came out at Nyon in 1849 and was called *Lola Montès Mémoires accompagnés de lettres intime de S.M. Le Roi de Bavière et de Lola Montès*. It catalogued Lola's sins, purported to throw fresh light on her relationship with the King, and bluntly called her a strumpet, a courtesan and a prostitute. All Europe talked about the Papon book since it was published in French, English and German, circulating widely and becoming a *succès de scandale*.

It was full of intimate touches about the King and Lola. As Papon put it in one of his letters to the former King: "Nothing is hidden from me, neither of the past nor the present; your cabinet, Sire, Lola's bedchamber, are still but glass for me. I enter both one and the other when I please." While working for the Countess in Munich the smooth, worldly and insidious Papon had taken careful soundings on what went on at the Barerstrasse and the Residenz. Beyond that he had picked up evidence against her in London, Geneva,

Paris, and even as far away as India, devoting months to tracing her history.

"It is not with joy that I unveil these disgraceful mysteries . . . or make myself the historian of royal turpitude," Papon wrote in telling the King that the Countess had made a fool of him, that youths had used her garden entrance while he had used the front door; that she had madly squandered state money and taken advantage of every opportunity to deceive him. He pictured her kneeling on a mosaic prie-dieu bemoaning her sins; groaning at the foot of the cross of pearl and ebony that the King had given her; twisting the chaplet of agate and silver in the icy fingers with which she rolled her cigarettes or struck soullessly on her guitar. She dared not be alone; repose and solitude made her mortally afraid, sorrowful and somber. "What, then, is the secret of this unknown and terrible life?" Papon wrote.

He reminded Ludwig that he too had been baffled by the Countess's enigmatic nature and had asked him for enlightenment. But neither one could explain it, and when Papon pressed him about her bills he said: "What consoles me, what fortifies me and encourages me, is the fidelity of the *incomparable*." On that occasion the King gave him 20,000 francs to pay her rent, her coal merchant and her servants and to redeem her plate from the pawnbroker.

It was the same story all over again when they got to Switzerland. According to Papon, the Countess went from one amorous adventure to another, and spent the King's funds with abandon. Papon wrote of the six rings she had bought from a Geneva jeweler, and the twenty summer dresses with other baubles that she had picked up in two hours. He felt outraged when she insisted on buying an assortment of animals that caught her eye in a menagerie in Geneva, going into raptures over a catacoa, two American parakeets, a tiny wistitis and a number of monkeys. He thought it characteristic that he could scarcely tear her away from an owl, an eagle, an antelope and even a rhinoceros.

153

Papon described the Countess as an original, the inheritor of conflicting traits. She knew Andalusia like England, France like Scotland, Russia like Poland, Prussia like Bavaria, and conversed with ease of Paris or Berlin, Cracow, Seringapatam, Seville or St. Petersburg. She quoted Latin without hesitation but he considered her German poor. He commented on her knowledge of Sanskrit and Hindustani, and said that she spoke French with an English and Spanish accent. Although she wrote and spoke Spanish, he was dubious about her grasp of this language.

The Marquis described his book as a narrative, written without hatred, without passion, and without satirical intent. But Lola found it a book filled with insolence toward a fallen monarch, not to speak of the savage attack on herself. During the dark winter days of 1850 she wrote many letters to the King about Papon's claims and charges, seeking to prove that she was in no way implicated in his blackmail scheme. With the help of a professional writer she turned out a book of her own entitled: *Lola Montez: or a Reply to the 'Private History and Memoirs' of that celebrated lady recently published by the Marquis Papon, formerly secretary to the King of Bavaria and for a period the professed friend and attendant of the Countess of Landsfeld.*

Lola accused Papon of being a "quondam pander," a man disappointed in his expectation of the reward he looked for, not in gratitude, but in gold. She compared him to Judas Iscariot, who for pieces of gold [sic] had betrayed his master. He sneered at Ludwig for calling those who had overthrown him revolutionaries. He said it was the "whole Bavarian nation, rising as one man against an irreparable outrage, against the most odious, the most wounding of insults that a king can offer to a nation."

Why had she been dragged into his dispute with the King in any event? Lola asked. Why rake Europe and India to find out and publish scandalous evidence against her? Had she not made Papon a chamberlain? Had she not paid him the ten thousand francs he demanded as the price for having his mother stay with her in Munich?

"Kings are mortal like yourself, Monsieur de Marquis Auguste Papon," Lola wrote, "and do not desire that their weaknesses be revealed to the public eye." She cited other kings and their mistresses and asked in what way the conduct of the King of Bavaria and Lola Montez differed from that of other monarchs and their mistresses—"women of the first wit, beauty, and intelligence." She had no apologies to make for her relationship with King Ludwig, said Lola, as she drew attention to the amours of Henry IV of France, Henry V, Louis XIV and Louis XV.

But Lola's seventy-six-page memoir, which she believed at the time to be self-exculpatory, turned out to be a disaster, and it faced her as she moved from place to place. In answering Papon's charges categorically she brought them into full view, whereas they might have passed unnoticed. But irrespective of Papon's destructive tactics she received strong backing in an article written by a well-known judge for the *American Law Journal* of 1848. Through her influence with King Ludwig she was credited with being responsible for great political changes in Bavaria. She had not used her power for the promotion of unworthy persons or for corrupt purposes, according to this publication. On the contrary, "political feeling influenced her course, not sordid considerations . . . on foreign politics she has clear ideas, and has been treated by the political men of the country as a substantive power. . . . Let Lola Montez have credit for her talents, her intelligence, and her support of popular rights."

This was balm for the Countess as she prepared to make another significant move in her life by returning to England along with the other exiles seeking sanctuary there after the great upheavals of 1848.

TEN

Marries Wealthy Englishman
—Flees Bigamy Charge

Tired of her continental wanderings and with fresh funds from Ludwig, Lola returned officially to England early in April, 1849. She had made one secret visit some weeks earlier without leaving any traces of her movements. On her second sailing, by the irony of circumstance her departure from Rotterdam came close to coinciding with that of Prince Metternich, who had fallen victim to revolution and was an exile from Vienna after years of rule in the tradition of the magnificos.

They were due to sail on the same ship but at the last moment the Prince received news that made him postpone his sailing. The long fight of the Chartists, a radical group pushing for parliamentary reform, had been refueled by the arrival of noted refugees in England after the storms that had swept the Continent during 1848. The spirit of revolution seemed to threaten Britain, too.

The Chartists planned a great demonstration for April 10, to assemble at Kensington Green and march on the Houses of Parliament.

The Government nipped in the bud this plan for the march, and appealed to the working class for support. Wellington took charge of the army in London and 175,000 men were enrolled as special constables to guard public buildings and government offices. Lord Palmerston personally directed the detachment defending the Foreign Office. The Chartists stopped at Westminster Bridge when faced by Wellington's troops. They soon scattered, but the impression prevailed that they were led on this occasion by foreign agitators.

Advance news of the planned demonstration caused Metternich to change his sailing at the last minute and he noted in his diary: "If the Chartist troubles had not prevented me embarking yesterday at Rotterdam I should have reached London that morning in the company of the Countess of Landsfeld—thank heaven for having preserved me from such contact," he later wrote.

Metternich had had a sordid flight and was short of money until Baron Rothschild sent him funds at the last moment. He had crossed the German and Dutch frontiers under an assumed name and it was not until he landed in England on April 20 that he was again Count Metternich, the man who had helped to reshape Europe after the Duke of Wellington had beaten Napoleon in the field. Now his flight to England was an embarrassment to the liberal regime of Palmerston, who was trying to keep Britain clear of the tide of revolution that had overthrown monarchies and conservative regimes in Europe.

Lola was subdued and weary as she sailed, with a youthful Swiss exile in tow. Her three faithful Alemannia had left her some time earlier in Berne, and she was heading into a new phase of her existence. Both she and Metternich could already see from vastly different points of view the fruits of the struggle in which they had shared. Her role might have been minor in comparison with that of the powerful diplomat who had influenced events in Europe for forty years, but it had not been so negligible that it had escaped his attention as a factor in the Ultramontane controversy in Bavaria and the abdication of the King.

Yet her return to England began a period of eclipse and anticlimax in her fast-paced life. She had been mirrored in the press as an empire shaker. Her power over King Ludwig had been analyzed from every angle. Her whip, her cigars, her figure, her magnetic blue eyes and white skin made her distinguishable wherever she appeared. Her name was well known from Dublin to St. Petersburg. Her romance with Liszt had added to her fame. The Dujarier case had already established her as a *femme fatale* and Dumas had put this thought into words that had penetrated the consciousness of a great many people.

But Ludwig's abdication was fresh in the public mind, and the political hierarchy in Britain watched Lola's course with interest and caution. For the time being she decided to keep out of sight but to seek the company of men of influence and power. She took quarters in Half-Moon Street and quickly set up a salon haunted by young men of fashion and titled Victorians who were drawn rather than driven off by the air of scandal that surrounded her.

Ambassadors who were in and out of London were disposed to call her their *enfant terrible*. Lola's diplomatic entanglements across Europe had brought her repeatedly to the attention of peers serving in the foreign field. Lord Normanby, who had since become Ambassador to France, had fond recollections of the bewitching young bride he had danced with during her early days in Dublin, and he was sometimes disposed to attend her receptions.

Edward Leveson-Gower, son of Earl Granville, who had served as British Ambassador in St. Petersburg, Brussels and Paris, had intimate knowledge of Lola's history. His family had always been interested in the theater, too, and in his *Bygone Years* Leveson-Gower told of his admiration for Rachel and for another "much less gifted individual but who, having captivated a King, upset two

Ministries, and brought about a revolution in Bavaria, was entitled to be looked upon as celebrated." He noted that on her arrival back in London she was causing "an even bigger sensation than that inspired by the Swedish nightingale Madame Jenny Lind."

But Lola's experiences in Munich had ravaged her, and her manner was dimmed by an air of melancholy. Leveson-Gower had expected more fire than he found, for she was tired, nervous and low in physical energy when he met her. It took her some time to recharge the batteries that had suffered such wear and tear, but her wit and intelligence were irresistible to him. She was freely discussed in Lady Holland's salon, which he frequented, and also at the Duke of Devonshire's. The peerage in general were interested in Lola, and the most alluring of the duchesses, in an era of outstandingly beautiful British duchesses, watched her warily. They saw her as a high flyer even in an age when license underlay the puritanical Victorian image. With Prince Albert the model consort at Windsor, all things German came under careful scrutiny in court circles, and Queen Victoria had been known to express the view that the battle in Bavaria had been between Lola Montez and the Jesuits, and not between the monarchy and the republican spirit. It was known that the Lady of Windsor, with royal relatives scattered across the map of Europe, was not indifferent to the fate of the errant Countess, particularly after she tried to storm a reception at Buckingham Palace. Lola's association with some of her Cabinet ministers was undeniable, and Benjamin Disraeli was a scathing critic of her arrogant behavior.

Lola fared best in liberal circles and benefited by the fact that England was having a political upheaval of its own. The Whigs had come into power and the Chartist movement was spreading. Trade unions were being organized and electoral reform was under way. Almost at once Lola became involved in political issues through her friendship with Lord Brougham, the Scottish jurist and political leader, who was married to the niece of Miss Emily Eden and Lord

Auckland. Lord Brougham happened to be a nineteenth-century swinger, brilliant, witty and an irrepressible radical. During his years as Lord Chancellor of Great Britain the reform coach rattled along with greater speed than the brougham that was named after him. His long life history was a constant fight for reforms which one by one came to pass. He was largely responsible for forty acts of law reform between 1828 and 1856. He helped push through the Reform Bill of 1831 and worked for the abolition of slavery. Measures to spread and liberalize education in Britain were brilliantly advocated by Lord Brougham and he was to a great degree responsible for the establishment of London University. With Sydney Smith he founded the *Edinburgh Review* and he was the "learned friend" in Thomas Love Peacock's *Crotchet Castle*, published in 1831.

There were a number of reasons why Lord Brougham should become the guiding star in Lola's circle of influential friends. She was ostensibly his ward through the Emily Eden connection. He had close knowledge of the operations of the East India Company and he understood Lola's background. As a reformer in all his instincts he was interested in the role she had played in Bavaria. He had followed the de Beauvallon trial in Rouen with close attention, because of his admiration for Berryer, whom he considered one of the three great lawyers of the day.

Lord Brougham was familiar with Paris in the days of Louis Philippe, and he often visited the Tuileries and conversed with the Citizen King. The life of the boulevards was well known to him, too, as the friend of Dumas and others who had been in Lola's circle in Paris. The ladies of the British peerage were divided in their attitude to Lord Brougham. He got on best with the strong individualists and Lady Jersey, Lady Rosslyn and Lady Darlington were among his favorites. His proud Scottish mother, Mrs. Eleanor Brougham, had dared to snub the autocratic Lady Holland and he was unimpressed by the great Whig dynasties of the day. Lady Grey, who had liked him at first, turned against him. He was as outspoken in royal circles as he was with his bohemian friends, such as Lady Byron, Leigh Hunt and Mrs. George Lamb.

Although as a youth Lord Brougham had studied political economy at Edinburgh University with Henry Temple, who later became Lord Palmerston, they tangled in many ways on political issues. Brougham emerged a flaming radical from the tutorial influence of Professor Dugald Stewart, a friend of Adam Smith's. Young Temple on the other hand stuck to the Tory principles of his inheritance and put them into practice when he became Secretary of War during the Napoleonic struggle. The two men battled endlessly on such issues as capital punishment, flogging in the army, slavery in the West Indies, the deportation of political refugees, freedom of the press, Parliamentary reform and injustice to prisoners. Lord Palmerston invariably voted with the Government against Lord Brougham and his fellow radicals.

The two peers were in conflict when Lord Brougham successfully defended Queen Caroline in the proceedings involving the Prince Regent's efforts to divorce her. Daughter of the Duke of Brunswick, Caroline had been forced by George III to marry his dissolute son, who hated her from the start and did everything he could to get rid of her. When he tried to divorce her on grounds of adultery with various menials, she had warm support from the public because of his own record as a profligate. The leaders of the opposition came to her defense and Lord Brougham functioned brilliantly as her counsel throughout the interminable proceedings. Having refused a settlement offered her on condition that she renounce the title of Queen, she was forcibly excluded from Westminster Hall on the day that her husband was crowned George IV. Lord Brougham fought for the abandonment of a bill in the House of Lords charging Caroline with adultery. When it passed by no more than nine votes, the King was persuaded to withdraw it. Lord Palmerston supported his monarch, and so did the powerful Lady Cowper and many of the more noted peeresses.

161

Already a reformer on many public issues Lord Brougham's name became a household word in the homes of the peerage as a campaigner for changes in the divorce laws. This had direct bearing on Lola's future when she became ensnarled in divorce and bigamy proceedings. It caused talk but did not surprise anyone when Lord Brougham brought the Countess of Landsfeld to the Ladies' Gallery to hear him speak on reform measures. It had been his function for years to hear appeals in judicial cases before the Privy Council and the House of Lords. He was in his early sixties when Lola came into his life, and for a time there was talk that he wished to marry her. This was manifestly absurd since his amiable wife, described as "sitting like an overgrown doll at the top of the table in a bandeau of roses, her face a perpetual simper without utterance" was as aloof from Lord Brougham's romantic interests as Queen Theresa was from Ludwig's. He was devoted to his children and divided his time between his wife's house at 5 Hill Street, London; Brougham Hall, his estate in Westmoreland; and Cannes, his favorite winter resort.

Lola was fascinated by Lord Brougham's scholarship, wit and reforming zeal, and they talked at length about Metternich, whose presence in London was upsetting the statesmen who wished to keep Britain clear of the revolutionary developments on the continent. Lord Palmerston was his most diplomatic self with the exiled Metternich but too many memories of working at cross purposes lay between the two men. The Prince was more drawn to Disraeli as a fellow conservative and one who made a point of flattering him, calling him in one of his letters the "greatest statesman and the kindest man in the world." The exiled statesman found satisfaction in briefing Disraeli on points he could use on continental affairs in debates with Lord Palmerston, and it entertained him to see in his morning *Times* how effectively his ammunition had been applied.

Metternich showed up constantly in London, Brighton and Brussels between 1848 and 1851, before he returned to Vienna and to fresh honors in his last years. There was no mistaking his majestic figure, lofty brow and thin lips as he sauntered about, swinging a gold-headed cane. He wrote to kings and statesmen but less and less to the women who had figured so prominently in his life. But they were not forgotten. Lola read with intense interest of the visits paid to him at Brighton by three aged figures from his past. All had been important in his life—the Duchess of Sagan; Madame Bagration, the "bel ange nu" painted by Sir Thomas Lawrence; and Princess de Lieven, who had been his love and his adviser for many years. She became his mistress at the Congress of Aix-la-Chapelle in 1818, and twenty years later, when she was fifty-two, she assumed the same role with Guizot, who was with her when she met Metternich at Brighton. Britain had become the refuge of the fallen notables of 1848. Louis Philippe, the Citizen King of France, was among them with his family and was a favorite of Queen Victoria's. She had always liked him.

Lola felt that she was part of the picture of deposed royalty as she took her place on the London scene. Ironically enough, for the first time in her life she now met Metternich. None who knew her doubted that she would face him unabashed and unafraid. Lord Brougham drove her to Richmond to call on the Austrian diplomat, who had settled in a house called the Old Palace, with a great library, impressive gardens and "everything worthy of him," in Disraeli's opinion. It would be difficult to fathom the impulse that had led Lord Brougham to arrange this confrontation, unless Lola had insisted on it herself. But, according to her account of the conversation, it gave her much satisfaction to see Metternich "with his claws cut and his wings clipped."

"Well, Countess," he said to her, according to Lola's recollection of the encounter, "I am astonished at but one thing—not at your winning a position as the head of the government in Bavaria, and the rebel party, but at your being able to keep it so long against all the batteries that were brought to bear against you."

163

Lola's response to this, according to her own version of the meeting, was audacious: "I always told the truth and acted above board and honestly, while you did the reverse."

The usual flow of gossip surrounded everything that the Countess did and her receptions were closely observed in official circles. Snuff boxes, fans and mugs stamped with her image turned up in many English homes, and her dramatic use of black—not drab Victorian black but gleaming Lola Montez black—affected the fashions of the hour. Her dashing hats and sure instinct for style were discussed freely in an overembellished age. As in Munich, aristocrats and bohemians gathered around her for good talk, music, excellent fare, and the excitement that she instinctively generated. She squandered money freely, but was filled with restlessness. Nothing seemed to satisfy her after the high days of her reign in Munich.

Lola spent much time at her desk, writing letters to Ludwig. She rode around London in a landau, often with her maid, when there was no young man at hand to accompany her. Inevitably her skill as a horsewoman attracted attention during her frequent rides in the park. The people close to the theater had not forgotten her, for she had been persistent in her gropings for fame as a dancer. Actors and journalists wandered into her salon from time to time, as well as august elder statesmen and the young bloods of the day. But she was a fallen idol with the press. Although the *Times* had given her serious editorial attention during her rule in Bavaria, it had swung back into strong denunciation when Ludwig abdicated. But her story held its own fascination for writers, and George Augustus Sala, who edited *Chat* and wrote a page of gossip for the *Illustrated London News* called "Echoes of the Week," considered writing her memoirs. Lola was responsive with him at first but he felt baffled when she insisted that she was the daughter of the Spanish matador Montez, one of her many flights of fancy.

"It was a hallucination which, curiously enough, was afterwards, to a certain extent, shared by Adah Isaacs Menken, who had the idea that her real name was Dolores, and that her father had been distinguished in the Iberian bull-ring," Sala wrote in his own memoirs. Adah was the black-eyed daughter of a clothier whose shop was close to the office of *Chat* until the Menkens moved to the United States. She resembled Lola Montez in many respects, from smoking cigars and committing bigamy, to being a friend of Dumas père, as well as of Swinburne and Dickens.

Inevitably Sala and Lola talked of the theater after he first ran into her buying cigars in a small shop in the Haymarket. He was the son of Claudio Sebastiano Sala, a Roman who had moved to London in 1776 and become a power in the theater. As she talked to Sala Lola's ambition for the stage revived. The mere thought of dancing again filled her with dismay, but her yearning for the limelight prevailed. Fanny Elssler was dancing at Drury Lane, and she knew that comparisons would be shattering to her. So Lola decided to play herself. Her old enemy, Benjamin Lumley, had gone and his successor thought it an excellent idea. Lola rehearsed carefully in a five-act play entitled *Lola Montez, or the Countess of an Hour*. It was based on her experiences in Bavaria, but the advertisement was quickly withdrawn when the Lord Chamberlain canceled the license. The Bavarian Legation had protested and the impression spread that the play lampooned foreign royalties. Prince Albert's feelings had to be considered where Germany was concerned. Lola's liberal friends challenged this censorship since the arts were involved, and there were cries of persecution.

Suddenly the irrepressible Countess was in the headlines again, and the old stories that she was an impostor were revived. She re-issued the public statement she had sent to the *Times* from Munich, detailing her own ancestry as she viewed it, when the same stories circulated there. But, in spite of her protests, the belief that she was passing herself off meretriciously as a Spanish dancer persisted. However, the failure of her stage ambitions in London did not dim her standing as a charmer, and her receptions on Half-Moon Street continued to have style and variety.

On a lilac-scented day in May, 1849, as she walked in Hyde Park she noticed George Trafford Heald, a handsome young man of impressive build who happened to be a cornet in the second regiment of the Life Guards, driving with a huge black Newfoundland dog in his carriage. After that when she walked alone in the park she was conscious of the same young man observing her closely as he drove past. Through a mutual friend she learned that he wished to sell the dog. Always interested in animals she decided that she would like to own this handsome specimen; perhaps she also wanted to meet its owner, but in any event she sent him the following note: "The Countess of Landsfeld presents her respectful compliments to Lieutenant Heald, and will be most happy should he be so kind as to honour her by joining a small party of select friends who will assemble at her residence tomorrow evening."

The Countess's formal invitations were rarely ignored, and after this reception they met daily and rode or drove together, impressing passersby with their combined good looks and superior horsemanship. Heald, who was rich and of good family, told Lola many amusing stories about the riders they passed. Her beguiling accent, her striking looks, and her imperious manner took the inexperienced young man by storm. She was used to army life and to soldiers, so that they had a common talking ground beyond his obvious infatuation. He did not stop to think that she had recently loved a man of sixty and cost him his kingdom, as he watched the statesmen, writers, actors, soldiers and professional dandies who circled around her. It was only a matter of a few weeks until he proposed to her, and on July 19, 1849, two months after they met in the park, they were married by the Reverend A. Alston in St. George's Church, Hanover Square.

Lola was cautious enough to see that there was no prior announcement, but an erroneous story spread that a member of one of England's oldest ducal houses was marrying a foreign countess. A crowd gathered in the street and watched a handsome equipage draw up. Lola emerged in a tide of satin. Her beauty seemed dazzling in the gray light of a murky day. Her high cheekbones and immense blue eyes, becomingly shaded by the darkest of lashes, were commented on in the press. Heald was described as looking ridiculously young, with a tilted nose, a downy blond mustache and whiskers of the most fashionable trim.

The statesmen of the day were somewhat shaken to learn that Lola Montez had landed a young Englishman of well-known lineage as a husband—not that she was a Nell Gwyn from the gutter, but in assuming the identity of a Spanish dancer she had turned her back on her own substantial heritage, with such men as General Craigie, Sir Patrick Edmonstone Craigie, and others of their kind involved. Ambitious young Disraeli watched her tactics with interest, knowing her to be the ally of Lord Palmerston, Lord Brougham and other liberal statesmen. His cynical view of her marriage was conveyed to his sister Sarah in a letter written in July, 1849:

Lola Montes' marriage makes a sensation. I believe he has only £3000 per annum, not £13,000. It was an affair of a few days. She sent to ask the refusal of his dog, which she understood was for sale . . . he sent it as a present; she rejoined, he called, and they were married in a week. He is only twenty-one and wished to be distinguished. Their dinner invitations are already out, I am told. She quite convinced him previously that she was not Mrs. James, and as for the King of Bavaria, (who, by the bye, allows her £1500 a year and to whom she really writes every day) that was only a *malheureuse passion*.

Lola was not unused to baronial splendor but she thought she was on substantial ground when she spent her short honeymoon with Heald at Berrymead Priory, the Gothic pile at Acton that had belonged to his father. Here Edward Bulwer-Lytton had lived in 1835 while he tried for a reconciliation with his wife Rosina, but it was a hopeless attempt as her anger and jealousy made the Priory a house of discord and misery. Actually it dated back to the time of Henry III and the family motto inscribed in mosaic on the hall floor *Nemo Sibi Mascitur* (No one is born for himself) gave Lola reassurance. It had many associations, literary and otherwise, that seemed piquant to the new chatelaine. Driving through the wooded grounds in a phaeton, viewing the beauty of the gardens in sun-

167

light and in moonlight, she felt a certain sense of peace about her future. Instinctively she began to plan the changes she would make to embellish her own image at the Priory.

The King had urged her to make a good marriage in Britain, and after the storm-tossed years she had a sense of security in the belief that her husband's income was at least $30,000 a year, a substantial sum at that time. She now felt that she could count on social status, a strong young man to love and protect her, money to spend and new clothes to adorn her fabulous person. A box at the opera and acceptance by some of the dowagers who had openly snubbed her now seemed to be within her reach. If Heald's intelligence was less impressive than his stalwart form, this did not bother the bright-witted Lola, who took each man as she found him, and prized the youthful passion expended on her by a soldier whose plumed helmet and glittering cuirass made him an impressive figure to her army-conscious nature.

Lola returned to London in high spirits, prepared to give her first dinner party as Mrs. Heald and to make social plans for the future. But she had not reckoned on the animosity she had stirred up in Miss Susanna Heald, George's paternal aunt, who had promised his dying father, George Heald, a well-known member of Chancery Bar, that she would look out for his inexperienced young son. There were four Heald sisters and four brothers, all unmarried, and eager to share in the large fortune and property that the noted lawyer had left. Susanna was their spokesman and two women more unlike than Miss Heald and the Countess could not be imagined. Young George, who had just come of age, was helpless in this clash of incompatible spirits.

Susanna, who eventually was likened to Betsy Trotwood by a contemporary writer, had been making a detailed study of the Countess's history ever since Lola had crossed her nephew's path and excited his interest. The trail had extended even to Calcutta, where she chanced on the unsuspected fact that Lola's husband, James, was still alive, and that their so-called divorce was nothing more than a legal separation. Miss Heald took swift action.

On August 6, 1849, less than three weeks after her marriage, Lola came face to face with the law as she stepped into her carriage, drawn up in front of 27 Half-Moon Street. Two officers from Scotland Yard blocked her way and announced that they were taking her to the Marlborough Street Police Office. For once in her life Lola was stunned rather than combative. She seemed to sense that she was in deadly danger, and she listened attentively to the charge of bigamy they recited against her.

"This is all nonsense," she told her captors haughtily. "I don't know whether Captain James is alive or not, and I don't care. It wasn't a legal marriage because I used a wrong name. Lord Brougham was present when my divorce was granted. But, oh, what will the King say?" Presumably Lola was referring to King Ludwig, and it was a fact that she had signed the marriage register Eliza Rosanna Gilbert at Meath.

The news spread quickly that Lola Montez was in trouble again and, according to the London *Times* of August 7, 1849, "the avenues of the court were thronged." Not only did the public come to look at the famous Countess, but members of the bar showed a lively interest in the case. The fact that Lord Brougham was involved in Lola's affairs focused attention on the hearing. Heald's father, too, had been a popular colleague. Beyond that, members of the bar associated Lola with the famous Dujarier trial at Rouen.

Once again she was the central figure in a court proceeding; once again she found herself in a difficult situation. She walked into court with an air of assurance, leaning on Heald's arm. Her costume, as always, was noticeably seductive. Her black silk gown and close-fitting velvet jacket showed that she had not lost her lissome grace. When she raised the blue veil attached to her large white chip bonnet, her extraordinary eyes seemed to a *Times* reporter "to spread a blue haze through the courtroom." Peregrine Bingham, the magis-

169

trate, gave her his close attention as she sat before the bar, with Heald at her side.

But the prosecutor went crisply to work, pointing out that Miss Heald considered it a duty she owed to her deceased brother to lay before the court evidence of bigamy in the Countess's entrapment of her nephew. Actually she was still the wife of Thomas James, at the moment Captain of the 21st Regiment of the Bengal Native Infantry and very much alive. Yet she had contracted another marriage "knowing that her husband was alive, or that every reasonable ground existed for believing he was alive."

A certificate was produced to show that James and the Countess were married in Meath, Ireland, on July 23, 1837. He was then a lieutenant of the 21st Regiment of the Bengal Native Infantry, but had since become a captain. Lola smiled softly when Captain Charles Ingram, who commanded the *Larkins*, the East India trader that had brought her home from the Orient, identified her, although he said that she had changed considerably.

While all this was going on Heald sat with Lola's hand clasped in his own. He squeezed it from time to time or pressed it to his lips as they whispered to each other. This show of ardor caused Miss Heald to shudder with distaste. The worldly barristers present were more amused then censorious, and Lola's own lawyer, named Bodkin, presented a haughty front when Thomas Howard Montague, clerk of the Consistory Court, produced the record of the proceedings in the suit of James *v.* James, dated December 15, 1842, and decreeing that Thomas James and Eliza Rosanna James be separated, but that neither party should have the power to contract another marriage during the lifetime of the other. When a copy of this document was handed to Lola she quietly admitted: "I don't deny it."

Frederick Danvers, a clerk from the East India House, produced a document with James's signature, showing that he was still alive and with his regiment as late as June 1 of that year. Bodkin said the situation was preposterous. He could not recollect a case of bigamy in which neither the first nor the second husband was a complainant. Lola's trump card was the fact that her young husband resolutely refused to support the charge against her. This bothered the prosecutor, too, who acknowledged that Heald was present merely to support and comfort the accused. "The proceeding is without the consent of Mr. Heald, who no doubt would if he could prevent it from being carried on," he said.

Both sat back quietly when Miss Heald's hostile face confronted them from the witness box. They stopped caressing each other as the prosecutor said: "Miss Heald has felt it to be her duty to the family of the young gentleman, who are highly respected, to take these proceedings, even without his consent; and no one, I think, will venture to impugn the motives or the purity of the intentions of Miss Heald in taking this step."

Lola's counsel thought otherwise and argued that had it been Miss Heald's object to prevent any family complications in the future, such as might have arisen from the birth of children, she could have laid the facts before them in private, and remained forever silent if they refused to separate. "I entertain no doubt whatever," he added, "that Miss Susanna Heald wished to ruin the Countess of Landsfeld, and that this was at any rate one of her motives in instituting police court proceedings."

Bodkin argued that although the Ecclesiastical Court might only have granted a divorce *a mensa et thoro*, or bed and board, his client had a "strong impression that a divorce bill had been obtained in the House of Lords." She insisted that Lord Brougham had put this through, and had been present when the divorce was finally granted.

"If such an Act of Parliament is in existence, no one knows better how to avail himself of it than my learned friend," the prosecutor remarked sarcastically. But in the end he asked that Lola be remanded until he had had time to bring certain witnesses from India to testify. When Lola's counsel pointed out that James might have died in the few weeks preceding the trial, Judge Bingham commented on the lack of evidence and freed her under two sureties of

£500 and another £1,000 for her reappearance at some future date.

Since Lola was never called to account then or in the future her guilt or innocence was widely debated. Lord Brougham stayed out of it all, and the assumption prevailed that she had not fully understood the nature of the decree, or had misinterpreted his part in the matter. Yet she was known for her keen mind and shrewd understanding of complex issues. Moreover, there was constant communication between London and India at this time, and she had military friends who traveled back and forth, and who had not forgotten that she was General Craigie's stepdaughter. But once again this court proceeding drew public attention to her identity, and reminded many that Lola Montez the Spanish dancer was also the child of Lady Craigie, for by this time the General had been knighted.

The Healds were told to remain in court after the hearing in order to elude the crowd that had gathered outside the Marlborough Street Station for a glimpse of Lola Montez. Her memory of the menace of crowds was still too fresh for her to appreciate this attention, and she knew that the image she had sought as an English matron, living in an aura of family respectability, was already shattered. Understanding the threat to her marriage and her future she surreptitiously left England with Heald next day, taking a ship from Folkestone to France.

ELEVEN

Love and War

As fugitives from the law the Healds made every effort to avoid
publicity. This was difficult since the face of Lola Montez was one
of the most recognizable in Europe unless it was heavily veiled. Besides, there were times when she could not refrain from courting
the limelight. For eighteen months they traveled from point to point
in France, Italy and Spain, with one return trip to England. Tales
drifted back of Heald's mad infatuation for Lola, of quarrels and
reconciliations, of violence and scenes in public places. It was less
than three years since she had figured commandingly in European
politics, and the high drama of her days in Munich seemed to emphasize the futility of her wandering life with Heald. They had
little in common but a mutual passion that was consuming and
eventually annihilating.

Lola had not changed and in course of time she tired of her ardent
young lover. Heald, who had dropped his army connections soon
after the divorce hearing, missed his clubs, his regiment, the sports
he had enjoyed, his friends and even his family associations, bitter

though these had become. The Marquess of Londonderry, Colonel of the Life Guards, recommended his resignation. The Queen consulted the Prince Consort and the Duke of Wellington, and the upshot was that instead of being gazetted he was allowed to resign voluntarily. Prince Albert had recollections of Lola Montez standing on a dinner table at the Beethoven Festival in Bonn, adding to the chaos that surrounded Liszt on that occasion. He knew that nothing would stop her from having her way, so there was something to be said for Heald. When the young officer decided later that he wished to rejoin his regiment Lord Brougham intervened on his behalf, but he was not reinstated.

Lola's sustained but innocuous correspondence with King Ludwig, most of which Heald saw, did not trouble him, and he had a brief encounter with the deposed monarch in France. But his insistence that his bride return to Ludwig the royal jewels that she still possessed infuriated Lola, and the gift of a ring soon after they arrived in France from England led to the first big explosion between them. His own engagement ring and the Heald family jewels, which he had lavished on her, were no match for the royal jewels that had come her way through Ludwig. And more than money Lola valued the jewels that added to her luster. It had been agreed at the time of her marriage that the King's annual allowance to her should end. She had done what he had advised—married an Englishman of substance with a sound family reputation. He had warned her to try to stay out of trouble and not to make scenes in public. The former King was not jealous; he merely wanted Lola to be happy, and as he traveled in Italy, France and Greece there were other pretty faces to study, youthful bodies to admire, and less tempestuous natures to while away the hours for him.

The Healds' continental travels, after their flight from England, entailed fresh trouble for Lola. When they left France and journeyed south through Italy they were recognized at Padua and again in Naples, where crowds gathered outside the Vittoria Hotel to gaze at the famous beauty who had won the love of their idol, Ludwig of

Bavaria. Lola had made the usual fuss, demanding better rooms that gave her the full sweep of the Bay of Naples, but her great pile of trunks had not yet been unpacked when Heald picked up a letter at the bank that caused them to leave in haste. It was a summons from Bodkin to return to England at once for fresh developments in the bigamy case. Since no steamer was available at the moment, they chartered a private vessel for $2,000 to take them to Marseilles, and from there they proceeded to England, landing with the utmost secrecy.

Lola was chagrined to find after their urgent race north that Bodkin had gone to the country and could not be found on her arrival. She trailed him finally to a tearoom in Ramsgate, only to learn that he had not sent for her. A ruse had been used to get her back within the jurisdiction of the courts. Warned by the lawyer of her precarious situation if she stayed in England, she and Heald sailed separately for Boulogne to throw their pursuers off their trail. Heald arrived last with their servants and their luggage. Lola had made ample preparations for her wedding trip and her fashionable gowns needed special treatment. But even before Heald showed up the vigilant New York *Herald* had picked up Lola's trail and on October 23, 1849, pictured her as having landed from the Folkestone packet on the 10th and gone straight to the Hôtel de Londres. She had with her the large black Newfoundland dog that had first brought her into contact with Heald. She registered as Mrs. Trafford and told the proprietor that she would await the arrival of her husband.

The townspeople soon learned who she was when she sauntered into the leading jewelry shop on the Grand Rue with her maid and produced an uncommon ring for repair. It had the royal Bavarian crown encrusted in jewels, with the name Gräfin von Landsfeld engraved on the inner side. Her identification became positive when letters bearing her title arrived and she had to declare herself at the post office. After that, people gathered around the hotel or observed her on her walks. The *Herald* reporter described the billowing gray

175

dress she wore with a gray cobwebby shawl. Her huge gray bonnet, with a cluster of orange flowers close to her black hair, sat far back on her head in the fashionable manner.

When Heald joined her they strolled around the port and studied the ships or took bracing walks along the seafront. Lola laughed like a child as she rode a donkey led by Heald. This seemed a great joke to two such accomplished riders. But behind the badinage she was concealing from him the fact that Bodkin had told her bluntly that he had confirmed the fact that no special act of Parliament covered her situation, and that she had misunderstood Lord Brougham's role in the case. He had been working, although unsuccessfully, for a change in the divorce laws. In short, Lola was in a serious legal situation. But she clung to the fragile story that she had been married at Meath under a variation of her true name—no novelty in Lola's history, since her names were legion.

After this she could scarcely pretend even to herself that she was not a bigamist, but Heald clung to the belief that the noted Lord Brougham could not have erred in so important a matter. However, the jurist's reforming zeal at times led him into curious byways, and Bodkin had had some trouble getting to him during this period of crisis. The situation between the young pair changed for the worse when Lola forgot herself and talked with great freedom to a reporter from the New York *Herald* who caught up with them in Barcelona. Not only did she describe in romantic terms the manner in which Heald had courted her, but she glibly told of having constant communication with the former King. Lola pictured him as a fatherly figure in her life, a kind old man who thought only of her well-being. She mentioned the pension he had allowed her and at the same time disclosed that in a pre-nuptial arrangement Heald had arranged for a life annuity, and had made provision for any children they might have.

All this was searing to her young husband's pride, but in Barcelona he had a stiffer blow when English friends arrived to tell him that Lola had indeed committed bigamy and that he must leave her at once. At this point the Healds had a blazing row when he accused her of having learned the truth from Bodkin and of withholding it from him purposely. Lola did not attempt to deny this charge, and as her fury died she became deeply depressed. Heald ceased to appear with her in public and spent his time with English friends. He grew thin and haggard and the newspaper correspondent who followed their fortunes in Barcelona commented on the rift between them. The story spread belatedly that Lola had stabbed him with a stiletto at Perpignan while they were on their way to Barcelona. They had planned to arrive by sea from Marseilles but in order to avoid quarantine in the harbor they had traveled by rail to Perpignan. Heald had failed to report this episode until he appealed to the British Consul in Barcelona for a visa to leave the country. At that time he produced a bloodstained waistcoat to substantiate his story of Lola's attack.

She stayed on in Barcelona, certain that Heald would return to her. Dreading extradition if she should go to France while the bigamy proceedings were still pending, she eluded the bold glances of would-be suitors in the Spanish city and moved about circumspectly, speaking the native language, riding every day and avoiding English-speaking visitors. When Heald's passion for her overcame his anger he sent her an abject letter of apology from Mataró, writing: "If you should ever have reason to complain of me again this letter will always act as a talisman." He told the representative of a French newspaper that English friends had persuaded him to leave Lola, against his own wishes. She took him back and again they were infatuated lovers until more trouble broke out in Madrid. He disappeared and she advertised for him as if he were a lost dog. She even gave a reward to the Frenchman who brought him back after a drinking bout. "Lola has been able to catch her faithless husband, and has brought him back to the conjugal roof," the *Fomento* of Barcelona reported.

In many ways he reminded her of her first husband—with his growing tendency to drink, a stubborn adherence to the fixed rules

177

of army training, and a Victorian view of a woman's role in life. She was bored with the narrowness of his interests, his conventional responses in all social matters, his thralldom to his family and his unreasonable jealousy. She would have no interference where other men were concerned, and if they chose to look at her with arrogant appraisal she saw no reason for his sullen resentment. Had it not been for his physical attraction for her, she might have dropped him as she had so many other men in her life. But the bohemian in Lola was constantly at war with her early training and the mixed impulses of her inheritance. She was tired of breaking the rules and dashing her head against obstacles, and during these wandering days on the continent, quarreling with Heald and indulging in frantic reconciliations, she lapsed into deep depression, a tendency of hers when she could not solve a problem.

Heald's family went to great lengths to rescue George from her clutches, and to keep the family fortune from getting into Lola's hands. In time he would inherit their respective riches as well as the property left him by his father and they had no wish to have Lola Montez share in this bounty. They sent legal emissaries and one of his own particular friends to reason with him and urge him to return to England. They even sent an attractive girl across the English Channel to offset Lola's influence. But when the heat became intense the young pair threw out a smoke screen by moving rapidly from place to place, leaving no traces behind them. Now and again the press found them in unexpected situations, usually because Lola had again been causing scenes. When traced they promptly packed up and vanished. They were variously observed in Madrid, Barcelona, Cádiz, Palermo, Naples and Nice, where Ludwig spent some time each winter after his abdication.

Whenever Lola was reported to be within range of the King, it was assumed that they were in communication, but most of the reports on this were speculative. These were days of obscurity and mystery in Lola's life. In *Les Contemporains* Eugène de Mirecourt, who did not like her, alluded to the birth of two children to the

Healds at this time, but she always denied this story and there was nothing to substantiate it. Up to the last days of her life she was plagued by a succession of girls who claimed to be her daughters.

Lola seemed to find a certain excitement in the rackety life they led. In between storms of tears and angry gestures there were interludes of good companionship, of fun and wit, and excitement at the gambling tables. She stood up better to their disorderly life than Heald did. He felt disgraced when he met a fellow officer. He shrank from references to Queen and country. Yet Lola was like a drug he could not give up. His physical decline and heavy drinking were self-evident, as she lashed out at him with her sadistic impulses. They were seen at the races and in gambling casinos, and the Comtesse de Marguerittes, a chronicler of the day who ran into them at the gambling tables, thought that Lola looked like a Rubens painting in a ruby-red velvet gown that showed off her startlingly white skin and jet-black hair. She showed no animation until the stakes mounted but her mood changed to high excitement as the play went on.

The Comtesse viewed her as a "desperate gambler" stretching greedily for the gold that came her way, and refusing to stop when her companion told her that she must leave because he had no more money to give her. She rapped him on the head and haughtily remarked within the hearing of spectators that anyone accompanying her to the tables should have money at his command. The Baroness did not realize that the man with her was Heald, but she had observed Lola's operations in Paris during the days of Dujarier.

In November, 1849, they decided to risk Paris, although the bigamy issue had not yet been settled. Heavily veiled, Lola sat in an upper box at the opera watching the ballet *La Filleule des Fées*. Not even Victor Hugo or George Sand, two of her friends, were aware of her presence until a whisper ran through the theater that Lola Montez was in the audience. The press had trailed her again. She left early, and in a swirl of lifted skirts dashed through the mud in her velvet slippers to reach her carriage instead of waiting for it

179

to draw up at the entrance. However, a few nights later she appeared publicly at the opera with Heald. Both were handsomely dressed, and their carriage was drawn by four white horses and manned by ornately uniformed footmen and coachman. Far from hiding herself from view at this point, Lola had decided to make flashing public appearances. But she also made the mistake of giving a press interview that threw light on her embarrassing situation. She said that her bigamy case had not yet been settled and that her English lawyers would prolong it for years, since she had plenty of money to make this possible.

Her indiscretion brought quick action in London. The Marlborough Street magistrate issued a written order for the immediate presentation of the additional evidence that had been collected in the case. The Countess was asked to appear in person or forfeit her bail. When this news reached her she decided to return to Spain, saying that she was making this move for her husband's health. The Healds were next heard of in Cádiz to which she made a mad dash to catch up with George when he left her on Christmas Day after a furious quarrel. He headed first for Gibraltar, with Lola in pursuit, but when she reached Algeciras on a French packet she found that he had already sailed for England.

But this was not the end, for he was soon back with her in Paris. They took a long lease on a mansion in the Beaujon region, close to l'Étoile. Lola then went on a spending spree, buying furniture lavishly and charging it to Heald. At peace for the moment, the Healds were having breakfast one morning when the owner of the house arrived with a troop of relatives to remove the contents of the wine cellar that came with the house. Lola had already warned this militant lady to stay away while she was in possession, and she flew into one of her rages and ordered her off the premises. When her uninvited guest addressed her sneeringly as the uncrowned queen Lola pushed the woman through the door, only to have her face scratched and her shins kicked. This brawl brought the Countess once again to the attention of the police.

This was the final fracas so far as Heald was concerned. He left precipitately for England, surrendered to the demands of his relatives and staved off the Marlborough Street action by having his marriage annulled. Once more Lola was on her own. The security of marriage and the Heald inheritance would no longer enter into her calculations, but for the time being she had money and a wealth of valuable jewels. She was also back in the environment where she had once found her greatest happiness.

The boulevards had not changed. The press was still engaged in mortal combat. The artists and writers were deeply involved in a different social picture, with Prince Louis Napoleon functioning as the nation's ruler. But the magic was gone. Wherever Lola went she was reminded of Dujarier, and a visit to his tomb started a train of mystical visions that depressed her. Some of her old friends were glad to see her again; others avoided her. A. Augustin Thierry noted that the "tunic of Nessus had attached itself to her shoulders." Dujarier's tragic end, the fall of King Ludwig, her frantic chase across Europe as Mrs. Heald reminded her former associates that she brought ill luck into the lives of men.

After moving to another house on the Champs Élysées Lola dropped from sight for a time that winter. There were reports that she was writing her memoirs. When told that her letters from King Ludwig would bring her a fortune she proudly spurned the suggestion, but with the help of a professional writer she put together some recollections for Antenor Joly of *Le Pays*, writing about her early days in India in the blue *cahier* of the French student.

Journalists gravitated automatically to Lola and visiting writers from the United States, interested in her both as a beauty and a political rebel, flocked to her receptions. They were eager to hear what she had to say, and how much she would talk about the fallen monarch. Many distinguished Americans in arts and letters were visiting Paris at this time, and her circle of friends from the United States widened through a banker named R. Green who handled her finances. By chance he bought for her some shares in the Eureka Mine in Nevada—an investment that would pay off handsomely in the future, but she had no inkling at the time of its importance. All of her new friends from across the Atlantic were talking about the Gold Rush, but she was scarcely conscious that she would soon be in the thick of it. However, the feeling that she should visit America persisted and various efforts were made to interest her in this idea.

As always when she was coming out of one of her depressions Lola flaunted her beauty and put on an extravagant show, making dramatic appearances in public places. With her customary passion for spending she drove around town, buying furniture, carpets, mirrors, objets d'art for her new setting. She entertained on an elaborate scale, kept a carriage and staff, and lived on a scale far different from that of her earlier days in Paris. The company she kept was different, too. She had seen little of her old literary friends until a hot day in June when she was one of the twenty-four guests at a reception given by Victor Hugo to honor Daniele Manin, who had led the patriotic movement in Venice as president of the restored republic of St. Mark in 1848 and in 1849 had masterminded the defense of Venice. He was now in exile in Paris. It was the old revolutionary touch to which she had become accustomed, and Lola in flowing white robes with flowers in her hair was in her element. Dumas and Gautier, who had seen little of her since her return to Paris, embraced her and studied the changes that events had wrought in Lola, who was now thirty-one. They were quite marked and it was evident that she now used heavy *maquillage,* but she still glowed with sex appeal and talked more fluently than ever.

After this she saw more of her old associates, went driving with Eugène Sue and appeared at the opera and the races. But her ornate equipage brought jeers that reminded her of Munich, and except to attend the opening of Dumas's *Pauline* she slipped out of sight again. Her big splashes usually were followed by total eclipse as her debts mounted and she was caught in the familiar network of creditors at her door. Even Claudius Jacquand, who had painted the

Healds together, was concerned about being paid for his work. After one of their rows Heald insisted that the canvas be cut in two, since he did not wish to appear with Lola. Jacquand would not hear of this, so Lola decided to hang it in her bedroom facing the wall, and jestingly told her friends: "My husband ought not to see everything I do."

The painting was about to be hung in an exhibition at the Louvre and Jacquand was anxious about its fate but was assured that Heald would pay for it. Suddenly all of Lola's household possessions were seized for debts as she was having them moved secretly out of the house. Once again she disappeared—this time to visit England and boldly confront George or his relatives, for she was now desperate for funds. She was also curious to know what had become of the elusive young guardsman. Lola attempted to storm his hostile family at Berrymead Priory but was coldly turned away. Back in London, she used all her wiles on George's closest friend to break him down but he told her bluntly that he was just as determined to conceal Heald's whereabouts from her as from his own family. It was no secret that he had become a hopeless dipsomaniac and was keeping out of sight. Susanna had had him declared incompetent, and his affairs were being handled by lawyers. There was no way in which Lola could breach this barrier, and the London papers described her as being destitute, and trying to raise funds through her former husband or his family.

When these efforts failed she returned to Paris and appealed to Ludwig to restore the income she had given up when she married Heald. The King had been following her tempestuous course across Europe with some concern, and when he heard that her house on the Barerstrasse was to be sold by Maximilian's order, he revisited it and rescued some of Lola's pet furnishings. He also listened to her appeal for help, and with a fresh flow of money that she said came from the deposed King she settled in another house in Paris, this time on the Rue Blanche.

For a brief period her constant companion at the races and in the fashionable cafés was Prince Bahadur, Ambassador from Nepal and a member of one of India's most powerful families. Lola knew a great deal about the Bahadurs and their flair for fostering education and the arts in India. She was outraged when this handsome Indian, Oxford-educated and inheritor of an ancient culture, was spoken of in Paris as the "educated barbarian." She had met him in India and they talked Hindustani together with ease and fluency. They made a striking pair wherever they appeared, and when the Countess showed up at the opera and ballet wearing a priceless Kashmir shawl threaded with gold and diamonds everyone knew that it came from the Prince, who also lavished jewels on her.

With her memoirs due to come out she decided to celebrate this event by giving a formal reception in her new home on December 6, 1850. Her current companion was the worldly Michel de Coral, a man-about-town whose name appeared on her invitations as host for the occasion. Although most of the men who escorted Lola around Paris were friends rather than lovers, de Coral was one of the few who established himself in her life, with what seemed to be the final disappearance of Heald. Once more she was trying for a salon in the old style, with music and poetry reading, good wines and knowing cuisine, encompassing a wide assortment of guests and the interplay of different languages.

To give her reception an official political tone the Countess had invited statesmen and diplomats of stature as well as the usual scattering of talented bohemians and hangers-on at the European courts. A number of Americans mingled with the Central European counts and barons, the Russian grandees, the English peers, the French aristocrats. Among them was Henry Wikoff, whose adventures and espionage activities would become well known on both sides of the Atlantic during the Civil War. At the moment he was recognized chiefly as the special friend of Fanny Elssler, but he made himself charming to all beautiful women who crossed his path. He corresponded for the New York *Herald*, picking up gossip and along with other correspondents from American papers appearing frequently in the same circles as Lola.

Wikoff's adventures in France, England and Spain were melodramatic in the extreme. He came to be known as Chevalier Wikoff after receiving decorations from Louis Napoleon of France and Queen Isabella of Spain. Lola found him courtly and knowledgeable, but she did not live to learn of the embarrassment he would cause President Lincoln by implicating Mary Todd Lincoln in the disclosure of state secrets that led to a congressional investigation.

No one was surprised to see him at Lola's party celebrating the publication of her memoirs. On the night of the reception her house on the Rue Blanche blazed with lights. Uniforms and decorations spruced up the gathering, and officials of the East India Company moved about in the wake of their hostess, who played her role in a soft key but emphasized her semi-regal connection. Her white moiré gown was deceptively simple and ultra-fashionable. Her scarlet lips matched the dash of color in the wide sash decoration that King Ludwig had given her. Otherwise she was all in black and white, with a camellia in her hair, after the fashion of the hour, instead of the scarlet carnation she wore when affecting the Spanish role. The evening's music, the catering, the glamour of her own presence, the variety of her guests, turned Lola's official evening into a personal triumph. But her social revival was short-lived. The memoirs that were to have been so sensational in their revelations had an abortive debut in *Le Pays* and ceased after the dedication to the King had appeared as a prologue.

Antenor Joly had originally arranged to run Lola's autobiography, but when Lamartine took over *Le Pays* he dropped it. The manuscript then went to *Le Figaro*, but the editors were afraid to run it, or possibly it was merely dull and not the sort of material they had anticipated about the King and the Countess. With the change in policy at *Le Pays* it was whispered around Paris that Lola had been bought off. No canard ever directed at her made her more furious than this, since it was a matter of pride with her that she had refused numerous offers to sell the King's letters. In her dedication to Ludwig she wrote blandly:

In publishing my memoirs my purpose is to reveal to a world still engulfed in a vulgar materialism Your Majesty's lofty thoughts about art, poetry and philosophy. The inspiration of this book, Sire, is due to yourself, and to those other remarkable men whom Fortune—always the protector of my younger years—has given me as councillors and friends.

Shortly after her disappointing debut as an author Lola was a victim of the influenza epidemic that raged in the spring of 1851. Not only did she come close to death but she thought she was communing with Dujarier again, and she could not shake off this obsession that beset her as she convalesced. All this was boring to de Coral, Count Blum and Prince Como (Carissimo), three worldly suitors who did their best to draw her out of her absorption in the mystical and her memories of Dujarier. During her illness the past was stronger than the present, and the streets, the cafés, the hurrying crowds, the sight of a vendor were more than she could tolerate in her weakened condition. She refused an invitation to attend a July 4th celebration by resident Americans at the Trois Frères Provençaux, of searing memory.

The loss of her hair from fever was a blow to her pride, and her emaciation became so severe that she used all sorts of ruses to fill out her sunken contours. Her haunted eyes and shriveled arms made her almost unrecognizable for a time. Even her bosom became flaccid, and when she was finally persuaded to join in a stag hunt in the Arménonville Forest her hunting costume, which she wore magnificently on other occasions, was padded to simulate her well-known curves, a device she despised; and a wig under a dashing hat concealed the fact that her own hair had fallen out. But she disliked these tricks, even at a time when they were fashionable. In general Lola was cold to the hunt, for in spite of her sadistic instincts with men, she could not bear to see animals being killed.

Badgered again by creditors, under par physically, feeling herself to be a failure in all respects, she did some serious thinking about her future at this time. Having had a King to command, having been abandoned by two husbands, she found that the assorted admirers who surrounded her in Paris—some of whom were all too eager to support her in style—could no longer hold her interest. For once Lola's physical energy was flagging. The fate of her writings, the charge that she was mercenary where King Ludwig was concerned, and the trouble Auguste Papon continued to cause her with his threatening operations convinced her that she must try to recover her status as an artist.

Each major move she made in these years was directed by the stars, and the message she received at this time was that she should shift her course entirely and make her own way again through her art. As she shook off the effects of her illness she prepared for a European tour under the management of an entrepreneur named Roux. But she was told that she must improve her technique before undertaking this engagement. She was not only in wretched shape physically, but her consistent neglect of her art was all too evident now. This time she took herself in hand and went with unfailing regularity for three months to the Jardin Mabille, where Charles and August Mabille gave her their full attention. Charles Mabille had danced with Augusta Maywood, the first of the American professional dancers, and he knew what would be expected of Lola Montez if she toured the United States. He trained her in six special dances, regional in spirit and choreography. The critics invited to view her work at his studio were willing to concede at last that Lola Montez had a certain unique quality as a dancer. They were still unwilling to compare her with the great names in her profession, but she had made progress.

Her tour was dimmed by the fact that as she was leaving for Brussels word reached her that Heald had drowned in Lisbon harbor. The first report was that he had been caught in the backwash from a passing yacht that had overturned his skiff at the mouth of the Tagus. Too drunk to swim he had drowned by the time help reached him. Like everything else in Lola's life even the death of Heald remained something of a mystery. Other reports had him drowning in the Solent, or dying of consumption at Folkestone in 1856.

Lola wept with abandon when she learned that her path once more had been crossed by violent death. Although she had always regarded Heald as a weakling, he had had much physical appeal for her. Of all her lovers he had come closest for a time to fulfilling her hope for an established family life, children and social approval. In spite of the fact that she had defied all the conventions many times over she still had occasional dreams of the established family pattern to which she had been exposed in her early years, although not necessarily in her own home. Yet nothing satisfied her and she needed the constant stimulus of the limelight to keep her from profound boredom. She was thirty-two years old and played out physically, but her spirit revived as she turned once more toward the sure way of earning money and attracting public attention—the stage. Beyond doubt she enjoyed the excitement, the applause, the publicity and perhaps even the rows in which she engaged with such dash.

As she toured France and Belgium she drew large crowds and was treated like a prima donna by audiences attracted by her history rather than by her art. She was essentially a personality, however much she longed to excel as an artist. Only in Prussia did she find herself up against a stone wall, and she was quietly ousted from the principality, where her propensity for causing trouble was well known.

By November, 1851, she was back in Paris, worn out from the strenuous pace set for her by Roux, who collected 25 percent of her earnings. She fainted several times on the stage from exhaustion, but she had earned enough money to pay all her bills and to leave the way clear to visit the United States. Fellow artists, scholars, lecturers, writers, adventurers, rebels of all kinds, were touring the rapidly developing continent in the 1850's, and Lola had often talked to her American friends about trying her luck in the land of independence. Jenny Lind was having fabulous success. Why not Lola Montez?

Phineas T. Barnum was building up his galaxy of stars at the time and Lola's role in Bavaria had attracted his attention, but he viewed her as a curiosity rather than as a dancer. His agent, Le Grand Smith, who circulated among the writers in Paris and London, was determined to lure Lola into the Barnum periphery. She was told that flowered arches would decorate the pier on her arrival. Garlands would be strung along her path, as for Jenny Lind. Her carriage would be drawn by willing hands to her hotel through cheering crowds and showers of rose petals.

The Countess listened skeptically. Barnum had made the initial mistake of referring to her publicly as "notorious." Outraged by this, she reminded Smith that she had coped with kings, statesmen and poets, and could stand up to the Napoleon of show business. Barnum, accustomed to flattery, did not like her attitude and, according to Lola, he threatened to ruin her if she visited the United States. Their negotiations were dropped but Lola urged Roux, who wanted her to fulfill more engagements in Europe, to get her an American contract. All of her American friends kept urging her to take this step. James Gordon Bennett had given her so much publicity that they felt sure the public would be eager to see her. His reporters had followed her across Europe with persistence and friendly interest, whereas other papers had been censorious and destructive.

When Peter Goodrich, the American Consul in Paris, engaged Edward Willis to manage Lola, arrangements for an American tour were quickly completed. As the brother of the well-known Nathaniel Parker Willis, editor and writer, he had many links and was working in Paris as a dramatic agent. He had attended some of Lola's receptions and quickly saw the possibilities of a tour that would emphasize her political history. Ambition burned high within her again at the thought of a new country to visit, a new public to inter-

189

est. Once more she would try to earn her living on the stage—a quest that she always pursued when life turned dull or funds ran low, or she longed for the prominence that had become the breath of life to her.

After a succession of high-paced parties that wore her out, Lola was eager to get away from her sporting friends in Paris. They had given her a final rush that bored rather than exhilarated her. A long sea voyage in preparation for the buoyant air of Thomas Jefferson's country was just what she felt she needed. She knew that she had nothing further to hope for in Europe, and that her path would now be downward unless she made a big change in her way of living. Nothing seemed worthwhile since the days of her ascendancy in Munich and she longed for wider horizons.

TWELVE

A New Land

The Countess of Landsfeld hoped to change her image for the American public and to be accepted as a political reformer who had played a part in the great upheaval in Europe. Although her wit and intelligence were quickly recognized by discerning men, she could not escape her fate as a dazzling beauty committed to passion, violence and uproar. Her fame as a voluptuary had preceded her, and she was soon a *succès de scandale* in New York, Washington, Boston and New Orleans. Her gifts as an artist were not sufficient to tide her over the shoals of scandal, a feat smoothly achieved by Fanny Elssler, who was retiring from the stage that year.

Lola could not change her nature, and her quarrels with managers, her tantrums and scenes were alien to the American spirit. But from it all she emerged dramatically beautiful, impudently eloquent, and determined to have her way at any cost. She got off to a poor start. The time of her arrival had been ill chosen. She had been badly press-agented and had been vilified in advance, so that New Yorkers were looking for a tiger woman as well as a great beauty when she stepped ashore on December 5, 1851, from the same ship as Louis Kossuth, the Hungarian statesman who had led the insurrection of 1848 in his country, and had since been imprisoned in Turkey, to which he had fled.

Flags flew, tens of thousands of New Yorkers jammed the streets, and a tumultuous welcome awaited him as he landed. The beautiful Lola, another political rebel whose arrival had been heralded in advance, was little more than a shadowy presence as the guns roared and Kossuth was deliriously welcomed at Staten Island and Castle Garden. Since both had been involved spectacularly in Central European politics, their attitude to each other on the *Humboldt* came in for comment. Lola was the toast of the ship and she charmed other men on the way across with her wit and knowledge of world affairs, but she had no chance to make an impression on Kossuth, who was seasick most of the time and had little desire to be linked in any way with the ill-fated dancer. All the revolutionaries knew that Lola Montez had a nimbus of disaster.

After listening to his address at Staten Island she called Kossuth a humbug. She had already decided on shipboard that he was self-centered and morose. Although they greeted each other civilly at public functions each regarded the other with suspicion. Lola later blamed Willis for having booked her on the same ship as the Hungarian firebrand. But she was not wholly ignored when she came into view, her looks slightly impaired by wear and tear and her arduous tour of Europe. Her interviewers marveled at the grace of her figure, the magnetism of her enormous eyes, and the smooth pallor that contrasted so dramatically with her black hair. Dressed in the height of fashion and sinuous in her movements, her powers of seduction were quite apparent to the observant press.

With ease and assurance she fielded all questions about King Ludwig by saying that she had never been anything more than his political adviser. She denied that Dujarier had been her lover, although this was a relationship that she had proudly proclaimed in court at Rouen. She was blank about her marriages and bigamy trial. Lola

192

laughed off questions about her whip, her pistol, her encounters with the mob in Munich, and she was noncommittal about her romance with Franz Liszt. But she bowled over her interviewers with her deceptive air of candor as she pointed out that if she were all that their questions implied, she would not be trying to make a living on the stage.

Lola was not the first theatrical star to conjure up a fictitious history for professional purposes, and she rattled off her usual story about having been born in Seville, with aristocratic antecedents. She said she was twenty-seven, when in actual fact she was thirty-three. Her accent was commented on, but it struck the press as being more French than Spanish. Some even found the Irish lilt in it that had been noticed in Europe. She wound up the interview with a graceful tribute to the people of the United States, and said that she was glad to be in a country where freedom and independence were assured.

Lola's charisma worked with the men who interviewed her, but her name had appeared too often in the leading European and American papers for the public to be wholly fooled about her. Ridiculous cartoons of her with King Ludwig had traveled across the Atlantic, and an assortment of mezzotints and lithographs were scattered around the city at the time of her arrival. She was shown in a dashing pose with riding costume, gauntlets, crop and plumed hat. There were other pictures of Lola in circulation that stirred her to anger, and she completely disavowed them. She indignantly denied the story that a group of Parisian roués had earmarked a large sum of money for her to dance in the nude and pose for pictures.

Before leaving France she had made up her mind to move with discretion in her new environment. She had met enough American women in Europe to know that they were both chic and intensely moralistic. But, although she had lived in many countries and was familiar with a great diversity of types, she had trouble finding her bearings in the United States. Wherever she appeared there was great interest in her presence, and men looked at her appreciatively, a form of flattery that she never ignored. But she was not wholly at ease on the American scene and found more kinship with the Central European barons and counts who soon gathered around her than she did with native Americans.

As an initiate of the Dujarier circle in Paris she knew the importance of winning the press, but Horace Greeley, often the friend of political rebels and a backer of Kossuth, was cold to her from the day of her arrival. His influential paper, the New York *Tribune*, gave her a mere nod as "this woman who has obtained an unenviable notoriety throughout the world on account of her romantic disposition and singular conduct." She had a true ally, however, in James Gordon Bennett. Always sharply alive to the European scene, he played her up in the *Herald* and treated the complications that followed her arrival with a note of chivalry missing in the other papers. Introducing her formally as a "celebrated danseuse, Bavarian exile, and European political reformer" the *Herald* soon noted that "the movements of Lola Montez since her arrival have not been marked with any very extraordinary degree of popular enthusiasm. But she is an extraordinary star of the first magnitude and may be expected soon to make her debut on a scale of the most magnificent dimensions."

However, it was only a matter of days until Lola, established at the Howard Hotel and holding court for the Europeans who visited her, was involved in a tangle of legal difficulties. She was being presented to the public as an impostor, a King's discarded mistress and a neoclassical Aspasia, a passing tribute to her power and intelligence. Lola had lived through ridicule and humiliation of every kind, but she had not counted on the petty frustrations that now met her at every turn. The *Herald* kept pounding home the message that many of the stories told of this "great female republican, and many motives attributed to her . . . are for the most part exaggerated."

Things might have been different had Barnum been in charge

of her tour. But by the time she arrived in New York he was insisting that he had never wanted her, although he considered her a spectacular piece of property. Lola, in turn, was calling him a monstrous humbug, the characteristic that she most detested in her fellow human beings, although at times she admitted to being one herself. "I had too much amour propre to be shown up like a woolly horse or a white Negro," she said with scorn, ignoring what Barnum had done for Jenny Lind, and concentrating on the more freakish aspects of his showmanship.

She was soon convinced that he had joined forces with Roux, who had arrived from Paris, established himself at Delmonico's, and brought a $65,000 suit against her for breach of contract. Through the well-known law firm of Howe & Treadwell he made public the terms of a contract that he said Lola had signed with him in France on August 26, 1851. He charged that she had failed to complete the tour after traveling to France, Belgium and Prussia.

Lola promptly countersued, claiming that Roux had distributed an absurd biography of her, presenting her as an *enfant terrible*, and that he had worked her so hard on her European tour that she had collapsed on the stage from sheer fatigue. Roux kept on her trail so that for a time she was in a state of siege in the Howard Hotel. But she soon recovered her poise and held court in a flower-filled suite. Admirers clustered in the lobby, hoping for a glimpse of the delectable Lola, and theatrical figures paid her their respects. She was offered a private theater box and the free use of the newly established telegraph. Lola functioned in high style and served her guests champagne and Tokay.

The New York streets seemed flat and colorless after the marble magnificence of Ludwig's Munich, the ancient aura of Paris, the dense substance of London. The effect was almost arcadian, she thought, as she drove north to the distant village of Bloomingdale. But the children looked bright and interesting rolling their hoops and skipping along in pantalettes and flaring skirts, wearing wide-brimmed hats. The men seemed handsome and worldly in their tall

195

hats, skin-tight trousers and narrow-waisted overcoats. Washington Square with its Georgian houses, shining door knockers and bright little gardens, struck a familiar note.

But aside from these graces Lola felt that life in New York was squalid when she had to move out of the Howard Hotel in the middle of the night and take lodgings in White Street to elude the persistent Roux. Willis, who had accompanied her to America as her manager when she quarreled with Roux and the Barnum prospects evaporated, was soon dismissed by the Countess in a fit of temper. She refused to pay him, accused him of mishandling her funds, and insisted that she had taken him on in Paris only because he seemed to be adrift and she felt sorry for him.

His brother Nathaniel, the tall and handsome editor of the *Home Journal*, tried to heal the breach between them but came under Lola's spell himself. He happened to be sensationally involved at the time in the divorce suit brought by Edwin Forrest, the actor, against his wife, Mrs. Katherine Forrest. The actor had beaten the editor in Washington Square with a gutta-percha whip as the seducer of his wife and had named Willis co-respondent. Columns of testimony on this sensational case filled the newspapers, with literary and theatrical personalities deeply involved, as well as the leading lawyers of the day. Mrs. Forrest was exonerated in December, 1851, just as Lola was ready to open her engagement in New York.

It was poor timing for her American debut, with public attention focused on Kossuth, on the Forrest case, on Louis Napoleon's coup d'état, with Paris in a state of siege. Lola was well aware of the need for publicity to arouse interest in the sale of tickets for her forthcoming performances, and just before Christmas the *Herald* cheerfully predicted that "Lola Montez, lacking only the sanctification of the church and a pair of wings—the bright-eyed Lola, the piquant, witty, handsome and sparkling Lola, will also, with the departure of Kossuth, come out, like the moon emerging from a total eclipse in a clear sky, and the more brilliant from the late obscurantism."

Lola was conscious at every turn that the vicious charges from Papon's pen that had followed her across the Atlantic, with her own ill-considered reply, were doing serious damage to her professional reputation. The combination of his revelations and her explanations served merely to point up the more lurid aspects of her life and to draw attention to her eccentricities and extremes of conduct. This was soon apparent to her as she talked to lawyers and writers in New York and appraised their reactions.

She had visited the deposed King in Rome before sailing for America and had discussed Papon's machinations with him. She was glad to find that Ludwig had settled peacefully into the life of a private nobleman and was not unhappy away from the cares of government, whether in Rome, Nice or Munich. As they walked in the gardens of the Villa Malta they discussed the new political upheaval, the collapse of Lola's marriage, and her decision to go to America.

Just before Lola had landed in New York, the *Albion* of November, 1851, commented that her intimacy with Ludwig was well defined in the first Book of Kings, Chapter 1: "And the damsel was very fair; and she cherished the king and ministered to him, but the king knew her not." It should be evident to any reflecting mind, this writer had added, that their association was a "sort of King David arrangement with the Countess exercising great power over the mind of the King of Bavaria and controlling his royal government."

This was the point of view that Lola constantly projected. It was also in keeping with her talent for meeting the special needs of any man she thought worth her while. The *Albion* further noted that "in spite of all her faults, Lola did some good in her unquiet way. The King was perfectly right when he said, 'Had her name not been Lola, but Loyola Montez, she would have still been in Munich.'"

Thus the stage was set for her appearance on Broadway. Tickets for Jenny Lind had brought as much as $225, and some for Kossuth's lectures had sold for $1,000 after endless ballyhoo. Bidding was lively at the auction held in the lobby of the Broadway Theater two days before Lola opened on December 29, 1851, in *Betley the Tyrolean*. The *Herald* reassuringly announced that if the Countess failed as a dancer she was still a politician, a statesman, a liberal, a republican. The theater was packed from the pit to the ceiling and standees were jammed together in the foyer for her opening. Her audience included many celebrities and was almost wholly masculine. No more than thirty women were in the audience.

Those who had come expecting a sensational performance found nothing either electric or voluptuous about Lola as an artist. She had been cast as a simple mountain girl in Tyrolean costume, dancing against a full choreographic display of marching men. Attired in a tight-fitting black velvet jacket with gold braid, a short striped skirt and a red cap with feather reminiscent of her Alemannia uniform, Lola looked so young and guileless that one of the critics was struck by her "innocent air so much at variance with her reputation . . . it was the most modest performance of public dancing we have seen for any length of time."

It was obvious at once to the critics that her technique was poor, and that she seemed to have difficulty keeping time to the music. Her old failing was apparent at once, in spite of all the coaching she had had in Paris. Her dancing was erratic and impulsive, although her movements away from the stage were the personification of grace. She knew that things had not gone well, and she blazed with fury behind the scenes. After that the orchestra was told to watch her steps and follow them, lest she be caught in mid-air, as she often was. Lola chose to blame these artistic lapses on the presence of a lurking Jesuit planted in the orchestra to throw her off balance and proclaim her ineptitude. This became something of a phobia throughout her American tour, and whenever things went wrong she reverted to this bogeyman.

Even the *Herald* could not extol her performance as a dancer and Bennett regretfully wrote: "As a danseuse, she is decidedly inferior to Cerrito, Madame Augusta and others, but there is a nameless grace of nature about her person and movements, which, with her history, gives her an attraction that a better artist could not command, but which is not destined to be everlasting."

Things went better on the second night. Lola managed to maintain a steady rhythm, and she won the approval of the large number of women who had shown up once they were assured that there was nothing shocking about her performance. Box seats had sold for $100, and it was a fashionable audience. Her curtain speech conveyed some of her charm, and bouquets fell at her feet. But once again the ghosts of Taglioni, Cerrito, Elssler, Ciocca and others were to haunt her. Once again she was to read in cold type that she was no dancer. By this time she was beginning to believe it; too many people had made the point for the underlying fact to be ignored. But she never failed to rush to her own defense on moral or professional grounds, in this way often drawing attention to episodes that otherwise might have passed unnoticed. Her association with Dumas, de Girardin and Dujarier had given her great familiarity with the press, and she turned instinctively to editors for support, although except for Bennett the New York papers were blistering her reputation. *Harper's Monthly* noted that "Lola, it seems, resents highly any imputation upon her good name. Her indignation is adroit."

Her tendency to get into print seemed to be quite uncontrollable, and since so much of what appeared about her was false, there was also much to explain away. But fresh waves of scandal rose around her and she was in desperate straits for money. She had left her lodgings on White Street without settling up, which led to more legal complications. This time she took quarters in a house on Waverly Place, which brought her within a stone's throw of the very heart of fashionable New York—Washington Square, where the old Dutch families lived. When she strolled past the Georgian houses, New York matrons watching her through their lace curtains recognized this exotic figure as the tiger lady from Munich.

Lola was reported to be reviving some of the style of her old bijou palace, with a setting of gold and purple Napoleonic pieces on

Waverly Place. Her canopied bed with floating nymphs was much publicized and she was pictured spending her nights in drunken revelry. This was far from being the truth since Lola, however dissolute, was reasonably abstemious, although she kept her guests happy with champagne, Tokay and brandy. Her smoking was no myth, however. She kept it up ceaselessly, throwing away her cigarettes after two or three puffs, and thereby giving credence to the story that she smoked as many as five hundred a day. Nor did she hesitate to smoke in public, an unheard-of indulgence in the 1850's.

The Bavarian picture was recreated briefly when a group of students, in the tradition of the Alemannia, serenaded her, no doubt another publicity ruse for her play. She toasted them in the old way from her wrought-iron balcony. This was picturesque but it did not endear her to the staid dwellers close to Washington Square. Her presence caused so much commotion that neighbors objected to having the scandalous Lola Montez entertaining men at all hours of the night. On January 14, 1852, the police were called in to eject her from the premises. Before they arrived, however, her lawyer, Benjamin Galbraith, had settled the matter amicably and Lola drove off with her maid and trunks to a boardinghouse on Chambers Street.

Outraged and defiant, she whipped off a mea culpa manifesto for Bennett to use in the *Herald*, which he did on January 15, 1852, just as she was thrown out of her apartment on Waverly Place. "I know I have erred in life often and often—who has not?" Lola wrote. "I have been frivolous, ambitious, but never vicious, never cruel, never unkind." She was making an appeal, she added, to a liberal press and the "intelligent gentlemen who control it" to help her "regain the means of an honourable livelihood." At this point Lola's anger boiled over and she wrote:

I have been traduced and slandered and vilified more I think than any human being that has lived for a century. If all that is said of me were true, if half of it were true—I ought to be buried alive. Recently I have been dragged

200

before the public in the New York press by individuals in cards and other publications. I disavow, I repudiate all these vile defenses and their authors.

This was followed by a lengthy discussion of the role she had played in Bavaria, in which she insisted that in her conduct toward King Ludwig she was influenced only by a wish to be helpful to him. Her habit of making detailed notes on public events, men of affairs and political movements, had caught his interest when she first met him in Munich. Showing surprise that she should be so well informed on European affairs he suggested that she stay on as his guest. "I talked to the King as I always do to anyone—truthfully, frankly and without concealment," Lola wrote. "I told him of errors and abuses in his government."

Because of this Karl von Abel had said of her: "She is King," and Ludwig had agreed. Lola added that she had been deprived of her property by Jesuits and Austrian power. She signed this communication Marie de Landsfeld Heald, and it was read with great interest by New Yorkers who, on the same day, were treated to a dispatch from Thurlow Weed, one of the city's leading politicians, then in Paris. He assured Bennett that Lola Montez "is by no means as bad as she has been represented and even less frail than hundreds of European ladies in high life who pass without scandal."

The whitewashing of Lola had begun. She was about to start on a tour. She had dismissed Willis and was being advised by Joseph A. Scoville, a wit and roisterer known as the Reverend Scoville, although he had nothing to do with the cloth. He had moved to Lola's hotel to act as her defender, and since he was genuinely popular in newspaper circles as an irreverent but knowing character, he softened her relations with the press.

Scoville had won some fame as a wit on the New Orleans *Times-Picayune*. He had been private secretary to John C. Calhoun when he was Secretary of State, and had been dubbed a "reverend" as a jest when he substituted one Sunday for a preacher in a Swedenborgian church. This was Scoville's only connection with a church,

201

and he had a much closer affinity for the bottle, but his wit and learning interested Calhoun, who told Bennett about his solitary sermon. Both men were amused and Bennett wrote about him as the Reverend Scoville, a title that stuck. In the early 1850's he edited a sprightly little paper called *The Pick* from offices at 24 Ann Street. He championed Lola in this publication, as he did around town. Through him she met Walt Whitman, Adah Isaacs Menken and others then on their way to fame. Lola was frequently seen with him in Pfaff's and other cafés frequented by people in the arts.

Scoville showed Lola that she was being presented in the wrong way to the American public. Unlike Roux and Willis he did not try to drape the scarlet mantle across her more visibly than it already was. He drew attention to her style, wit and intelligence, and tried to persuade those who would listen that she was the soul of propriety, and that the tales about her conduct on Waverly Place were ridiculous. In fact, she made a point of not being alone with a man at this time, but of keeping a duenna on guard. Lola always managed to have a maid in attendance.

She relied on the wit and understanding of this dark-eyed, clever Southerner who listened attentively to her tales of political intrigue in Europe. Nathaniel Willis also gave her professional advice, as his interest in her developed, but her lengthy reply to Papon, which included her answers to the charges he had made, was being distributed so widely by New York booksellers in 1851 that she had unwittingly opened up a hornets' nest, and brought the Jesuit question into high relief. Lola pointed out to Nathaniel that the Jesuits had not run her out of Bavaria; on the contrary she had helped to oust them from Ludwig's kingdom. Arguing with the indignant Countess, Willis was struck by the fact that some devil seemed to get loose in her, in politics as in love, until her insatiable spirit broke bounds and caused chaos.

Lola was ill-advised to play up the persecution angle as she toured American cities. Bigotry flourished at the time, and she was convinced that the power of the Roman Catholic Church led to censorship behind the scenes. She fought this battle over and over again, often with straw men, since it had become an uncontrollable phobia with her. She could not understand why she came under such heavy fire when Fanny Elssler had toured America triumphantly and without similar abuse, although Fanny's flamboyant history in Europe was well known. Her illegitimate children, her affairs were common talk on both continents and they too involved the courts of Europe. But Lola overlooked the fact that Fanny was a superb dancer, and was accepted as a great artist.

Jenny Lind was another overwhelming example of a European star winning her way in America, and just when Lola was snatching at fame the *Herald* noted that Lola was "somewhat smarter, wittier, fairer, taller and younger than Jenny Lind, though not near so pious or saintlike in temper or demeanor." Wherever Lola went on her tour she was faced with the image of Jenny, being feted and admired, the darling of the public who could do no wrong. Her marriage to Otto Goldschmidt while Lola was under fire was played up as one of the great romances of the day. And when Lola was evicted from the house on Waverly Place, Jenny was described that same day in the newspapers as viewing the picture of "Washington Crossing the Delaware," then being exhibited at the Stuyvesant Institute in New York.

The contrast was painful and it was recalled that Jenny's prudishness had caused her to refuse to sing in Munich while Lola was in power. But Lola's spirit was strong and buoyant. She believed in herself, if few others did. If Fanny and Jenny had been borne through the streets by human hands, with showers of flowers raining down on them, she would impress the politicians of Washington and the scholars of Boston with her intelligence and her reforming zeal. It irritated her that men like Roux and Le Grand Smith should view her only as a man-killing spectacle.

She started with Philadelphia and appeared at the Walnut Street Theater on January 19, 1852, in a poor production that had not been well rehearsed. Fresh from her latest brush with the law in

New York she lacked her usual dash. When she danced between the acts in her old European manner, her failure to synchronize her steps with the music evoked a storm of hissing. This roused her temper and threw her further off balance. Backstage she talked violently of Jesuitical hanky-panky in the orchestra. But the City of Brotherly Love had failed to find her either gifted or of more than passing interest.

In Washington, on the other hand, she received a genuinely warm welcome, and was briefly in her element, finding herself at the seat of government. She established herself at the Irving House and held court, receiving as many as seventy-five callers a day. Among them were the most hard-headed of the legislators, who thought her conversation witty and informed. She was as well posted on the upcoming national election in the United States as she was on the attempted assassination of Louis Napoleon, the latest news from Europe. Senators, congressmen, diplomats crowded around her and found her a "very well-bred and very clever woman."

True to form she never missed a chance to give a glowing account of her own history, and she exculpated herself with such conviction that the unwary were carried away. The *Herald* noted that in her conversations with the nation's lawmakers she "had vindicated her character and history with considerable success—her statements being very plausible." She was invited to visit the House of Representatives, and a reception was held in her honor. Ludwig's lost adviser later recalled that she had seen tears in Millard Fillmore's eyes when she talked to him.

Lola attached a good deal of importance to the impression she made at the capital. She knew what each city she visited stood for, and here she was determined to play up her political sagacity and to meet America's statesmen on solid ground. She instinctively took more pride in her political sophistication than she did in her dancing, and some of these same men had crossed her path in Europe. But her femininity came first and she decided that she had been underplaying her role since landing in the United States, partly as a sop to what she had learned to believe was the puritan spirit of America. Too many advisers had been trying to curb her style. Now she decided to be her own dramatic self.

For the time being she abandoned her elegant black effects and appeared in showy Paris gowns—red satin, gleaming with brilliants; figured brocades that tightly outlined her bosom and burgeoned gracefully below the waist in the widening line of the early hoops. Small bunches of ringlets fell from her smoothly coiffed hair, and her bonnets were always sensationally right for Lola— simpler than fashion decreed, more dashing, and always worn with an instinctive sense of style. As she drove through the streets she was recognized as the most sensational beauty of her day.

She was rapidly recovering her looks after her devastating illness. Her curves were rounded again. Her face had a touch of melancholy, with her cheeks slightly sunken and her eyes looking more enormous than ever. But her chin was firm and delicate and her mouth as provocative as always. A fashionable audience turned out for her opening, including members of the diplomatic corps who knew a great deal more about the Countess than most Washingtonians did. Warmed by the reception she received, she danced effectively, if without much inspiration. For the first time since landing in America the improvement in her technique from the hours she had spent with the Mabilles in Paris was apparent. The patriotic note was strongly emphasized in Lola's performance, for this was the nation's capital. She passed muster with the critics and all went well until her last night in Washington.

As bouquets rained down on her and the audience applauded Lola noticed one man in a front seat thumbing his nose at her. Like lightning she rushed to the footlights, glared down at him and exclaimed in her husky tones: "Sir, I did not come here to be insulted."

A deafening burst of applause followed, and the culprit was grabbed by those sitting close to him. Washington's most regal hostesses leaned forward in their boxes, and senators reacted quickly to trouble. General Roger Jones of Iowa jumped up on an orchestra seat and shouted for order. Others followed suit, with much scrimmaging and confusion. Finally General Jones and a number of witnesses were marched off to the Watch House to be questioned by the police.

When Lola had cooled off she came out again, looking tense and unsmiling. The audience quieted down to hear the curtain speech that had become a habit with her. "Ladies and gentlemen," she said, "I return to you my most grateful thanks for your kindness to me during my sojourn in your magnificent and extraordinary city." It was her final gesture in the capital but she knew that she had erred where she wished most to make an impression.

Once again her ungovernable temper had betrayed her and led to a scene. She was in a subdued mood when she moved on to Boston, for some of the veneer had been wiped from her image as she left the capital. But when she arrived on a cold March day she learned that the Howard Athenaeum had already been sold out for her opening night. The demand for tickets had been so great that hundreds had been turned away.

By actual count only thirty-four women showed up, but many of Boston's most thoughtful and scholarly men were in the audience, as well as the rowdies who had turned out to see her famous shape. Lola's history as a revolutionary appealed to the more advanced thinkers. Boston was hospitable to dissidents of all kinds who crossed the Atlantic to make themselves heard. It was used to the best as well as the most eccentric, and its scholars were slow and precise in their judgment. The Boston *Herald* soon announced that the "extraordinary success and popularity of the Countess de Landsfeld in the metropolis of the Puritans had brought out her leadership." But the critics again found her wanting as an artist. She was described as making a mockery of the "art which had been cultivated by Taglioni, Cerrito, Elssler and others, while her attempts at acting were ludicrous in the extreme."

But Lola was suddenly raised from the depths by running head-on into the blue laws of New England, and becoming something of a heroine with the more advanced thinkers of her own sex. Frederick Emerson, a member of the Boston Grammar School Committee, had invited her to visit the Wells School, the Latin School and the English High School. It was customary for visitors from abroad to see these exceptional schools, and when a friend of Lola's whose daughter attended Wells School made the request it was granted at once. The pupils at all three schools were fascinated to have the glamorous Countess not only watch their exercises, but take part in their French, Latin and Spanish lessons. They were charmed by her beauty and ease with languages. Her gestures, manners and speech suggested a far-off world, and although they were used to being visited by world celebrities she brought authentic drama into their classrooms. When leaving Wells she bowed and thanked the girls for their welcome and they reciprocated, which was the established etiquette for visitors at Boston's noted schools.

But some of the mothers, knowing the dancer's reputation, were deeply concerned, and when Epes Sargent, the bright young editor of the Boston *Transcript*, attacked her on moral grounds the Countess was in trouble. He could see no justification for the schoolchildren's being exposed to this pernicious woman. He reviewed her history and dredged up every possible charge against her with damning effect. Emerson replied testily that the Countess had in no way forfeited her claim to the courtesy usually granted to those distinguished in her profession.

Sargent happened to be an ambitious young man who was then engaged in building up the *Transcript*. He was something of a poet and he wrote prolifically on spiritualism, in which he had become involved. Challenged by this individualist, Lola responded in kind and aroused considerable sympathy among the proper Bostonians.

"Did your fellow citizens think it improper to accept the capstone of the Bunker Hill Memorial from Fanny Elssler?" she wrote furiously on April 1, 1852. "Do you think, Sir, that one of those children would have had an impure or improper thought connected

207

with my visit if it had not been put into their heads by yourself?
. . . There are men who would stand before the Venus de Medici
and the Apollo of Belvedere, and see nothing in them but their
nudity. There are men like Paul IV who would object to the painting of the Last Judgment, and throw a bronze drapery over the
statue of Prudence."

Lola charged her misfortunes directly to a "sly, Jesuitical in-
famous design to unsex her—to deprive her of that high, noble
chivalrous protection which is so uniformly accorded to women in
this generous country by men." She added that as soon as it became known that she would visit America "all the journals from
Canada to Mexico were flooded with communications of the most
blackguardedly nature." One by one she ticked off the more picturesque charges—that she tamed wild horses, horsewhipped gendarmes, knocked flies with pistol balls off the bald heads of alder-
men, fought duels, threw people overboard for the sake of saving
them from drowning, and similar implausibilities.

Their efforts had failed, Lola wrote, for she felt that she had
been well received on the whole. It was with "scalding tears"
that she had returned to the stage, determined to succeed legiti-
mately as an artist. Who could doubt her statement at this point
that she had turned down offers of a personal nature that would have
made her fortune? But in attempting to succeed as an artist she had
not tried "to buy the good opinion of journals" and it was false to
say that she had ever posed as being other than an *artiste*. She made
light of the *Transcript*'s view of her as a dancer, but concluded her
much-discussed manifesto with her inevitable itch to defend her
character:

Americans are no fools, sir . . . you cry out against me as an intruder (fie
on you, sir, for an ill-bred snarling cur, unworthy to stand in the portal of
public opinion) . . . never give circulation to aspersions on the character of
a lady of which you know nothing, which are false in themselves and which,
for my own part, I defy any man living to prove.

208

News of Lola's clash with the Boston authorities spread quickly across the country and brought a fresh wave of comment from Europe. The leading American papers emphasized the folly of paying so much attention to a wandering Countess who seemed to be in quest of publicity at any cost. Once again Bennett came to her defense in the *Herald*. He published her lengthy manifesto in full, as if it were a royal document. He commented editorially that the Countess had denied all their imputations against the purity of her character and had acknowledged a life of eccentricity, but not of immorality or vice. She claimed to be a republican, but she was not a "red republican," in Bennett's opinion. He noted that she opposed socialism and internationalism with equal fervency. But her success and popularity since her arrival had brought into the open a host of powerful assailants determined to wipe her out, he added.

Bostonians read Lola's defense of herself with interest, and many who had felt neutral about her were aroused to action. For the rest of her stay in the city she had solid support. Her political sophistication, linguistic skill and knowledge of letters had made an impression, and the just-minded felt that she had been unfairly attacked on the school issue by a young editor intent on creating a sensation. She had devoted a good deal of time to conversing with well-known Bostonians, and her grasp of political issues, both in America and Europe, had impressed them. In Washington and Boston she had deliberately tried to make this count and to avoid the echo of personal scandal that always followed her.

The severity of the attack had roused the women of Boston, too, and the free thinkers among them came quickly to her defense. Whether from curiosity or sympathy her final matinee was a tremendous success, with an impressive number of respected matrons present to applaud Lola the scholar, the fighter, if not the dancer. She left New England feeling that she had gained ground professionally. Beyond doubt she had stirred up a storm.

On her way back to New York she staged a battle royal with her manager, and in a rage she canceled her next engagement. She was not satisfied with the *Carnival at Seville*, in which she had appeared. But he drew up a new contract which both signed. It stipulated that she should appear at the Broadway Theater in New York in the story of her life, to be prepared by C. P. T. Ware. She had to promise that she "would cause no explosion, revolution or volcanic eruption in the politics or religion of this country." Two things were clear to everyone involved—that Lola was hurting herself seriously with her Jesuitical bugaboo, and that she was in need of better stage presentation and fresh material. She had made $10,000 on her tour, and expected to earn $50,000 more before she finished.

But, although restored to grace and accepted again as a resident at the Howard Hotel, by the end of April she was tangling once more with the Jesuits and was defending her reputation in the *Herald*, with a few piquant questions added: "Who had me twice shot at?" "Who placed a fanatic upon my stairs at midnight with a poignard in his coat?" "Who had me poisoned with arsenic?" And, harking back to Europe, "Who had tried to waylay my coach out of Munich to drive me into imprisonment at Spielberg, like Silvio Pellico, the Carbonarist?"

The month of May was filled with further tribulation for Lola, when *Lola Montez in Bavaria*, the Ware production, closed after a disastrous five-night run. It pictured her as a dancer, politician, countess, revolutionist and fugitive. The backdrop was her little palace on the Barerstrasse, and King Ludwig was introduced, but in a totally inoffensive way. Lola was again pronounced a failure as an artist, if not as a woman.

In her suite at the Howard Hotel she continued to function dramatically as a woman, with a constant stream of Europeans paying court. An interested observer was the Comtesse de Marguerittes, the French singer and diarist who was touring the United States that year. No one knew more about Lola's life in Paris than this writer, who had been in and out of the salons of the literati for many years.

But the visitor who excited most comment among her friends was Prince Bobo, emissary from Faustin Élie Soulouque, the Negro General who had been elected President of Haiti in 1847 and now called himself the Emperor of Haiti. In his new role he invited the Countess to be his guest at the royal court. Prince Bobo, striking in looks and attire, did his best to persuade Lola to accept the Emperor's invitation. She was on the verge of promising when Scoville and some of her other advisers urged her to stick to the terms of her tour. But she and Prince Bobo made a dashing pair when they appeared in public in New York.

It seemed impossible for Lola to keep out of the headlines, and early in 1852 she was the focal point of another rumpus at her hotel when, during one of her evening gatherings, she turned furiously on the Prince of Como, whom she called Carissimo. The Prince had been one of her suitors in Paris but had drifted off to another interest. He was now in close attendance on Mrs. Katherine Forrest, but since she happened to be out of town at the moment he sought to console himself by visiting Lola. Several other European counts were on the scene, and she was plying them all with champagne when the Forrest case came under discussion. Instantly Lola championed Forrest, but Carissimo heedlessly observed that she should be the last person in the world to attack Mrs. Forrest, particularly in the presence of someone like himself who had knowledge of her "conduct and unenviable notoriety in Paris and elsewhere."

Before he knew what was happening the Prince was having his ears soundly boxed. He fled from the room. Lola slammed the door after him and threw the key to another of her guests, asking him to call for help. Meanwhile the Prince had found a fellow Italian in the bar downstairs and had persuaded him to go back with him and confront the fury.

Lola's maid had just come in from walking the dogs and the two men followed her and pushed their way through the outer door of the suite. There were screams and shouts in various languages, with Lola's imperious voice in the ascendant. The dogs barked and jumped about excitedly. Guests all along the corridor looked out to see what was going on. Scoville, who was at the party, flattened both Bobo and his friend with neatly timed punches, and helped them on their way down the back stairs.

The police were involved before it was all over, but Lola charmed them by inviting them to a dinner on the stage after one of her performances. Scoville, a sophisticate in local politics, thought it would be tactful to invite some Tammany gentlemen, too. They pronounced her a Royal Squaw and various civic clubs offered her their protection. With all this going for her on the local scene, Scoville decided to make the Countess the star of a "Grand Picnic and Cotillion Excursion in the beautiful and romantic woods and groves of Yonkers on August 26, 1852." This was a semi-political affair intended to honor Scoville who was popularly known as "Mr. Pick." To all intents and purposes it was a Tammany Hall picnic, with Greeley, Barnum and other public figures in attendance.

In or out of his cups Scoville was the best of company and if anyone could smooth Lola's path with the press it was he. The situation was serious, for she was threatening to sue all the papers, even the friendly *Herald*, and she had already brought suit against the *Times* for $65,000, charging libel in its presentation of her European history.

Lola was no novice at rustic picnics; she had enjoyed them in Ireland, England, France and Bavaria. But the Tammany roisterers were a new experience. The day began with a downpour as advertisers, subscribers and readers of *The Pick* boarded barges at various wharves, along with ward politicians. The official barge *Hero* had to wait at Christopher Street for Lola to appear, a picture in summer muslin carrying a parasol instead of a whip. She swept disdainfully past Greeley and Barnum and stayed out of sight until the Grand March began, with Atkins' cornet and quadrille band setting the pace.

It was not quite like running King Ludwig's Cabinet, but Scoville saw to it that the Countess had good press exposure all day, and that the reporters had a chance to interview her and take note of her wit as well as her charms. When the passengers landed at Yonkers she separated herself from the rabble and drove up the hill in a carriage to Kellinger's Hotel for lunch, passing the trudging Greeley, Barnum and other celebrities who also had separated themselves from the hordes bound for the picnic in the Grove. Things grew merry as the day advanced, with dancing, feasting and drinking, and Lola whirled around a few times in the quadrille. She was loudly cheered as she gracefully climbed the bandstand to present a silk banner to the Pick Club, and when the time for toasts arrived there was much applause for Bennett, and groans for Greeley and Henry J. Raymond, editor of the *Times*.

When evening came the barges went back by moonlight with their roistering passengers, but Lola returned to New York by train with Mr. Pick. It all provided newspaper copy for Scoville, who trumped up a fictitious dialogue between Greeley and Barnum on the subject of Lola Montez, and ran a cartoon of the Countess dancing with a Tammanyite. She found the company of Mr. Pick refreshing and was glad to have his protection from the press. The day had been a success. It was nineteenth-century press agentry, but it mellowed the picture for Lola, who withdrew her suit against the *Times* and talked no more of this form of action.

She was soon a welcome figure at cafés popular with actors and writers, and she shone conversationally during this period of restoration. Lola squandered money as fast as she made it and she talked to Cornelius Vanderbilt at Pfaff's about visiting the gold fields of California. She was already planning a trip to San Francisco, which was becoming a strong theatrical center. Scoville urged her to try New Orleans on the way, a city that he felt sure would welcome Spanish-speaking Lola.

But traveling south she tore loose again in St. Louis on a March day in 1853. She was appearing at the Varieties Theater, then managed by Joseph M. Field, the comedian and producer. Young Kate Field, his daughter, who would win fame for herself later as a writer

213

and actress, wrote to her aunt: "Well, Lola Montez appeared at father's theater tonight for the first time. The theater was crowded from parquet to doors. She has the most beautiful eyes I ever saw. I liked her very much; but she performed a dumb girl, so I cannot say what she could do in speaking characters. She is trying to trouble father as much as possible."

Before she had finished the Countess had horsewhipped the manager of the theater and smashed his nose with a candlestick when he dared to criticize her work. The woman who had played the dumb girl in *Yelva* so appealingly had let loose a tornado of abuse as well as some hearty blows at the management. She was long remembered in St. Louis, and was in a subdued frame of mind as she traveled on to New Orleans. She had been well primed by Scoville on how to behave in the city of romance, flowers, religion and revelry. It seemed unlikely that her past history would endear her to the people, so the impression was spread by press agentry that the Countess was a penitent, anxious to work for the poor, and eventually to take the veil.

There may have been some sincerity in this attitude, for she had been subject to strange swings of mood since her illness in Paris and Heald's death. But the final effect was to ensure large audiences when she appeared at the opera house. Lola responded to the warmth, style and strong Gallic tone of New Orleans, and her stage appearances were well received until she was again involved with the police. Her maid had left her and sued for unpaid wages. When a policeman arrived at the theater with a warrant the Countess, who shrank instinctively from any paper handed to her, drew the dagger she used with her Spanish costume and brandished it in his face. A fellow actor seized it but by this time she had reached a high pitch of excitement. She rushed from the room and drank from a small bottle marked poison. Like the dagger it was only a prop, but she played the scene to the limit. When her rage and hysteria subsided she went quietly to the police station for a hearing and talked her way out of any prosecution.

Although she had arrived in New Orleans with considerable fanfare, her departure was characteristic. She had been studied with interest and admiration for her style and good looks but no one regretted her departure. As she left for California she had a new maid to cater to her whims, a young girl who was the daughter of a quadroon mother and a planter father. Her name was Hyacinth, but after studying her remarkable eyes thoughtfully Lola changed this to Periwinkle, pinning down another shade of blue. It was a subject on which she was sensitive. Her own eyes had been described as everything from navy blue and turquoise to "sixteen varying shades of forget-me-not," the illusion she had created for Lesniowski, her newspaper admirer in Warsaw who had catalogued her charms with precision. Actually they were closest to a sapphire blue, as exceptional in shade as they were in size and expression, and changing constantly with her fluctuating moods. It was her custom now to bring out their full beauty with the accompanying shades of blue she used in veils, hats and gowns. Periwinkle would cater to this whim with full understanding as maid and constant companion to the Countess in the days that lay ahead of her in the American West.

THIRTEEN

The Golden West

Lola's romantic history in California was already being shaped as she took ship for the West from New Orleans. On her journey across the Isthmus two suitors who would compete for her had wooed her on the ship. Samuel Brannan, who had led the colony of Mormons to California in 1846, and had established the *California Star*, San Francisco's first paper, found her irresistible. He was a power in local politics, a married man of sporting instincts, who saw in Lola a rare acquisition, a worldly beauty, reckless in spirit, a companion to flaunt.

But it was Patrick Purdy Hull whom she came to love even before their arrival in San Francisco. His Irish wit, his endless flow of stories, his political outlook all appealed to Lola. Beyond that, he reminded her of Dujarier—in his looks, in his way of making love, in his broad approach to political issues. After sharing in Zachary Taylor's campaign for the Presidency he was sent west to take the census in California, and he stayed on to become a well-known newspaperman and part owner of *The Whig*. He was a familiar figure in the growing city and Lola was aware that she had interested a man who could push her interests in the West. He opened her eyes to aspects of political life in America that had not occurred to her, and he never tired of listening to her tales of her life in Paris with the learned revolutionaries. Hull was proud and reserved by nature but he was bowled over by Lola's intelligence as well as by her bodily charms.

The journey itself had been exciting and strenuous for Lola, with its jungle atmosphere and reminders of her early days in India. When they reached Aspinwall, close to Chagres, she was struck by the forests that rolled clear down to the blue waters of Navy Bay. All night long the click of castanets and the beat of fandangos could be heard from the ramshackle wooden inns of this point of transit. Lola stayed at City Hotel, the best in town, but so crowded that many of the guests slept on canvas cots lining the porches. Her trunks, her maid, her dogs added to the confusion, and her passage through was remembered, for Lola Montez could not go anywhere without leaving her echo.

But she indignantly denied the account given by a traveling Englishwoman in *The Adventures of Mrs. Seacole*, a chatty little book with an introduction by the well-known journalist W. H. Russell, of the *Times* of London. He had been writing for the *Times* from 1841, and Lola's background was no mystery to him. Mrs. Seacole described her as a good-looking, bold woman, with bad eyes and a determined bearing. She was struck by the fact that Lola seemed to be dressed ostentatiously in masculine attire. Her velvet-lapeled tailored coat, her elaborate shirt front with turned-down collar, her spurred and polished boots all conveyed the idea to Mrs. Seacole that she was looking at another George Sand. Her hat and riding crop completed the picture, in strange contrast to the "French unmentionables" that she also listed as part of Lola's outfit.

All this happened merely to be Lola's customary riding attire, but the point that stung in Mrs. Seacole's narrative was her statement that when a man in the street pulled her long coattails in

passing and made a ribald comment she lashed him across the face
with her whip. No sooner did this appear than Lola categorically
denied each point. She said that she had never in her life worn men's
attire except when she disguised herself to return to Munich after
her flight. Nor had she been in Cruces, where Mrs. Seacole had
mistakenly placed the incident. Nor were the Englishwoman's dates
correct for the period of her passage across the Isthmus. "If I were
to collect all similar falsehoods which I have seen in papers or books
about Lola Montez, they would form a mountain higher than
Chimborazo," the Countess commented with a touch of bitterness.
But, in view of her propensity for swinging her whip, the story,
true or false, was circulated widely.

The Panama railroad ran only twenty-five miles at this time, and
passenger cars clanked along between coconut palm and date trees,
heavily draped with flowers and vines, through densely forested land
and stretches of oozing marsh. At Gorgona they had to ride by mule
over an old Indian path, with paving stones often standing on end.
Brannan noticed that Lola handled her mule with great skill. She
rode like a man as well as sidesaddle and refused his help, except
for arranging about guides and the handling of her luggage. This
was a constant problem for the Countess, with all her costumes and
jewels that had to be conveyed from place to place.

She had several days at Panama waiting for her steamer, and she
commented on the wretchedness and squalor she saw on all sides.
Her knowledgeable companions filled her in on much of the native
history, since Lola had an avid mind for facts, and never forgot that
she had presented herself to the world as the friend of the people,
wherever she was. Her regal self and her democratic self were sometimes at war. She paced the deck or played euchre with politicians,
businessmen and gold prospectors, often to the music of fiddles and
banjos, as they sailed up the Pacific coast. Her habits and her fas-
cinations were observed with interest by William M. Gwin, the
Senator from California who would figure prominently in the
Civil War, as well as by Brannan and Hull. The moonlight, the lap-

ping ocean, the exotic Lola had worked magic with Brannan and Hull. The stage was already set for her arrival in San Francisco.

She became part of the early history of the city from the moment she stepped off the sidewheeler *Northerner* on a May day in 1853. She was strikingly well adapted to the high-paced life of the Gold Rush days. Her own romantic history, her looks and political views made an instant impression on the vigorous men who were building up their fortunes in California. Although she arrived as the Countess of Landsfeld, disposed to be haughty and aloof, she soon emerged as the tigress Lola Montez, creating her own special aura of violence and discord, yet with an inner core of charm.

Her arrival had not been heralded but she was quickly recognized as she came ashore. Her figure and style were unmistakable, although at thirty-five she was beginning to show the ravages of her way of life. She was fashionably dressed, but in a subdued way. The usual crowd was at the wharf, celebrating the arrival of one more steamer loaded with passengers speaking sundry languages. Wives and children were embraced by waiting men. Newcomers in quest of gold stepped ashore—lawyers, merchants, scholars, dandies and ruffians all bent on the same goal. Politicians from the East walked briskly down the gangplank with businessmen. An English journalist who had come to study the promise of the Far West took note of Lola in passing. Aside from the passengers, the bags of mail on the ship were of prime interest to the waiting crowd.

As Lola raised her voluminous skirts and twirled her parasol to walk through mud to a waiting carriage, her presence acted like tinder on the watching crowd. Men rushed toward the equipage, unharnessed the horses and dragged it up the wharf. Hull picked Lola up and swung her into place. The procession moved through the windy streets toward Russ House, picking up new followers as the Countess bowed, waved and threw kisses to the crowd. The hand-drawn carriage had become something of a Barnum tradition for visiting stars, and she shone brightly in this galaxy, if not under the great showman's aegis.

The hotel lobby and the street outside were soon jammed with admirers waiting for her to appear, but she had not liked some of the suggestive comments she had heard along the way. Lola had decided to proceed with caution and dignity in her new environment, until she had established herself. She stayed in her suite for the first five days, receiving important visitors and discussing plans for her performances. Officialdom came first as the Governor, judges, lawyers, local politicians, merchants and a few stray diplomats called and welcomed her to the Golden Gate. Brocades, pictures and souvenirs of the King were quickly taken from her trunks to give the Countess the setting in which she liked to receive her guests, as she offered them champagne, caviar and good conversation.

To the local press she was a "lioness who had swayed potentates and editors and public opinion, who had surmounted ill-natured criticism." But it was only a matter of days until fresh waves of scandal surrounded her as the Papon charges and juicy accounts of her history in Europe gained circulation. She exploded with the customary stream of denials and Hull was able to help her by bringing his newspaper friends to meet the famous Countess. The Gold Rush had lured them from all parts of the country and some from abroad. Lola knew their value for publicity purposes, and in spite of her many battles with the press she found these hardy pioneers amusing and original. Fred Woodworth, who fostered the arts in San Francisco and often arranged concerts to be held in his piano warehouse, gave the Countess his approval and professional backing, as well as supplying her with a piano. She was soon playing, singing and dancing for the benefit of her guests. She was also smoking cigars, much to their amusement.

Lola had no intention of associating herself with the wild girls who were a well-understood element in the blossoming city. She knew the type; she had been close to them for years, but she would never let anyone forget that she had been King Ludwig's adviser and a power in European politics. She was unlike any star who had toured California up to that time, for she was a combination of dancer, virago, wit, political rebel and aristocrat, hard to handle, unreasonable in her demands, unrestrained in her impulses, flaunting the democratic banner, yet showing at times the instincts of an unregenerate snob.

Lola was always at home in the company of men who lived hard and dangerously, and the air in San Francisco was, as Bayard Taylor put it, "pregnant with the magnetism of bold, spirited, unwearied action." She understood the adventurous and gambling spirit that motivated many of them, and she quickly appraised the types around her. The Gold Rush had thrown together Beau Brummells and tramps, scholars and dullards, the virile and the weak, the rough-hewn and the suave, the decadent and the godly, the extroverts and the withdrawn, the drinkers and the sober, the geniuses and the morons. Nearly all talked of gold, of new strikes and ridges. Because women were still scarce on the coast men were responsive to any likely quarry, and Lola's history made her fascinating to some of the prominent men of the city as well as to the rakes.

The stir and excitement around her were exhilarating after her confused days in the East. She enjoyed the sunshine, the early-morning mists rising over the bay, the flowers, the picturesque attire of the men. With her knowledge of languages she was quick to identify the various accents she heard. The population was divided between the Hispanic-Californians of early settlement, the native Americans from the East, and the great influx from foreign lands. She singled them out—Chinese and Russian, Moor and Turk, Czech and German, English, Irish and Scotch, and everywhere the Spanish intonations for which she felt a special affinity. Some came from Chile, Peru and the Sandwich Islands, and Alexander Abell, who had been consul for the islands, was one of her friends.

Inevitably European adventurers found their way to Lola, and she was soon observed on Montgomery Street with a variety of men —some wearing ruffled shirts, Prince Albert coats, fancy waistcoats and close-fitting trousers over polished boots; others in the rugged attire of the mining fields. In spite of the plank sidewalks and deep mud Montgomery Street had a certain pageantry of its own. New buildings were going up on every street, and promenading was fashionable, in spite of the rutted roads. Here and there the prefabricated houses sent out from Boston set up the illusion of German, Belgian, French or English settlements. Along Stockton Street and in South Park, where Senator Gwin lived, Southern traditions and hospitality prevailed in houses surrounded by iron fences in an area modeled after London's Berkeley Square.

There were strong reactions to the Compromise of 1850 which had postponed the Civil War for a decade but had not satisfied either the slavery or the antislavery advocates. However, with California newly admitted to the Union as a free state it forged ahead with great momentum. Each group in the heterogeneous population cultivated its own social rites, so that there were bull fights, cock fights, gambling, racing and all manner of other diversions, as well as balls, extravaganzas and theatrical productions. Operatic and stage stars were cherished, and the San Franciscans expected something special from Lola Montez. They were well aware that her acting and dancing had been deplored in New York and in most of the capitals of Europe, but they prided themselves on their independent judgment. In this environment her Spanish links were in her favor, and her beauty was of prime appeal.

But she had been in the city only a short time when word spread of difficulties behind the scenes as Lola prepared for her first public appearance. She was heedless of time, arriving hours late for rehearsals and usually bringing along an escort who backed her in her critical comments on the scenery and other technical details of the production. When her manager tried to oust one of the European counts who invariably showed up wherever Lola chanced to be, she held up the rehearsal until he had apologized. On another occasion she sprang at him with fury until fellow artists interfered. All this preliminary commotion was thought to have been staged to ensure a lively sale of tickets, but Lola's history as a whole suggests that she simply could not control her sudden impulses, for she made these moves at times when she must have known that their effect could only be destructive to her own prospects.

The American Theater was packed for her opening night in the West. The best seats had sold for $65; the second best for $25. The city's most fashionable and substantial residents turned out as well as the sports and speculators from the gold fields. She was rapturously applauded, with many curtain calls. Masses of flowers were thrown at her feet, and she responded with all the grace of her European training. But her acting had run true to form.

The play was *The School for Scandal* and her Lady Teazle was condemned by the critics for the artificiality and awkwardness with which she played the Sheridan role. All Lola's natural style seemed to evaporate when she tried to act. Her own intensity got in her way. It was much the same when she danced, for her erratic sense of rhythm was invariably at odds with the music. One critic observed that as Lady Teazle she lacked the "dignity, subtle wit, voice and repose needed for Sheridan."

On her second appearance, in the play *Yelva*, she took the part of a dumb girl in pantomime, and introduced her famous "Spider Dance" between the acts. This was a curious exhibition vaguely modeled on Fanny Elssler's "La Tarantule." To many it was a repulsive dance; to others it was straight erotica; to Lola it was profoundly tiring, for she performed it with such intensity that she was wholly spent as it ended.

She looked her loveliest as she pirouetted into view, her long slender legs in flesh-colored tights, for she no longer danced without the requisite maillot. Her glossy hair, wreathed in flowers, fell to her shoulders. Her skirt consisted of tiers of tinted chiffons creating the illusion of a spider's web, entrapping her as she spun around, constricting her steps. With the music slowing down she struggled to free herself and shake off the spiders lurking in her chiffons. As the dance grew more frantic she shed the spiders and stamped them underfoot. They were stage props made of whalebone, cork or rubber. When the music changed to a jig Lola spread out her hands and

223

feet like a spider and leaped from one side of the stage to the other. The effect was as grotesque as it was riveting. It all ended with fire and abandon, as she stamped on the last of the fallen spiders. Sometimes she did the dance in pantomime without the props.

Her audiences were invariably aroused by this strange dance. There were shouts and bravas from the men as well as straight applause. She had learned that a sagging program could always be enlivened by the "Spider Dance." Critics felt that it also helped to conceal her deficiencies as a ballet dancer. She varied her steps and mimicry from one performance to another, shuddering with horror as she sought to dislodge the spiders and fight her way out of the web that had been woven around her. Under fire for this dance she defended it as an artistic production, Spanish in origin, and totally misunderstood by her critics.

The Countess had little success with *Lola Montez in Bavaria,* one critic saying that she did her own history a disservice in this production. People clamored to see the play, believing that it would give a realistic view of her life as the King's adviser. It was as disappointing to the San Franciscans as it had been to her audiences in the East, and she battled behind the scenes about the Bavarian settings and scenic details, slapping and then firing her agent.

As surely as her curves were lost in the "Spider Dance" they were displayed to the best advantage in the "Sailor's Hornpipe," which she danced with flair and accuracy. Her tight tarpaulin trousers and snug jacket were highlighted with flashing beams and for once her steps were in total accord with the music. When she appeared in the *Maid of Saragossa,* her entre-acte dance was "El Ollé," and this brought thunderous applause. But there were always carpers in the press who insisted that the great Lola Montez could not dance. She now had Patrick Hull behind her, however, to see that she never lacked attention from the newspapers. When she appeared in a benefit given for the first Hebrew Benevolent Society she was warmly applauded by the San Franciscans, and soon she became the friend of all its firemen with a benefit she played for the San Francisco

Firemen's Fund on June 18, 1853. When she did her "Spider Dance" the firemen threw their helmets onto the stage. In taking her curtain calls she filled one of the helmets with flowers tossed at her feet, held it close to her famous bosom and exclaimed: "I have the firemen's hearts as well as their hats." Other popular stars performed that night, but Lola was the one who counted, with her castanets, her spiders and her vivid presence.

Fire was an ever-present hazard, and San Francisco had already had five serious fires when this benefit was held. It netted $30,000 and the Countess became the firemen's idol, a useful lesson she had learned in New York. It also helped to establish her in the community, for although she gave only five performances in all at this time, she moved freely around the city and became its most conspicuous personality. But Lola, with her imperious ways and her great success with the firemen's benefit, had aroused the envy, or antagonism, of some of her fellow players. She had no sooner launched her "Spider Dance" than she was savagely burlesqued by Caroline Chapman in a sharp-edged production *Who's Got the Countess: or, the Rival Houses.* The play as a whole was a parody of Lola's espionage activities and love affairs. She was called the Feminine Musketeer, a throwback to her association with Dumas. But the talented Miss Chapman's most biting effect was her burlesque of the "Spider Dance" in a skit that became famous as *Spy-Dear.*

The author was Dr. William Robinson, popularly known as "Uncle Billy," whose family was identified with the showboats on the Mississippi. Dr. Robinson wrote skits, songs, parodies and sketches of all kinds. Lola was stunned by this attack, for she had visited the Robinsons on Telegraph Hill soon after her arrival and had used her gift for exquisite needlework in the repair and production of stage costumes. She thought that she had established both personal and professional rapport with Mrs. Robinson, until she saw the relentless parody of her quarrels with her agent and manager, her awkward dancing and her role in European politics. Mrs.

Robinson regarded actresses with some severity although she had married into a noted theatrical family, and her impressions of Lola emerged in some of the parodies.

Caroline Chapman, who played Shakespearean roles with young Edwin Booth and tossed off the Robinson skits on Lola Montez between the acts, kept up this travesty for years, adding new sketches based on Lola's adventures in the West and in Australia. Caroline's brother, William B. Chapman, shared in the vendetta, and the theaters in the mining towns became well accustomed to the Chapman parodies of Lola Montez. Although the San Franciscans found momentary amusement in *Spy-Dear* they soon resented this treatment of a famous guest. The benefits Lola had given had been effective. Moreover, she had important backing among the politicians, and some of the leading lawyers and judges were her friends and defenders. From the time of the Dujarier trial in Rouen and Lord Brougham's sponsorship in London she had always been of interest to members of the bench.

Her efforts to propitiate her own sex did not flower in San Francisco, and she was soon the most discussed person in town. She laughed at stories that she bathed in lavender water and dried herself with rose leaves, but there was no denying the fact that she smoked cigars and cigarettes, rode like a man, swaggered through the streets with her riding crop, and invaded masculine haunts with the verve and enterprise shown a century later by members of the Women's Liberation movement. Anything forbidden was a direct challenge to her, and she thought nothing of walking into the dining room of the International Hotel without an escort, or of visiting saloons that were out of bounds for discreet women. The gambling places to which Brannan introduced her were fascinating to Lola, with raw gold dust the stakes, and a flamboyant assortment of men gathered around the tables. He took her also to bull fights and to the races at the newly opened Pioneer Course. She sat in the grandstand watching a horse that bore her name win, and later she rode in an exhibition race.

Lola was quickly recognized wherever she went, for the city was flooded with lithographs and daguerreotypes, cartoons and illustrations of her in many guises. Fashions were named after her, but conspicuous though she was, she had none of the flamboyance of attire shown by the buxom demimondaines of early San Francisco. Her décolletage was carefully modulated with a view to propitiating the city's most imposing matrons when she was being officially entertained. The handsomest and best-dressed women in town had to concede that the Countess of Landsfeld was in a class by herself. Out of a population of fifty thousand, only one-sixth of the city's residents were women, but some important dowagers were emerging on the social scene.

Another notable belle who had come from the East and appeared in many of the same haunts as the Countess was Mrs. Rose O'Neal Greenhow, later a famous Confederate agent but at the moment a Virginia hostess of note who had traveled west after the death in San Francisco of her husband, Robert Greenhow. He had been working for the State Department settling land claims for the government. Many able lawyers were busy trying to straighten out the confusion over titles and there was endless litigation between rival claimants, leading to fist fights and brawls. Greenhow, a brilliant linguist, had fallen through a plank sidewalk in San Francisco and died of his injuries, leaving Rose a widow with three children. Senator Gwin and other members of the Southern colony at Stockton Park made much of her. She was handsome, stately, a favorite in Washington drawing rooms and a close relative of Dolley Madison's. She had many British friends, notably W. H. Russell, the newspaper correspondent, and Lord Lyons, who would serve as British Ambassador during the war years.

Mrs. Greenhow and the Countess of Landsfeld were unquestionably the most dazzling ladies on view in San Francisco at the time. Both had style, presence and political savoir faire, and knew many famous men. Both dressed beautifully and cut a swath wherever they appeared. But their paths diverged, and as the Countess lay dying in New York in 1861 Mrs. Greenhow was beginning to show her hand in Washington as a master spy for the South.

Another matron of consequence who took note of Lola during this period was Mrs. Amelia Ransome Neville, daughter of Colonel and Mrs. Leander Ransome, who had moved from Connecticut to California and were quartered at the Presidio. Two years earlier Mrs. Neville had visited England and had been presented to Queen Victoria. She knew the Earl of Cardigan, who had led the Charge of the Light Brigade and she had dined with the Duke of Wellington, an experience she shared with Lola. She had heard much in England about the Spanish dancer, so she watched with interest and reported in her book *The Fantastic City* that there was "light gossip" about the Countess in San Francisco and that everyone spoke of her startling beauty, her perfect figure, her magnolia skin, and large gray (sic) eyes filled with expression. Mrs. Neville continued:

She would promenade Montgomery Street in a short black velvet jacket over a flaring skirt of silk, a broad hat with black lace falling over the brim. Word would go down the street, "Lola Montez," and everyone stared in the most discreet manner possible. It was known that she had once struck her riding-whip across the face of a man too bold in his admiration.

But Lola was soon seeking new fields. She was stung by the ridicule of the Chapman parodies. She was having trouble with Brannan, who prevented her from seeing as much of Hull as she wished. For the time being she was in love with Hull and she decided suddenly to marry him, after seeking the advice of a fortuneteller, a natural gesture for the superstitious Countess. No advance notice of the wedding was given but Woodworth and a few close friends were in on the secret. Even the bridegroom was not convinced that Lola would go through with it, but forty friends arrived on horseback or by carriage, traveling along the Mission Road over which she had driven to the races so often with Brannan. The Governor and a number of well-known politicians crowded into the Mission Dolores in the shadow of Twin Peaks, the old adobe church where Father Junípero Serra said mass in 1777.

228

The Countess ordered the door closed, so that none could intrude. She was quietly gowned in gray, with a fashionable gray bonnet, and her hands clasped a nosegay of orange blossoms in a tiny vial. Her marriages had been curiously different—the first in a little church in Ireland; the second in a fashionable church in London; the third, on July 2, 1853, in a Catholic chapel along the Mission Road.

When the brief ceremony ended guests who had stood outside the chapel during the service crowded in to embrace Lola and congratulate Hull. A wedding breakfast and reception followed, with the Governor, the Mayor of San Francisco, senators, judges, writers and leading merchants present. Lola was toasted time and again but not by Sam Brannan, who did not attend the wedding and was sulking in anger and frustration. Lola now signed herself Marie de Landsfeld Hull. The variations of her name never ended.

Immediately after the wedding the Hulls set off on a tour to Sacramento and the surrounding mining towns. They had assembled a small orchestra, with Miska Hauser, a well-known violinist who had already been exposed to Lola's tantrums, and other musicians picked up from local places of entertainment. They went first to Sacramento in the *Arrow* on their wedding day, and Lola set her own goal for the future when she announced to the ship's captain as they drank champagne that she would like to settle in California, and make her home in the mountains where she and her husband could hunt and fish and enjoy the rugged mountain life.

But her reception in Sacramento rocked their marriage from its start. They stayed at the Orleans, the best hotel in town and prepared for Lola's appearance at the Sacramento Theater. Everything possible had been done to embellish her surroundings, although hard chairs and benches took the place of the plush-covered seats by that time customary in most of the theaters where she appeared. The gaslight chandeliers were new and the backdrop showed the craggy lines of the Sierra Nevada. Sacramento was emerging fast from its tentlike aspect at the height of the Gold Rush. Brick houses were being built, and levees protected the town from heavy floods. The saloons and gambling halls were filled constantly with roistering men, and performers were apt to be heckled and jeered at unless they pleased the lusty taste of the miners. But there was great expectation when Lola arrived. Here was a novelty indeed, and her appearance at the hotel confirmed the impression that she was strikingly beautiful.

She dropped the role of actress and confined herself to her "Spider Dance," the "Sailor's Hornpipe," "El Ollé" and a Swiss dance which involved some yodeling that was out of character for Lola. The bawdy shouts that greeted the "Spider Dance" shook her poise, although Hull assured her that the miners were good fellows, out for a rousing time, and that she must not make a scene in these surroundings. But on the second night her "El Ollé," danced in diaphanous veiling instead of in Spanish costume, brought roars of laughter and ridicule. If she had intended her costume to be seductive she had taken the wrong cue. Completely out of step with the music, she stopped Hauser and the little group he had assembled from saloons and gambling dens, and faced the audience. She stamped furiously on some of the bouquets that the management had provided, and harangued the audience in husky tones, her eyes blazing, her body quivering. Lola announced defiantly that far from being afraid of them she despised them, but a shower of vegetables drove her off stage.

A cabbage as large as a football scattered the musicians. The manager persuaded Hauser to return and play. He launched into "Yankee Doodle," his key piece, to quiet them down. Lola decided to return and she went solemnly through her entire dance, regardless of Hauser's diversionary medley, and without any suitable accompaniment. The uproar continued until the manager fled outdoors. When the audience stormed the box office for refunds and found it closed vandalism began. Stage props were wrecked. Benches were overturned. The wooden chairs went sailing through the windows.

Hull rushed Lola back to the Orleans, but the mob followed her there with an impromptu band of pots and pans. Suddenly she was caught up in the evening's excitement. Using her old technique she appeared on her balcony, this time with an oil lamp that illumined her white face and showed that she was unafraid. She shouted down to them that they were blackguards, puppies, cowards and loafers. Her feeling for melodrama was better than her dancing.

The miners were silenced by her spunk, and by the words that flowed so fluently from her lips. They burst into laughter and cheers. Lola saw that she had won them. Her face lost its somber, threatening look and she smiled down at them in her most seductive manner. One miner threatened to climb the ladder and blow out her lantern. This was no Romeo and Juliet act. She was wildly angry and slipped back into the shadows. But a few sips of champagne in her suite changed her mood again, and when Sacramento's newly formed vigilante group arrived on the scene she was back in view, throwing kisses at her tormentors and answering their obscenities with a vocabulary of her own.

This sort of thing seemed to be almost as inevitable in Lola's life as her endless hours with her mirror—to be the center of attention, to be the focus of interest in any group, to play a high hand in face of danger. Whatever her surroundings, or her social status at the time, she remained true to herself—the brainy wanton responsive to untamed impulses, the great lady with her face now and again in the gutter.

Some angry words with Hull had sparked her up, for the picture was growing dim between them. Although he understood how to amuse her with his stories, his Irish wit that matched her own and his interest in public affairs, he tended to be rough-edged himself. When they appeared publicly on the street next day—Lola, spectacular in a billowing black dress and a monster bonnet shirred with pink on her proudly lifted head—Hull was sulky, angry and jealous of Lola's instinctive response to the most virile men in sight. The riot of the night before had been more than he had bargained for, and he had not liked her performance on the balcony. He cautioned her on the way to behave the second night, fearing the collapse of her tour. A claque was planted, the house was papered, and careful preparations were made to avoid another débâcle.

The theater was sold out for Lola's second night, but the vigilantes were on hand to keep order. Some of the more influential women of the region had turned up to defend the visiting celebrity and show their disapproval of the riot. John A. Sutter, on whose land gold had first been found in that region, although it had since been taken over by squatters, showed up as Lola's defender. The manager of the theater led the Countess by the hand to the front of the stage to make her apologia. It was characteristic, and rested on her monomania that planted troublemakers were assigned to wreck her performance.

"Two or three individuals insulted me grossly by sneering and laughing at me," she said. "I was more sensitive, perhaps, than most artists upon such an occasion, for the reason that I am persecuted and followed by certain persons and their agents, because I made political enemies in Europe who follow and annoy me upon every occasion."

Lola added that she thought women were more respected in America than in any other country in the world. The men were chivalrous and gallant and would not insult a woman gratuitously. She explained that in stamping the bouquets underfoot on her first night she was merely trying to annihilate her spiders, and not to spurn the offerings. She demonstrated the vigor with which this had to be done, saying it was just chance that the flowers were destroyed.

Ending on a light and jesting note Lola won her audience and there was deafening applause. She endeared herself further to the people of Sacramento by giving a benefit for the manager of the theater, and another for the local fire companies. She was already well established as the firemen's darling, and three companies in full regalia attended the performance and staged a parade back to the Orleans Hotel, where they serenaded the Countess with their band.

Without hesitation she came out on her balcony and unfurled an American flag into the hands of a handsome fireman. The group was then invited by Hull into the hotel saloon for drinks, and things grew noisy as the evening proceeded, with Lola arousing her husband's anger by her concentration on the fireman.

After the furore in Sacramento the impression spread that much of the fuss was worked up by knowing press agentry, that claques were planted in her audiences, and that her stormy ways were timed to promote the sale of tickets for her performances. But this was only half true. With his knowledge of the newspaper world Hull understood how to promote a firemen's benefit, or to draw in the Mayor for a Lola event, but he had learned that there was no controlling her impulses and he could never anticipate which way the wind might blow.

The final gesture before leaving Sacramento to tour the mining centers was Lola's challenge to a local newspaper editor to a duel of her own devising—pistols or the choice of two pills in a pillbox, one to be poisoned, the other not. The editor had dared to suggest that these half-mad scenes were deliberately worked up to sell her as an attraction. She snapped back that he had lied in barefaced fashion, and although not an advocate of women's rights she was prepared to counter his attack. The editor ignored the challenge, but the incident amused the public, and a local *bon mot* soon came into currency among the miners, who shouted, "Pistols or Pizen," when a fight was brewing.

Hull was exhausted and resentful by the time they reached Marysville. The temperature was 106. Lola was being unreasonable, both with her husband and her maid, Periwinkle, who strove to humor her whims and to keep her perfectly groomed and ready for every emergency. The theater in Marysville was one of the better ones on their tour, substantially built, topped with a dome, and with comfortable seats. The residents were discriminating in their tastes and reacted best to the Shakespearean productions that Junius Brutus Booth was fostering in California. They disliked Lola's

233

"Spider Dance," and they considered Hauser an indifferent violinist. The musicians, who had not been paid, were disorganized. Hauser was nursing bitter resentment against the imperious Countess.

The general air of disdain with which she was received in Marysville stirred her up again, but this time instead of fury she tried hauteur. Hull pointed out the stupidity of this attitude in a frontier town; it served only to make her ridiculous. By this time she was battling with her husband, with her musicians, with her audiences, and it was clear to her that she faced another disaster—one from which she could not find her way out. She turned bitterly on Hull, whose jealousy reached into her past as well as her present. Any mention of Ludwig drove him wild, and he was beginning to see Lola as many of her critics did. He was familiar with the country they were touring; he understood the temper and tastes of the people. In the opinion of Lemuel Snow, one of Hull's closest friends, a "more mismated couple never lived."

When Snow first met her in Sacramento she was wearing a pink dress and a black-and-pink bonnet, and he thought her "positively the most wonderful creature I had ever seen up to that time" but the enchantment dwindled rapidly as he came to know her better. He watched her through a series of moods and felt that she was always the actress. "I have seen her eyes fill with tears over tales of human suffering in the camp," Snow recalled. "Again I have seen her wild with rage, stamping her feet and spasmodically working her hands together when she fancied anyone had slighted her."

Lola could be a frightening spectacle when she went into one of her tantrums, with her entire body quivering, her eyes blazing, and her hands ready to strike. The disintegration of her marriage to Hull was no surprise to Snow. He saw it coming after the riotous scenes in Sacramento that had shaken up his friend. The chill they encountered in Marysville and Lola's constant references to her lost King, made Hull silent and sulky. Always inclined to drink heavily, he spent more and more of his time in saloons. It was all too clear that Lola was tiring of him. It took her only a short time to burn up the consuming flame she brought to each new affair, but Hull was a husband, and this presented its own complications. He watched attentively as men's eyes were turned constantly in her direction, and he came to recognize the ease with which Lola responded to their admiration. She had worn him out with her demanding ways and her unreasonability, but he had not yet fully recovered from the bewitchment she exercised.

As their funds ran low they quarreled over investments. Hull had always been suspicious of gold gambling operations. Lola had led him in this direction, when his own inclinations ran to the world of journalism and the ownership of papers. But a serious break in their relations occurred in Marysville when an emissary arrived from King Ludwig with a gold comb engraved with the Bavarian crown. At the same time the Countess was notified officially that Queen Theresa was dead.

This was a significant moment in her life and Hull, who could not endure her communications with the former King, accused her of all kinds of deceit, and of being silly enough to think that Ludwig would now wish to marry her. Lola promptly threw her husband's clothes from an upstairs window and clawing madly with her nails pushed him down the hotel stairs. He vanished from her life for the time being, although he had served her purpose and had helped her with her press and theatrical connections, as well as being a lively companion.

Grass Valley was the last engagement on her tour, and here she paid off her troupe and reached another turning point in her life.

FOURTEEN

Grass Valley

Lola was tired of life, of herself, of her failures and the triumphs that quickly turned to chaos, when she decided to settle in Grass Valley. "Well done, after traveling the world over, to settle at last in a California mining town," said the *Golden Era* when it was learned that the uncrowned Queen of Bavaria had decided to give up the world for a quiet life in the mountains. Old friends in Europe found it hard to imagine Lola Montez living in a small town in the fantastic West, even though the air she breathed would be richly dusted with gold.

The purple slopes of the Sierra Nevada, capped with snow, reminded her of Bavaria and Switzerland. Grass Valley lay in the foothills, sunny and sheltered, with its mountain streams, its blaze of wild flowers, and the tall pines that scented the air and towered in silhouette against the clear blue sky. It had the richest mines in the state, and for a time was known as the Gold Capital of America. Digging was at its height when Lola arrived, with more than a hundred mines in operation within a radius of six miles.

236

Its fame soon grew for another glittering asset—Lola Montez. In his *History and Directory of Nevada County* Edwin Bean wrote that a "historical sketch of Grass Valley without passing word at least of Lola Montez, would be a sort of *Hamlet* with the demented Dane left out." She brought into this community fresh life, some demented doings and a variety of kind deeds that shed some new light on her own many-faceted personality. The town had four thousand inhabitants and fewer than three hundred women, but it was the kind of mixed population that Lola understood and enjoyed. The rush for gold had brought in all types—some cultivated, knowledgeable and idealistic; others raffish, daring and enterprising. There were Harvard graduates, ministers' sons, poets and Chinese laborers; senators, judges, lawyers and fugitives from justice. A number of criminals had been shipped in from Australia, and highwaymen galloped through the mountains. The Indians, Negroes, Chinese and Mexicans mingled with men from nearly all the countries of Europe.

Lola liked the frantic babel of tongues. She had listened attentively to its component parts in San Francisco, in Sacramento, and now in the town she had chosen for her home. She was not saying goodbye to the worldly life. There was constant traffic between Grass Valley and San Francisco, in spite of the difficulties of the journey. But the strong appeal of the region for Lola was the fine mountain riding in which she could indulge, the pungent air, the clean sweep of the sierra winds, and the sun that shone so constantly. She confessed to Mrs. Dora Knapp, a neighbor who had helped to persuade her to settle in Grass Valley, that she was utterly tired of the fast life she had led, and that she sought a new existence. Here she might find exhilaration rather than boredom. Her interest in a local mine and her close association with Johnny Southwick, a well-known promoter, whose fortune from the Empire Mine was at its peak, also influenced her. Lola's worldly sense had not deserted her, but in the small mining town she hoped to be free of the quarrels and scenes that surrounded her life in the theater. Gold was the prime topic of conversation as panning went on in the rivers, and the rising fortunes of the new state made news around the world. Preachers countered the worldly manifestations of the Gold Rush with the word of God, as gambling flourished and sex was publicly exploited.

Lola had made money touring, since she always drew crowds. She invested in the Empire Mine, which was Southwick's chief interest at this time. It was the stock she had bought in the Eureka Mine of Grass Valley while she was still in Europe that had first drawn her attention to the region. Hull had sold his newspaper interests in San Francisco and thrown his profits into gold-mine shares. Their financial interests were closely interlocked, but the collapse of Lola's tour led to serious complications. No one ever knew how she squandered her money, but as fast as she made it, her profits were gone and she ended up in debt, and pursued by creditors. Then the golden fountain would geyser again, and she would go on a wild spending spree until not one penny remained.

Hull and she were briefly reconciled after the uproar at Marysville, and they took a furnished cottage while looking around for a permanent place to live. They rode in the mountains, slept under the stars, and Hull shot quail and pheasant. The sunsets, the invigorating mountain air, the vitality of the miners, excited Lola. She was surprised to find this small mining town so beautiful and so civilized. It had none of the barren air she had expected, and the creek that ran the length of the town was as refreshing as the vistas she had of the mountains. The days of tenting were in the past, and substantial houses were being built close to the mines.

She was anxious at first to propitiate the women of the region. They were sharply divided between the matrons of standing and the raffish types who gathered around camps. It was clear at once that her own status would be unique and that she would associate mostly with the rebels, the bohemians and the individualists. No one who ever lived in Grass Valley drew as many celebrities from the outside world as Lola; yet, though well-known from San Francisco to Vienna, she was persona non grata to the established matrons of the local community. "Trollop and wild jade," wrote the editor of the Sacramento *Union*. "Brilliant and capricious" was another newspaper verdict.

She made up her mind to avoid stage appearances in her new setting but there was so much demand for her to appear professionally that she did her "Spider Dance" once more in the local Alta House. She was enthusiastically received and after a few performances appeared at the Dramatic Hall in Nevada City and at the National Theater in Downieville, where she met John W. Mackay, then on his way to fame as the Bonanza King; and a handsome German baron named Kirke Adler, who would figure briefly in her life as one more conquest. His interest was in hunting and horticulture, rather than in mining, and he and Lola had much in common. She found him knowledgeable about the life she had led in Germany, and as they rode together in the mountains he kept her entertained with his scholarly knowledge of the birds and flowers of the region. Both had strong feeling for the rugged mountain life and Lola liked to tell of the time a masked highwayman surprised them while they were bagging pheasants along a mountain trail.

Her rocky relations with Hull did not improve as she spent more and more time riding in the mountains with the Baron, who had dropped his title and was known simply as Dr. Adler. Her husband was not only troubled, but he was heavily afflicted with bronchial asthma, that seemed to grow worse with the dust of the mining country. He was ill, sulky and beset by a racking cough. Lola nursed him sympathetically during the worst of his seizures, and saw to it that invalid dishes were prepared for him by their cook, but they were worlds apart when they set off for San Francisco on a trip beset by misfortune.

On their way to Sacramento the stagecoach in which they were traveling hit a tree stump and overturned. This was not an unusual occurrence in such rough terrain, and Lola suffered only a few bruises. The driver had managed to keep the horses in control, and

239

the trunks and boxes filled with gold were soon back in place. But they had a more serious accident at sea while sailing from Sacramento to San Francisco. Their sidewheeler the *Antelope* was cut almost in two in a thick fog by another steamer, the *Confidence,* which went on without stopping to give aid. The passengers were finally rescued by a third steamer and Lola was credited with showing great pluck and efficiency in getting them transferred. Her cabin, in the bow of the steamer, had been almost sliced off and was partly submerged. The passengers were finally driven to Benicia, where they boarded the Stockton boat. Hull had been hurt in both accidents, and had to go straight to bed when they settled at the California Hotel.

Back among the fleshpots, Lola set up court at once, and one of her first visitors was the handsome and ubiquitous Nathaniel Willis, who had both plagued and pursued her in the East. Her European escorts swarmed around her again, and as she shopped there were cries of welcome for Lola. She bought lavishly for her new home in the valley, and paraded around in a fashion that annoyed her husband. He was back with his drinking friends and men of the press, and he now viewed Lola as all too ready to break into a stag gathering, share in off-color stories, flourish her cigar, and respond quite visibly to the approaches made by men.

Hull had accepted all this in the days of their courtship, but now that she was his wife he counted on more decorous behavior. A young bear cub that she had bought broke up one of their dinner parties in a fashionable restaurant, creating chaos and enraging Hull. One of their last public appearances together was in a theater where Caroline Chapman burlesqued her once more. This time Lola was ridiculed as an "Actress of All Works," but her presence in the audience in an arresting costume, and her good-natured acceptance of the satire, swung public opinion in her favor. Caroline had a chilly reception on her second night, and Lola had a friendly send-off when she left for Grass Valley with two wagons piled with household articles, and a small menagerie of dogs, her bear and a

240

parrot. But this was the end of her marriage. Hull was seen only briefly again in Grass Valley. He worked for a time on a paper in Marysville, and they were subsequently divorced in San Francisco. Lola went on to other romances, other adventures.

For a time she stayed at a boardinghouse run by Mrs. Harriet Robinson, a miner's wife who had been on the stage and was her contemporary. Traveling actors invariably put up at Mrs. Robinson's when they visited Grass Valley, and it was there that Lola first met Mrs. Mary Ann Crabtree, mother of the famous Lotta Crabtree, who ran another boardinghouse nearby. Mrs. Crabtree's husband, John, had given up his New York bookshop to share in the Gold Rush, but he did not flourish, and she followed him rather despairingly from place to place. It was her custom to spend some time in Harriet Robinson's cheerful ménage when celebrities arrived. Lola was warmly welcomed in this bohemian circle, but she was also defended in Grass Valley by Mrs. Knapp, a respected member of the prevailing establishment.

The Countess's boardinghouse days were only a temporary expediency until she took the house that was to become famous in the history of Grass Valley. It already had a somewhat questionable reputation as the home of Jennie-on-the-Green, so named because of the green baize table tops on which faro had been played and there had been much big-time gambling. Jennie was a frontier character, stout-hearted, well used to violence and swashbuckling ways. She added a verandah and plain pillars to this cottage on Mill Street, covered the plank walls with flowered paper, and had curtained alcoves where the gamblers could relax after their play at the tables.

No one thought it strange that Lola should take this house, and install in it some of the treasures that had been sent over to her from Germany by Ludwig's command. She sank at least $5,000 in improvements, with the help of Johnny Southwick. The house was remodeled. Its plain pillars were supplanted by more graceful ones in accordance with the contemporary sweep of Greek Revival architecture across the country. Carpenters and various craftsmen were brought from San Francisco to give the fine workmanship to Lola's remodeling that she demanded. It took two months to replace the primitive windows with small-paned French windows. Glass panels and sliding doors gave space and light to the white cottage surrounded by sycamore trees. Lola was able to create a spacious drawing room by the use of sliding panels, and a marble fireplace was the focal point of the dining room, where she entertained as if she were still on the Barerstrasse.

She had tried to recreate the scene in a small way, with goldleaf decorations, fine paneling and delicate Empire wallpaper. A bust of Ludwig in a niche in the hall set the stage for arriving guests. Her carpets and lace curtains had come from Munich, as well as her Louis XVI gold-leaf cabinet. A love seat she had shared with Ludwig, console tables and her nine-foot mirrors, once so essential to her existence, were part of her décor, and her swan bed with its silken canopy was still her resting place. Ebony tables inlaid with mother of pearl, then fashionable, were a Victorian touch beside her sofa and chairs upholstered in crimson and gold.

Lola added a wing at the back of the cottage for the kitchen, bathroom and wine cellar. The bathtub caused almost as much talk as Millard Fillmore's at the White House. It was a novelty for California, although it was still of the primitive order and kept her servants running back and forth with cans of water. Lola had achieved only minor splendor but her décor seemed impressive in its frontier setting. She gave a Christmas party after moving in, and was the star of the evening, playing carols on her melodeon, singing with some abandon and drinking champagne. Rubies glittered against her white skin. Her gown was of ruby-red velvet, cut low, and the men gathered around her could not take their eyes off the enchantress. Echoes of Munich were in the air.

Queen Theresa's death from cholera had been significant news for Lola, who considered herself the uncrowned queen of Bavaria. It was no surprise to her to learn that the Black Lady who presaged death for a Wittelsbach had been seen in the Castle of Aschaffenburg before the Queen's death. This legend went back to a princess who had died a century earlier, and all Bavaria knew her as the Black Lady who brought doom to the reigning house. Lola was well versed in the mysticism that surrounded the Wittelsbachs, and her own passion for wearing black was commented on in this connection.

She had not been settled long in her new home before she gave a reception, and Wednesday became her regular night for these gatherings, which brought guests from San Francisco and Sacramento, as well as the surrounding valley. Hampers of delicacies arrived regularly from San Francisco and were served in the European manner. Champagne flowed liked water, and her wines, carefully chosen by Dr. Adler, were chilled to the right degree. Her maid's plain cooking was expanded to choice cuisine with the skilled touch of a French chef who had worked at one of the mines. Lola wore her jewels and her most ravishing gowns at her soirees, as they were called in Grass Valley, although they were always "receptions" in her terminology. It took little persuasion to get her to play, sing or dance. Cards and chess were always in evidence, and in a minor way she revived the social image of her life in Munich —but without its focal point, the King. There were all-day celebrations on Christmas, New Year's and Independence Day.

It was customary for German, Russian and Polish counts and barons to attend these gatherings, and two of her favorite guests were nephews of Victor Hugo. When they left California she gave a big party in their honor. Lola prided herself on focusing her gatherings on the larger interests of the world. The latest books from Paris and London were always on hand for discussion. Each guest was expected to give something of himself to uphold the tone of this curious salon in Grass Valley. The latest *bon mot*, the raciest, newest story, the prevailing mood of the hour in each of the countries she had known came into play.

Lola was a born communicator when in the mood, and in a moment she would drop her frivolous manner to discuss legal issues with Stephen J. Field, who later became a Supreme Court Justice, or with William M. Stewart, one of her lawyer friends from Marysville headed eventually for the Senate. Always at her best discussing politics, she took sharp issue with the sons of Henry S. Foote, Governor of Mississippi, and with Preston S. Brooks, who would become famous by bludgeoning Charles Sumner in the Senate over the antislavery issue. Lola had strong feelings about the right of every man to be free.

She found it gratifying to have some of the more rugged men of the West around her in contrast to the dandified types that continually crossed her path. She had never given up the illusion of conducting a salon of her own, and the frontier spirit appealed to her. Perhaps alone among the great beauties of the era Lola was equipped to swing the various elements into harmonious juxtaposition.

Sam Brannan, who by this time was divorced, attended her parties now that Hull was out of the way. Touring artists visited her on their way through Grass Valley. Both Edwin Booth and Laura Keene were entertained by Lola and she gave a musicale in honor of Ole Bull, the Norwegian violinist. Donning her Spanish costume that night she danced her "El Ollé" for a more appreciative audience than she had found in Sacramento. Her fellow artists, particularly those identified with the foreign scene, treated the Countess with deference, although they knew how difficult she could be behind the scenes.

Lola took pains to honor them all when they came to Grass Valley. She regularly attended the professional entertainments given at Alta Hall, which by this time had footlights, good scenery and plush seats. When the Montplaisir Ballet Company visited Nevada City, she made a point of riding over muddy roads to attend their performance. Realizing that her presence might prove to be a diversion she tried to slip in quietly, but she was recognized at once and cries went up for Lola. She appeared briefly on the stage to

244

wild applause, but stilled it to make a short speech wishing the ballet company well. In spite of all her tantrums and scenes, she was occasionally a professional at heart.

Stephen Massett, the composer and poet, recalled a merry evening at Lola's "picturesque little Villa." He found Southwick acting as host, and he was struck by the assortment of dogs, bears, parrots and cats on the premises. They played cards, and had songs and music until dawn. Both Massett and Alonzo Delano, poet and newspaperman, dashed off verses about Lola, a custom long ago established in her life by Ludwig. The dove cote and wine cellar that Dr. Adler had built at the back of the house gave it all a Bavarian air.

Lola lavished special care on her garden and passersby became used to seeing the great star, who had lived in palaces and the luxury hotels of the world, groveling in the mud, planting, weeding, shaping and pounding the earth around her plants. She gardened as furiously as she rode, letting off energy until she was tired, when she would throw aside her tools and collapse in a state of total exhaustion. It seemed to onlookers that she had created a small paradise out of the rich soil.

Lola's neighbor Mrs. Knapp observed that she was the first person in the region to catch the grotesque beauty of the cactus. "I believe hers was the first collection of growing cacti made for ornamental purposes among the thousands that have been made in California," she commented. But Lola also cultivated rose bushes, flowers and shrubs, and often came back from her mountain rides with roots and bulbs to plant. Her attire was as diverting to her neighbors as her gardening operations. She usually wore rough mining clothes while she worked in her garden, but an hour later she would appear on the street in a simple calico dress, with a sunbonnet pinioned with flying streamers, and the demure air of a schoolgirl. Most often she was seen in her trim riding clothes, or in Quaker gray, a color that she used to good effect with touches of blue to bring out the beauty of her eyes. Lola looked her best on snowy

245

days wearing a hooded fur coat in the Russian tradition. One of the Nevada newspapers pictured her "flashing like a meteor through the snowflakes and wanton snowballs" to the tinkle of silver bells in a bright red sleigh drawn by a span of horses.

In the evening she wore the gowns from Europe that she had finally unpacked from her many pieces of luggage. But whatever she wore Lola had style and a sense of fitness. She differed completely from the women who were making a business of flamboyant attire in the Gold Rush days, and her figure commanded attention in any type of costume. Her jewels were all thought to be of royal origin although other men besides the King had decked her with gems.

Lola was under constant observation by a gold miner named Edwin Franklin Morse, and he dictated his impressions later to his daughter, Mary Phillips Morse, as part of his reminiscences. He was one of the few men immune to her physical charms, but he was impressed with what she had done with Jennie's property and the garden she created. He was convinced that it was Johnny Southwick who had persuaded Lola to settle in Grass Valley, and he wrote: "Lola was no fool, and she knew a good thing when she saw it; and that good thing was Johnny Southwick, while his money lasted."

Morse was a tall, skinny miner whom Lola called the Greyhound. They often chatted with each other in neighborly fashion, for he lived almost across the road from her, in the Robinson boardinghouse. Lola did not invite him to her great parties, but he was always well aware of what was going on and he reported hearing Ole Bull play on the night of his musicale. He commented on how constantly Kirke Adler mooned around the stables, worked on the wine cellar or spent hours with his beautiful hostess when the servants were out.

A fresh wave of scandal enveloped Lola when word spread that Adler, out hunting by himself, had been shot in the woods. No one knew whether his death was accidental or a suicide, but it was a depressing experience for Lola, as she added one more to the list of men close to her who had a violent death. She had not gone with him on this occasion, but she was a familiar sight galloping over the mountain trails until night fell and fantastic sunsets lighted her way home. She seemed to glory in the freedom, the excitement of these wild rides, often taken without a companion. On a May day in 1854 she was nearly killed when her horse threw her as he leaped a ditch. The *Shasta Courier* reported: "Lola Montez, the eccentric and beautiful and daring, was recently thrown from her horse into a stream of water, by the effort of the animal to leap a ditch to enable his fair mistress to gather a bunch of beautiful flowers. She escaped unharmed, but was in great danger for a short time."

Lola soon had a clash with the church. Both the Methodists and the Presbyterians opened their doors about the time that she settled in the valley. The Roman Catholics and Congregationalists established themselves and the African Methodists had a church of their own. The Episcopalians were just getting under way. The Methodist minister, whose name was Wilson, preached a thundering sermon aimed at Lola and her "wanton circle" after she had done her "Spider Dance" at one of her soirees. The word traveled that her light chiffons had barely covered her gorgeous figure. Some of her neighbors nodded approval in church as their pastor described her as a "shameless devil in the guise of a beautiful and fascinating dancer."

This was a direct challenge to Lola. She donned her "Spider Dance" costume, threw a cape over it and sought the parsonage.

"Well, Mr. Wilson, how much of a devil am I?" she asked as she stood before the minister and his wife and dropped her cape.

In addition to a short chiffon costume she wore her maillot and her ballet slippers and was more covered up than she often was in her evening gowns. Lola had faced up to the church before, and the minister quailed, as her blazing eyes were turned with full effect on his. He had nothing to say, but with one of her swift changes of mood she softened, chatted with him briefly and was served tea. She engaged his interest at once with her conversation and she later sent a contribution for his church. This was characteristic of her inconsistency.

But her encounter with a local editor ended less amicably than her brush with the church. On two occasions she threatened Henry Shipley, a Missourian who edited the Grass Valley *Telegraph*. When her Kanaka houseboy ran home one day and told her that Shipley had shoved him aside in a local store and called him a "damned nigger" she tucked her whip under her shawl and accompanied the boy back to make his purchases. The editor saw her coming and suspected her intentions. He disappeared and Lola stood guard while the boy did his buying.

The second occasion was more serious. On a November day in 1854 the *Telegraph* ran an oblique reference to her that made her furious. Actually the paragraph, reprinted from the *New York Times*, did not refer directly to her, but in characterizing a European royalty it mentioned the "Lola Montez–like insolence and effrontery" involved. She dashed along Mill Street with her riding whip in one hand and a copy of the *Telegraph* in the other. Before she got to his office she met Shipley in the street and crack went her whip. She curled it around his head and face while he warded it off with his hands and tried to snatch it away from her. But Lola was as expert as a fencer; her footwork was fast and sure. As Shipley bolted into a nearby saloon she broke her whip and threw both parts after him. The miners who had gathered around from the saloon ignored her. They were not anxious to stir up trouble with the local editor or involve themselves in one of Lola's rows. She bought them drinks and talked to them persuasively, but they laughed at her, and so did Shipley, who treated the incident as a joke. After she had cooled down she wrote to him accusingly, calling him a blackmailer, a man of feeble intellect who had dared to accuse her of hypocrisy and effrontery.

The public lashing of a well-known editor shook up the people of Grass Valley. It was the first time she had been seen swinging her whip in the mining town, although everyone had heard that this was part of her history. It was one more black mark for Lola, who had succumbed again to what seemed to be an uncontrollable impulse. The California papers in general came to her defense, and the *Golden Era*, which always treated her gently, said that Shipley was meddling in affairs that did not concern either him or the public. "Let Lola Montez alone, so long as she is not at present on the stage," was the message. Before long Shipley resigned, drifted about for a time and ended up a suicide, another violent death across Lola's trail.

Nor did she escape the suspicion of espionage during her stay in Grass Valley. This too was part of her public image, and no one doubted that she liked to dabble in political affairs, whenever she could. Even on the local level she was surrounded by experienced politicians. But letters found in an old trunk long after her death stirred up the suspicion that she was in on an abortive plan to foment revolution in California and establish an empire over which she would rule—a far-fetched vision, even for Lola.

All this was less strange than it seemed, since various elements were at work in California to swing the state to the South as the Compromise of 1850 went into effect. There was much intrigue going on, with the settlement of land claims, the bitter feeling of the Spaniards after the Mexican War, and the nation as a whole heading toward the Civil War that had been postponed for the time being because of the Compromise. Mrs. Greenhow was among the intrigantes, although she would not show her hand until the war actually broke out. Her work in California was subtle and remote in its implications, for she was close to the prominent Southerners who were settling in San Francisco. Her husband's work on the land claims brought her significantly close to government operations. Like Lola, Mrs. Greenhow believed in influencing men in order to gain her ends.

Although the newspapers on both sides of the Atlantic constantly suggested that Lola's love affairs were tied up with espionage activities, the pattern never emerged with any clarity in spite of her strong fight against the Ultramontane. In general she allied herself with the liberal point of view, but many of the rakes who surrounded her had court connections and Lola was never indifferent to the nobility. The number of times in which she was helped out of difficulties in European capitals by British officials, in spite of her tarnished reputation on the home front, suggested to many that Lord Palmerston gave her his backing. But there was no consistency in her operations, since she sometimes seemed to foster conflicting interests.

Lola lived in a period when women of presence and intellect meddled freely in political affairs. Her own love affairs gave her an unfair advantage at times as she listened attentively to the confidences of well-known men. In Grass Valley she had time to dwell on these memories but it seems unlikely that she envisaged any great future for herself in this setting. As she talked to her lawyer friends who were already heading for political power she was well aware that the nation was ripening for war. She listened attentively to men who were for and against the extension of slavery, and Lola was always articulate in her defense of the black man, with full freedom for everyone. She never forgot about Lord Brougham's long antislavery fight.

There was much about her that baffled her neighbors and even her closest friends. She received an endless stream of letters from Europe and wrote many herself, although they were skimpy and almost illiterate for one so highly educated in the worldly sense of the word. Her trunks, containing a wealth of old stage costumes and jewels, took up considerable room in her house. It was common talk that she had $30,000 worth of treasures under her roof. The local children longed to get close to those trunks, although their mothers were wary of Lola until little Lotta Crabtree came under her wing. After that she would have them in for parties, dressing them in some of her finery, dancing for them, and feeding them Viennese pastries.

Lola was as fond of children as she was of pets, and watching a group go past to school every day, she had been struck by the bright little redhead whom the world would come to know as Lotta Crabtree. Mrs. Crabtree had entered Lotta in a small dancing school for children. It was next to a saloon, and sometimes the children could scarcely follow the music for the racket. Mrs. Crabtree had come to know Lola through the Robinsons and she readily agreed to let her help Lotta with her dancing. She taught the child some rudimentary ballet steps, the "Highland Fling," the "Sailor's Hornpipe" and the more popular dances in her own repertoire. Lotta was amazingly gifted and had a better sense of rhythm and timing than Lola had at any stage of her career. Soon she took Lotta riding with her into the hills and taught her some of the graces of the larger world, in addition to working on her diction. Lotta was impish, dimpled and bright, and she came to adore the Countess, who was always ready to produce her stage costumes from her trunks, or let her dance to her German music box.

Mrs. Crabtree, who was something of a termagant herself, kept a tight rein on Lotta, but she refused to listen to the warnings she received about letting her little daughter go about so freely with the notorious Countess. On one of their rides they visited the mining camp of Rough and Ready, four miles from Grass Valley, and it became part of Lotta's history that this was the spot where she first danced in public. When they stopped at W. H. Fippen's blacksmith shop he played a tune on his anvil. Lola picked up the seven-year-old child and swung her onto the anvil, where she showed off her steps to the accompaniment of anvil strokes. A crowd gathered to cheer the little prodigy, and the anvil, which had been brought across the country by covered wagon, became a historic possession.

251

After this it became a mark of distinction for the small fry to be seen riding with the Countess. Lola spent some of her nights in Grass Valley at the bedside of sick children whose families could not afford to have nurses, and there were times when she rode over the hills to take food and medicine to an ailing miner. She always gave food to the Indians who came begging at her door. These gestures were remembered long after her death, and the Grass Valley *Telegraph,* with another editor, treated her with more understanding: "Lola is no ordinary person. She is possessed of an original mind, one decidedly intellectual and highly cultivated. She delights in change and excitement."

Lola spent hours over her needlework, when she was not reading, or dreaming, or gardening, or riding into the hills. Her housekeeping was well looked after by her staff, and Periwinkle was always at hand to brush her hair and dress her as carefully for her parties as if she were preparing her for the stage. But in Grass Valley she showed that she could be practical as well as decorative, although during most of her life, from her early days in India, she had been waited on hand and foot, with servants and coachmen at her command. She had always been skilled with her needle but she now laid aside her superb needlepoint to fashion simple frocks for the local children from calico bought in Grass Valley. She knitted heavy underwear to suit the climate, and Caroline Chapman, her tormentor, later treasured an exquisite sampler made for her by the Countess. There was nothing helpless about her, and she did her best to fit into the frontier life, rmembering not to wear her Parisian gowns to the local dance hall, or to serve French cuisine to local visitors. For once in her life Lola, who had made her own kind of pitch for democracy, tried to avoid the semblance of being a snob.

Her menagerie both interested and dismayed her neighbors. A bear was her star boarder, tied by a silver chain to a post when he was not locked up indoors. When he was small Lola would walk him along the street on his chain, but as he grew he became for-

midable. It was not much of a novelty to keep wild animals in
California or Nevada. Wildcat and bulldog fights were common,
and there were savage contests between bulls and bears. But Lola's
collection included what one of her neighbors called "baying
hounds, monkeys and a cursing parrot, as well as the bear Major."
Nothing was too much trouble for her where her animals were
concerned. Her houseboy was apt to curse them, as he tended them
in a shed behind the house when the weather turned cold. Lola
considered Major a protection, since he kept away visitors whom
she did not wish to see. She was also said to use him for intimida-
tion when the miners quarreled among themselves over boundary
lines. But when Major bit her hand as she fed him one day she
screamed with pain like any other member of her sex and had to
be rescued by a miner, who clubbed the bear until he let go. After
that the Greyhound across the street observed that the Countess
seemed to be afraid of her bear, and to stand well back while she
threw scraps of food to him. This was soon followed by a newspaper announcement that an "affably inclined bear" was for sale.
In the end Major disappeared from Grass Valley and from Lola's
life.

As these events crowded her, and Mrs. Crabtree took Lotta away
to join her husband in Rabbit Creek, Lola sank into one of her profound depressions. There was no overwhelming romance in her life
at the time, and her wildest gallops over the mountain trails failed
to soothe her. She spent hours by her fireside, writing letters, reading the new books that arrived from France, and studying the
principles of animal magnetism and extrasensory perception through
Andrew Jackson Davis's book *The Principles of Nature, Her Divine
Revelations and a Voice to Mankind*. Lola later disclosed that this
book had a profound effect on her and changed her whole life. She
was slightly affected, too, by the ouija board experiments and table-
tipping staged in Grass Valley by mediums who had come from
Nevada City.

She had always been responsive to mystical influences and to the eerie work of the spiritualists, preoccupied as she was with death, but Davis brought a new factor into her life. He was one of the gurus of the period, a clairvoyant cattle herder from Hyde Park, New York, who was the foremost advocate of the animal-magnetism cult then sweeping the country. Black-haired, handsome, young Davis preached "interior meditation and mental expansion." He pled for "universal peace, brotherly love, and social and national unity."

Day after day Lola studied this book, seeking to slip into the mood of mystical revelation. She would take it with her into the hills, and riders passing by would observe the Countess, dabbling her feet in a mountain stream, seemingly talking to herself, and quite unaware of the world around her. She was practicing mental expansion and reaching toward Dujarier's star, but her neighbors thought her demented. No one quite knew what was happening to Lola, but she ceased to care any longer for appearances. Her exquisite grooming became a thing of the past, and a tidy housewife who lived nearby said that she needed soap and water, as she studied Lola's famous neckline circled not by diamonds but by an unmistakable ring of dirt. Periwinkle's ministrations no longer helped except for big occasions. The Greyhound watched this decline with strong disapproval and added a note to his memoirs: "When carefully dressed and gotten up, she was still very handsome, but ordinarily she was such a slattern that to me she was frankly disgusting. She needed soap and water. . . . She had undoubtedly been a beautiful woman, but her charms were then beginning to fade. She still retained a slender and graceful figure. She had heavy black hair and the most brilliant flashing eyes ever beheld."

In the spring of 1855 Lola was roused at last from this long period of listless boredom and melancholy. Scandal, a small fire, the loss of many of her pets, including Major, had worn her down and she needed fresh stimulation. She was getting short of funds and her mining investments were in trouble. But beyond this she had a new love interest in her life—a young man close to the theater named Augustus Noel Follin—and this revived her faster than anything else. Shy, handsome, sensitive, this youth had joined in the Gold Rush when he was twenty-three, leaving his wife and two children in Cincinnati. He had been singularly unsuccessful and after five years he was struggling to make a living collecting bills in the daytime and working as a cashier in the theater box office by night. But he was known to many of the stars and he booked engagements for some.

Noel came under Lola's spell when he attended one of her soirees with friends from San Francisco. He was soon writing to his young sister Miriam, who would become well known later as Mrs. Frank Leslie, suffragette and owner of the Leslie Publications, that he had met the "lawless little meteor" who had been the mistress of the King of Bavaria, of Dumas and of Liszt. He had shown her a daguerreotype of Miriam and Lola had been charmed by it. His view of the Countess after their first meeting was graphic:

She lives in Grass Valley with a pet bear, a dozen dogs; birds, a summer house filled with the rarest flowers, all sorts of musical instruments . . . there is all the remnants of a lovely woman about her, her nose appears chiseled out of marble and her conversational powers are fascinating to a degree: I talked with her in English, French & Spanish, she speaks German, Italian, Portuguese and Russian in addition.

Follin, morbid and introverted by nature, felt out of his depth as he listened to Lola's worldly discussions with men who had shared in the university life of Harvard, the Sorbonne, Oxford and Munich, as some of her friends now in the gold fields had. Although he was only on the fringes of the theatrical world and lacked the bold spirit that Lola expected in her men, she viewed him not only as an attractive young man but as holding a key to her immediate future. She had worn out her welcome in California with her feuds and eccentricities and was now ready for something new. It was clear to her that through Follin she could promote her own career and his at the same time, and fulfill her long-cherished ambition to return to India, which was still in her blood; to tour the world, be-

255

ginning with Australia. She was tired of Sam Brannan and Johnny Southwick, whose health and riches were failing. Follin, unlikely though he seemed, was the right man at the right moment, and his theatrical associations enabled him to get bookings for the Countess, with considerable prodding from her.

The prevailing feeling in Grass Valley was that she was leaving because she had run out of funds. She had tossed away large sums of money on her lavish entertaining and costly way of living. She made one last tour of the region where she had found such freedom and exhilaration. A miner's wife went with her, and they camped in the old fashion, riding and fishing, cooking over their campfires, sleeping in the open.

At the last minute she rode to Rabbit Creek to see the Crabtrees, but Mrs. Crabtree was about to tour the mining towns with Lotta, and she refused to let her daughter join the small company that Lola and Follin were rounding up for their world tour. Lotta was disappointed. Her affection for her glamorous teacher had not waned, but the risks were obvious to her mother, and things were moving fast in the child's own life.

It was a simple matter for the Countess to close her house, have her furniture covered, and give her most treasured gold-leaf pieces to a neighbor for safekeeping. A large crowd turned out to see her off by stagecoach, and the prediction was made that when much else was forgotten her memory would be green in the valley to which she had brought such dash and excitement.

She had a two-month engagement to fill at the Metropolitan in San Francisco before sailing for Australia. Once again the San Franciscans turned out to see Lola Montez. The plush elegance of the theater, its gas chandeliers, crimson velvet seats and gold decorations brought her sharply back to the world of luxury and show. Her affair with Follin was developing at this time, and he sat like a shadow in the background watching her in *Lola Montez in Bavaria* and *The Maid of Saragossa*—a foretaste of the tour to come.

He was torn with remorse as he fell deeper under her spell, and he confided his doubts to his mother and half sister. "No hand can ever again make the clock strike the hours that are past," he wrote. "Lately I have become very melancholy in disposition." Finally he asked them to tell his abandoned wife that he was bound for Honolulu, Sydney, China, Calcutta, Bombay, Constantinople, England, then on to Paris and back to New York.

"I shall be gone two years or more," he wrote. "I go with the Countess Landsfeld, Lola Montez, as agent—if successful I shall make twenty-five thousand dollars. I have nothing to lose and all to gain; things are and have been very dull in California for months."

His disinclination to let his family know how deeply involved he was with Lola was apparent in his final note: "I hardly have the heart to write. I have tried to do so twenty times during the last week but could not. Now that the moment has arrived in *desperation* I send a few lines. . . . I dare not trust myself to say more. I should die if I did. God bless you. I love you. Noel."

FIFTEEN

Off to the Antipodes

Lola sailed for Australia on the *Fanny Major* on June 6, 1855. A shimmering pink dress billowing wide in the breeze, a picture hat with trailing streamers, a green parasol casting shadows over her white face gave her the bloom of youth that she had lost during her rugged days on the frontier. She waved gaily to the crowd that had gathered to watch her sail, and gave no sign of her own inner uncertainty. To all intents and purposes Lola was going around the world, with two years of travel ahead of her. But things went wrong from the start.

Thirty-three days at sea and a succession of rows and tantrums shook up her fellow troupers and many of the other passengers. Lola made little effort to exercise her well-known charm and Follin bore the brunt of her ill humor. He was constantly mollifying the people she offended. Her small group, all of whom belonged to the Metropolitan Theatrical Company in San Francisco, finally decided to let her strictly alone. In any event they saw that she was absorbed in Follin, when she was not lost in trancelike abstraction.

When she found a steward whipping her dog she drew a dagger and flourished it in his face. She insisted on being moved from first class, where he worked, into steerage quarters. She brightened when they sailed into the handsome harbor of Sydney, reminiscent of the one she had left. Almost at once they were in the familiar atmosphere of adventurers seeking gold, for Australia was having its own Gold Rush at the time, and immigrants were pouring in. It was a period of depression in commerce and agriculture, but the quest for gold was constant.

Lola's fame had traveled around the world and she was received with interest and some enthusiasm. Traveling stars were not yet a commonplace, and her experiences in Britain had been well advertised in Australia, so that conservatives viewed her with reserve. The moralities were more strongly emphasized than in the American West, so far as the stage was concerned, and she soon came under fire. News of ructions behind the scenes leaked out and her reception at the Victoria Theater in Sydney on August 23, 1855, was not enthusiastic, although the *Era* described her as looking charming and acting "very archly." She gave one of her curtain speeches and presented her King Ludwig in the play *Lola Montez in Bavaria*—a Londoner named Lambert—with a "handsome bundle of cigarettes—a very great compliment, as she is an inveterate smoker and seldom gives any cigars away."

She passed muster four days later in *Yelva, or the Orphan of Russia*, which she had translated from the French version. This was followed by a benefit, *The Follies of a Night*, into which she introduced the "Spider Dance." It was instantly condemned as being a "libertinish and indelicate performance." The Australian women snubbed the daring Countess, but men packed the theater to see her, in spite of all the condemnation of her technique.

The professionals in the company became restless and some scattered, unable to cope with Lola's whims. When she decided to move on to Melbourne two members of the company issued a writ of attachment as she was about to sail from Sydney. Mrs. Fiddes, with considerable professional experience, led the rebellion, with the company's finances at stake. The sheriff who boarded the ship to keep Lola from leaving could not find her until after they set sail. Then she sent for him to arrest her, but warned him that she was stark naked in her cabin and would remain that way. Thus challenged, the sheriff gave up and was let off the ship at the Heads. Later he was the butt of many jokes as he told this story about the Countess.

She settled at the Grand Imperial Hotel when she reached Melbourne, which was then the center of the Gold Rush. In many ways it reminded her of San Francisco. People of all nationalities walked the streets and again she could place them accurately as she listened to the various languages they used. The press was ready for her. The Sydney correspondent of the *Argus* had spread the bad news that the Countess was a terror and her "Spider Dance" a moral outrage. A local editor had already done a thoroughgoing exposé of Lola's history, so that the odds were stacked against her. Her old enemy Hauser had passed that way, too, and had been quoted as saying that only the devil could work with Lola Montez.

Wasting no time, she wrote to the editor of the *Argus*, protesting the attack on the "Spider Dance," which she said was a national one, witnessed with delight by all classes in Spain and by both sexes. With all the preliminary uproar about this dance Lola made one of her speeches from the stage and asked the audience if they wished to see it. They did, and there were hisses for the *Argus* and cheers for Lola. But a warrant was issued for her arrest, and things were settled only when she modified the dance. The town sports took up the issue, however, and the Lola Montez aperitif made with Old Tom, ginger, lemon and hot water was used to toast her at the Café de Paris in Melbourne.

She had found a young Frenchman to champion her at this point and both threatened the editor who had attacked her. She was in a fighting mood when they reached Adelaide, a center of the gold diggings at that time. The town was plastered with posters advertising a concert by Hauser. In a destructive mood she stalked around, tearing them down—her personal vendetta against the man she said had helped to break up her tour in the mining country at home. The Countess had official backing in Adelaide, however. Sir Richard Graves McDonnell, Governor of South Australia, and Lady McDonnell attended her performance and found nothing unwarranted about it. But her tour became increasingly disorganized as she moved from place to place. The establishment seemed to be against her but the diggers loved her. She went into the deepest shafts with precise knowledge of their operation.

The people of Geelong, a quarrying center forty miles from Melbourne, would have none of her. She was not allowed to perform at the Theater Royal on grounds of moral obliquity. It was announced that she was suffering from bronchitis after being exposed to a severe thunderstorm. The same resistance prevailed at Ballarat, another mining town, but here she fought back briskly when the editor of the Ballarat *Times*, named Seekamp, wrote about her in a scurrilous vein. He made no secret of the fact that he had drunk and caroused with Lola.

When she learned a few days later that he was in the lobby of the United States Hotel, where she was staying, she rushed downstairs with her whip and swung it at him in public view. But he had arrived with the same means of defense, knowing Lola's reputation with a whip. Soon they slashed back and forth at each other until onlookers pulled them apart. Lola had an ovation in the handsome Victoria Theater that night, and she won her audience completely with a curtain speech: "You have heard of the scene that took place this afternoon. Mr. Seekamp threatens to continue his charges against my character. I offered, though a woman, to meet him with pistols; but the coward who could beat a woman, ran from a woman. He says he will drive me off the diggings; but I will change the tables, and make Seekamp *de*camp."

It took another woman, however, to worst the Countess, and Mrs. Crosby, wife of the theater manager in Ballarat, whom she had harassed beyond endurance, battled her physically when she saw her raise her whip to strike Crosby. She had accused him of cheating her, but Mrs. Crosby knocked her down and broke her wrist—a novel experience for Lola, who had been the winner in all her battles with the whip. Her beautiful face was scarred and bruised for the time being.

In spite of her many encounters with men it was rare for Lola to have open conflict with members of her own sex. Those who did not admire her were apt to avoid her. She was generally feared or scorned by them, except for fellow professionals who had tolerance for the humbug of press agentry, and some of whom had hearty respect for the fame she had made for herself in Europe—provided they did not have to work with her.

On their return to Sydney Lola's interest in Major-General Charles Wellesley, younger brother of the second Duke of Wellington, wounded the sensitive and jealous Follin. Well aware that his brother had known Lola in London, young Wellesley, a married man on military duty in Australia, called on her and offered to show her the town. A number of his officer friends had been her escorts in London. All the better-known Britons resident in Australia were familiar with Lola's well-publicized history and she gave a highly successful benefit for the wounded at Sebastopol before sailing for home on the *Jane E. Falkenburg*.

There was no further question of continuing their tour around the world. They were in serious financial difficulties and creditors pursued them right up to the moment of sailing. Far from having made a fortune for himself and his family, Follin was in despair over their finances. He was still in love with Lola and jealous of her fluctuating interests. A moody man to begin with, he had passed the point where he could cope with her tempers, and his sense of guilt about his family was overwhelming.

They were off the Fiji Islands when he disappeared at sea on July 8, 1856. The mystery of his death was never cleared up. One version was that he had fallen overboard after a champagne party celebrating his birthday. Another was that Lola had pushed him to his death. The most generally accepted theory was that he had committed suicide. There had been a lively party the night he drowned, with champagne flowing freely, but no one admitted to being on deck when Follin disappeared. A scream from Lola brought help. She was found lying unconscious on the deck. When she revived she said that she had gone to her cabin to get some money she had in reserve to give to Follin, and that when she returned he was gone. Apparently she had then collapsed from shock. It was some time before the ship's officers realized that he was missing. The ship circled for a time, then gave him up for lost. Lola conceded the likelihood of suicide, but she was always vague about Follin's end. *The Golden Era* of August 3, 1856, said that as they were celebrating his birthday with a supper party he "stepped on deck to empty a glass, and being somewhat under the influence of champagne, a sudden lurch of the vessel pitched him overboard."

In any event the obscure Noel Follin came into view internationally as another of Lola Montez's victims. The European papers made much of the story. Her enemies believed that they had quarreled over money and that she had pushed him overboard, or that he had jumped in despair. She showed no sign of grief or concern when she disembarked after this fateful voyage. Lola was her most assured self, with a white cockatoo resting on her shoulder. Her collection of birds, dogs and other pets she had picked up on her travels was established in the house she took on Telegraph Hill. Since she had engagements to fill in San Francisco, she kept up a front. But whatever had occurred at sea her penitence in private was overwhelming, and she was never the same after Follin's death.

The loyal San Franciscans welcomed her back. The city was expanding in every way—in size, in sophistication, in open-mindedness to the world at large. It was not immediately apparent to them that the brilliant creature walking the streets so boldly with her white cockatoo was actually communing with the spirits and was lost in profound remorse.

She appeared in Grass Valley like a ghost from the past, death still stalking her course. She cut all strings with the little mining town and sold her house. By that time Southwick was an ill and ruined man, and vandals had made off with some of her possessions, as in Munich. But she sold what remained, except for the treasures she had left with the Robinsons. Later the scattered objects were recovered by this family, and eventually were displayed at the Mission Inn in Riverside, California. They included marble tables with mirrors nine feet tall; an inlaid chess table, historic because King Ludwig and Lola had used it for many games; a black lace fan with tortoiseshell sticks identified with the dancer who had made the use of the fan an art in itself; chairs and sofa upholstered with crimson and gold damask; console tables with mirror backs and ebony pieces inlaid with mother of pearl.

Lola kept her final theatrical engagement in San Francisco, opening early in August, 1856, in *Lola Montez in Bavaria*, which most San Franciscans had already seen, followed by *The School for Scandal*, which had never been her best medium. In turn she appeared in *The Morning Call, The Follies of a Night, Charlotte Corday* and *Antony and Cleopatra*. Junius Booth, under whose auspices she played at the Metropolitan Theater, was one of the first to detect the great change in Lola. He had played with her before and knew how difficult she could be. But now he found her almost humble in spirit. When he told her not to smoke in the theater she flared up for a moment and said that she would slap him. But when Booth told her that he would slap her back Lola subsided without protest. It was clear to him that she had lost her fire and was living in some world of her own. Laura Keene noticed this, too.

Lola's Australian tour had inspired another Dr. William Robinson satire, entitled *A Trip to Australia: or Lola Montez on the Fanny Major*. This was staged as the Countess had her jewels auctioned off, intending to give the proceeds to Follin's widow and children. San Franciscans were outraged, and they later packed the theater where Lola was playing, and boycotted the Robinson production. The San Francisco *Herald* warned the public to stay away from this vulgar representation of the manners and behavior of a visitor— "a ridiculous caricature of her person, and a coarse exaggeration of her peculiarities."

But Lola knew that her star was falling. While on Telegraph Hill she entertained in the old manner, but chiefly for members of her own profession. With Hull out of her life few politicians showed up at her gatherings, and the socialites left her strictly alone. The impression prevailed that she might be drinking, for although she had a book entitled *Beauty Secrets* published that year (1856) she was no longer the exquisitely groomed Countess of the past. Actually, she was communing with the spirits and was passing a good deal of her time with mediums.

As she declined, her old friend Adah Isaacs Menken was coming to the fore, and she seemed to be copying many of Lola's ways. She strode about with a whip under her arm and rode astride, racing along the coast to the ocean on a Tartar stallion. She smoked cheroots and drank her whiskey straight in public bars. In course of time she would become a bigamist, like Lola, and she was also a sensational beauty, with masses of red-gold hair and a melancholy charm caught by Swinburne in one of his poems. She was gifted in many ways and as the years passed she gave Chopin recitals, painted and wrote passable verse. Her stormy ways were always of great interest to Lola, who corresponded with her regularly. Their mutual memories went back to their early history in London.

Mrs. Crabtree and Lotta were on the scene in San Francisco during Lola's last days there, but Mrs. Crabtree was reluctant to let the rising star come under Lola's spell again. She disliked Lola's absorption in spiritualism and the publicity it had received when she was taken in by a fake medium. Lotta was doing well and was appearing with the Chapmans on a mixed program, billed simply as

La Petite Lotte. Before leaving the city Lola introduced her to
Edwin Booth and Laura Keene. She had not lost faith in the gifted
child, and although she did not live long enough to see Lotta's
Fountain, her gift to San Francisco, go up at Market and Kearney
streets, she was also spared the knowledge that by 1866 Lotta would
be burlesquing her in the Caroline Chapman manner at the Howard
Athenaeum in Boston.

The Countess was in Sacramento when her jewels were auctioned
off on Montgomery Street in San Francisco. The bidding was slow
and her pigeon's blood ruby, that had become almost a symbol of
Lola's fire; her diamond cross, directly associated with her life in
Munich; her brooches, earrings, watches, lockets, chains and rings
brought only $10,000. In the course of her lifetime she had re-
peatedly sold off valuable jewels, or lost them, or given them away,
according to her whim. The small sum raised at the auction was no
clue to the fortune in jewels that had been part of her life history.
But now her one desire was to raise money for the Follins. Her
sense of guilt over Noel's death was overwhelming. Her engagement
at the Edwin Forrest Theater in Sacramento had been disappointing financially, although she had been well received in the city,
the storms of the past all forgotten. But tickets sold for a dollar
only, where once they had gone for $35 each when Lola Montez
appeared. She knew that the shadows were closing in on her, and
she decided to move again. The stars now told her what she
should do.

On an autumn day in 1856, Lola sailed for San Juan on the
Orizaba, leaving Periwinkle behind to marry the man with whom
she had fallen in love. No one had been told where she was heading, but she was next heard of in St. Jean de Luz. She had left her
ship at Marseilles and traveled to the resort in the Pyrenees close
to the Spanish border. It was one of the fashionable watering places
of the period and she established herself at the Hôtel du Cygne.
Stirred up by reports in French and Belgian newspapers that she had
married an actor named Mauclerc, who had then thrown himself

from the summit of the Pic du Midi, Lola dashed off one of her letters of protest, this time to the *Estafette*. It was dated September 2, 1856, and her old friend Émile de Girardin, still editing *La Presse*, picked up the story with deep personal interest.

Lola's letter and Mauclerc's reply added to the mystery and gave the episode the flavor of a hoax. She wrote:

> The Belgian newspapers, and some French ones, have asserted that the suicide of the actor, Mauclerc, who, it is reported has thrown himself from the summit of the Pic du Midi, was caused by domestic troubles for which I was responsible. This is a calumny which M. Mauclerc himself will be ready to refute. We separated amicably, it is true, after eight days of married life, but urged only by our common and imperious need of personal liberty. It is probable that the tragedy of the Pic du Midi exists only in the imagination of some journalist on the look-out for sensational news.

Mauclerc's reply sent from Bayonne on September 9, denying both the marriage and the suicide, ran in *La Presse* and reminded Parisians that the Countess was back in France and that the shadow of death seemed to be hovering close to her again. But Mauclerc was briskly reassuring: "I have never had the least intention of throwing myself from the Pic du Midi, or from any other peak, and I do not recollect having had the advantage of marrying —even for eight days—the celebrated Countess of Landsfeld."

Neither one denied knowing the other and Mauclerc may have been a passing episode in Lola's life. But it was during this blank period in her history that she is thought to have gone through a marriage form with the deposed King. It was no secret in Grass Valley that after Queen Theresa's death Ludwig had asked Lola to return and marry him. This, at least, was the current legend, whatever basis it may have had in fact.

But the question remained—did the Countess go through a wedding ceremony with Ludwig in that same winter of 1856, in the chapel of the Residenz in Munich, with Polish cousins and some German nobles in attendance? Princess Ekaterina Radziwill, a Polish relative of Czarina Alexandra, wife of Nicholas II, accepted this as a fact and mentioned it in her book *The Tragedy of a Throne,* published under the name Hildegarde Ebenthal in 1917. She made the point that Ludwig II could dispose of a civil list of two million florins, thanks to the rigid economy of his father, Maximilian, but that half a million had to be paid to Ludwig I in the "exile to which the latter had retired after his voluntary abdication and secret marriage with Lola Montez."

The former King's family were reported to have treated the Countess with contempt and indifference, paying her out for past slights and her treatment of the Queen. She could not re-establish her old sympathetic relationship with Ludwig, and she was glad to escape, ill and ravaged, from an impossible sequel to a high-powered romance. Lola never cleared up this mystery. She spoke vaguely of having been married four or five times, but she continued to make only the most guarded and loyal references to the King. It was not until 1899 that San Franciscans first heard echoes of the royal marriage, if marriage it was. Like much else in Lola's history the story was fogged up with myth and doubt.

Whatever occurred between Lola's landing in Europe in the autumn of 1856 and her reappearance in New York early in 1857, her first concern was for the fate of Follin's widow and children. Abandoned and bitter, the younger Mrs. Follin would have nothing to do with Lola, but Noel's mother, Mrs. Susan Danforth Follin, was more receptive, and accepted an invitation for a meeting in a New York hotel. This Mrs. Follin was the first of three wives that Charles Follin, Noel's worldly father, who dealt in cotton, tobacco and hides, had had. Originally they had lived in the Vieux Carré in New Orleans and there were children by each wife—Augustus Noel Follin, Ormond Weyman Follin and Miriam Follin. The elder Follin was a wanderer, an adventurer and a scholar, speaking five languages. Lola had heard much about him from Noel, whose sympathies were entirely with his mother, now facing her in a hotel room in New York.

She flung herself at the older woman's feet and cried: "I have killed your son, I have killed your son." Her story was received sympathetically and both his mother and his half sister Miriam thought that Noel's widow should accept the Countess's help. They urged Lola to make every effort to see the younger Mrs. Follin, which eventually she did. Arrangements were made to enter Noel's daughter Caroline in Emma Willard's Seminary at Troy, and to send his son to a good school. Lola also made a will leaving her property to his mother in trust for his children. Again she had been guided by the stars.

But the chief beneficiary was Miriam, an eager girl who, as Mrs. Frank Leslie, would become one of New York's most influential dowagers in the late nineteenth century, the survivor of four marriages, a woman of power and drive. How much she learned from Lola no one will ever know, but as Minnie Montez she toured with the star, after some tutoring and elocution lessons to prepare her for the stage. Having lost Lotta Crabtree Lola saw the advantage of taking on this fresh young protégée of Creole ancestry. It was one of the strangest combinations in theatrical history, and the story soon spread that twenty-year-old Minnie was Lola's illegitimate daughter. This was nothing new for the Countess. She was used to such canards.

On February 2, 1857, the "sisters" started a week's engagement at the Green Street Theater in Albany. The audience caught its own reflection in a huge mirror curtain, a novelty in itself, although mirrors were both gargantuan and popular at this time. Lola was on familiar ground in Albany because on an earlier tour she had appeared in the local museum with a troupe of twelve flimsily-clad dancing girls. This time the big social issue of the day was the subject chosen—the antislavery movement. Minnie Montez played Jenny in *The Cabin Boy*, a two-act play by Edward Stirling. As the daughter of a French plantation owner and a slave she was auctioned off, with Lola rescuing her at the last moment. The play was in the mood of the day, with Harriet Beecher Stowe's *Uncle Tom's Cabin* shaking up the country and creating sympathy for the slave.

269

But Lola's highly developed sense of publicity went further when they started off on their way to Providence to keep an engagement, and ended by crossing the ice-choked Hudson by boat. The river had flooded after heavy rains, submerging houses, shops, and even the basement of the theater where they played. Cattle were drowned and the wreckage of dislodged houses floated between the ice floes. The journey could have been made on dry land, but Lola thought of Eliza on the ice floes and decided that it would be picturesque to cross the river by boat. She offered $100 to anyone who would make the trip with her.

The "sisters" sat half-submerged in the boat. Their stage costumes were washed away, but their gallant boatmen got them across and they were the first to land on the other side of the river after the storm. The men who had helped them ran into trouble on the way back, however, and had to be rescued as they were being borne down the river. *Frank Leslie's Newspaper*, which young Minnie would one day own and run, had a sketch of the "sisters" in their boat and noted that the "indomitable Lola Montez (and her sister) who had been playing a theatrical engagement at Albany, desired for some purpose known to herself to cross the river, and nothing daunted at the fearful danger before her, challenged some boatmen to take her across."

This miraculous event brought an audience of two thousand to see the plucky "sisters" at Forbes' Theater in Providence. Together they stirred up considerable theatrical excitement, and Miriam was described as being "quite as attractive, personally, as she was represented to be, and acquits herself well, on the stage, for a novice." They repeated their performance in Pittsburgh, and Minnie was surprised to find how tough her mentor could be in quelling hecklers as they toured together. Their repertoire included *Follies of a Night*, *Eton Boy* and *Lola Montez in Bavaria*.

Under the Countess's expert tutelage, Miriam was coached in the arts of beauty, symmetry of figure and harmony in dress. At the same time she picked up much knowledge about the theater, as well as about political conditions in Europe. It was all good preparation for the life that Miriam would lead—not as an actress, for she did not stay in the theater, but as a journalist, a social leader, a publishing dictator. By the summer of 1857, when Lola had moved on to other interests, Minnie was playing Tom Taylor's *Plot and Passion* in Albany, a not inappropriate title for her own future. She was advertised at the Green Street Theater as "Minnie Montez, sister of the famous Lola Montez." The two had much in common, but Lola was a fading flower and Minnie was heading toward full bloom.

SIXTEEN

Champion of Her Sex

Nearly a century before the Women's Liberation movement shook up the established order in the 1970's Lola Montez was projecting the views that prevail today in avowedly feminist circles. A memorable platform figure because of her unique history, she lectured on both sides of the Atlantic with a curious blend of scholarship and dim-wittedness, of common sense and vanity.

Quoting Plutarch, Erasmus and other authorities she challenged the masculine philosophy of woman being the "inferior human being, an insult to God who had created her the equal of man." "Let historical justice be done to the intellect of woman," said Lola, "and I am content to leave the history of her heart and moral life, without comment, to defend itself by contrast with that of the other sex . . . but woman—ah! she must be a saint, even while she hurls a tyrant from his throne, and does the rough work of war and revolution."

Lola as a lecturer was something of a novelty. Her talks had a certain charm, like herself. Even in the dingiest of halls she shed an ambience of her own. Her platform manner was irreproachable. Where her fellow lecturers were apt to present a picture of spinsterish austerity, or to be smothered in lace and trailing garlands of flowers, she was invariably gowned with the classical simplicity that did most for her figure and her bearing.

Lola knew that her own career on the stage was over when she turned to the lecture platform. It was becoming fashionable for earnest-minded women backing causes to promote them in this way. Elizabeth Blackwell was advocating sex hygiene. Frances Wright was backing free love colonies. Lucretia Mott and the Grimké sisters were in the field for the antislavery cause. Lucy Stone was beginning to lecture on woman suffrage. Mary Wollstonecraft had broken the ice with *The Vindication of the Rights of Woman.*

Although her femininity had been Lola's strength, her sense of power had given her a broad view of women's status with men. Her own particular cause was her spectacular self, but she could still add beauty, magnetism and experience to what she had to say, and men for one reason or another gathered to hear her speak. Few women in history have known more about men of different nationalities than she, but in these last years of her life, as she skirted forty, she heaped bitterness and scorn on men and urged women to demand what they wanted in forceful ways. Although the essence of femininity and seduction herself, she had lived a man's life in many respects, exercising full sexual freedom and asserting her own personality in violent and ambivalent ways.

The sting in some of her lectures was lost in the smoothness of her manner. Although her words were those of a fighter, Lola was never in any phase of her life more demure and orderly than when she lectured. Those who attended expecting fire and brimstone were astonished to see her move gracefully into view, the soul of propriety—no extreme décolletage, no whip, no tantrums. But her lectures, like herself, were paradoxical. In one breath she extolled artifice; in another she deplored all sham and stressed simplicity and character. Although she was insistent on the power and strength of

273

women, she was not sympathetic to the early efforts of the suffrage workers as a body. Jabbing at the pioneers who had convened at Seneca Falls in 1848, and in the 1850's were pushing the cause of women's rights, she said that men only laughed at a convention of scolds and paid no more attention to them than to a flock of chattering blackbirds.

With what seemed to be strongly personal reasoning Lola added: "One woman going forth in the independence and power of self-reliant strength to assert her own individuality, and to defend, with whatever means God has given her, the right to a just portion of the earth's privileges, will do more than a million convention-women to make herself known and felt in the world."

"Heroines of History" was Lola's subject on this occasion and her text was sprinkled with the classical allusions that she liked to use as garnish whenever possible. For four hundred years the heroism of women had manifested itself in the midst of convulsions and revolutions, she said, with some personal knowledge of the matter. Quoting Rousseau's comment that "all great revolutions were owing to women," she expressed her own view that the French Revolution was helped along by the combined power of intellect and beauty and not by the yells and violence cited by Edmund Burke.

The winners every time, said Lola, were those who united great personal beauty with rare intellectual powers. They had a "power stronger than strength," since the beauty and wit of women "controlled the councils of diplomacy and the state." With the memory of Munich still fresh in her thoughts she added pertinently: "And this is as true of modern as of ancient courts." Lola had been there in person.

Her own list of high-powered women had a wide range, taking in Zenobia, Aspasia, Olympias and Sophonisba as well as Queen Isabella of Spain, Queen Elizabeth I, Mary Queen of Scots, Catherine of Russia, Christina of Sweden, the Empress Josephine, the Marquise of Châtelet, Madame de Staël and Joan of Arc. She cited Madame Roland for her "genius and mental powers"; George Sand,

274

her friend and the "most powerful writer of France"; and in England Lady Montagu, for her wit and stimulating influence in the literary world.

However scholarly Lola aspired to be, it was soon clear to her that her most popular lectures were those devoted to beautiful women and their grooming. When she lectured on this subject at Hope Chapel in New York early in February, 1858, an amused reporter noted that few lectures given in that conventicle had been "half so intellectual nor half so wholesome, as the lecture our desperado in dimity gave us last night." The scent of roses still hung around her, he said. The audience listened attentively when she, one of the great beauties of the era, drew a composite picture of universal beauty: "Let her head be from Greece, her bust from Austria, her feet from Hindoostan, her shoulders from Italy, and her hands and complexion from England—let her have the gait of the Spaniard and the Venetian."

Pointing out that it had been her own fate to see the most celebrated beauties of the world, she proclaimed the women of Britain to be the most beautiful of all, selecting the Duchess of Sutherland as a natural queen, typifying the British aristocracy. She rated Lady Blessington, known in Italy as "the goddess," at the top of the list. The Duchess of Wellington was a "fine piece of sculpture and correspondingly cold, with little intellect or animation." Lady Blackwood and Lady Seymour were in her gallery of beauties, and she paid passing tribute to the Sheridan sisters, known as "The Three Graces of England."

Lola's views on marriage were somewhat cynically set forth in a lecture she gave on March 18, 1858, at the Stadt Theater on the Bowery after a showing of her play *Lola Montez in Bavaria*. She discussed the free love colonies in France and Italy and drew attention to the Mormons and other groups that, according to her, were promoting free love settlements in the United States. The audience, made up mostly of men, cheered enthusiastically when Lola finished, but the women present showed resentment when she made fun of the romantic love celebrated by the poets. "Love," she told them realistically, "has a comic as well as a sentimental and sighing side, and temporary separations are a refreshing antidote to boredom."

Lola was intensely critical of American men in her lectures on "Gallantry" and "Wits and Women of Paris." She noted that they were never at home except to sleep, and that they were so absorbed in the rise and fall of stocks that they had no affection to give to their families. The United States, she said, with typical inconsistency, was too busy and practical a nation to harbor the old spirit of gallantry that required leisure and the cultivation of romance. Thus love became a business like everything else she noticed in New York. Men manipulated pretty women as they did stocks, and the "panics they created in the social markets surpassed the revolutions and breakdowns in finance." Their gift for intrigue equaled that of the Frenchman, but although she found the American husband's "brain a ledger, and his heart a counting-room" she conceded a good deal of genuine truth and honest love of women among the "lords of creation in the United States though it often clothes itself in the language of extravagance and exaggeration."

The inconsistencies in Lola's lectures were no surprise to those who knew her, but when she took to berating the American woman for her vanity and devotion to dress, she was belying her own character and life history. "There is no country where the women are more fond of dress and finery than the United States," said Lola, "and history shows us that there is no such depravity of women as this vanity . . . if the insane mania for dress and show does not end in a general decay of female morals, then the lessons of history and the experience of all ages must go for naught."

Did Lola write this, or did some ghost? It was wholly out of character, although her own inner life was changing rapidly at this time. Her lectures were so much discussed that in 1858, the year in which she made most of her platform appearances, two books were published under her name—one in New York and the other in Philadelphia. *The Lectures of Lola Montez with a full and complete auto-*

biography of her life was attributed chiefly to the Reverend Charles Chauncey Burr. The autobiography was presented in the third person, but it was clear that he was quoting the Countess, and that she was trying to wipe out some of the misconceptions contained in her earlier memoir. The second book—*The Arts of Beauty, or Secrets of a Lady's Toilet with hints to gentlemen on the art of fascinating*— was signed by Madame Lola Montez, Countess of Landsfeld. Her lectures promoted her books, and her books drew audiences for her talks.

She was living restlessly in a rustic cottage at Nineteenth Street and Third Avenue while all this was in progress. Manhattan was stretching northward and the rumble of traffic on cobblestones reached her faintly as she passed her days in a setting of flowers and shrubs, with bird cages from which came streams of melody, and her usual collection of dogs. Her health was poor and she spent hours bolstered up in bed, surrounded by reference books to check the classical allusions for her lectures.

As autumn advanced Lola sank deeper into confusion and abstraction. She still pulled herself together for evening gatherings but the caliber of her guests kept sinking lower. Some of the hangers-on had been involved in local scandals; others were gamblers and refugees from the law. They were of all nationalities and they battened freely on the good fare and fine wines that the Countess still provided. She smoked without ceasing as they gathered around her in the basement dining room, where flowers from her garden scented the air. Some of the silver she still possessed bore the royal crest. Cards were played for high stakes, and lights blazed all night for these gatherings in the Morris-style cottage then gaining ground in America. Lola's spirits soared and sank, from sparkling wit to catatonic silence.

Her cynical guests teased her about the advice she was handing out to men in her lectures on the art of fascinating women. Obviously it was done with tongue in cheek. At the lectures the more worldly roared with laughter, knowing that the Countess was making fun of them, for surely none knew better than she the techniques that she lightly brushed off with sarcasm. They should assume from scratch, said Lola wryly, that women preferred triflers to men of sense. Their conversation should never rise above the level of balls, parties, fashions and the opera. They should load themselves with jewelry. They should show up as perfectly dressed coxcombs, with no recommendation but face, coat and impudence. They should boast of some scrape to suggest courage, and should never forget that a ready wit and a good pun were effective assets. Lola finished breezily: "You ought to know that there are four things which always possess more or less interest to a lady—a parrot, a peacock, a monkey and a man; and the nearer you can come to uniting all these about equally in your own character, the more will you be loved."

Women absorbed this lecture as avidly as they did her beauty secrets, but here she was on unassailable ground. She was avant garde in her advice on diet. She deplored strong coffee, hot breads, fried foods, peppered soups, fish, roasts, game, tarts, sweetmeats and ices, all of which were on her list of taboos. Her counsel was almost as spartan as that of Sylvester Graham, whose whole-wheat products were then changing the nutrition picture of the United States, or the macrobiotic enthusiasts of the 1970's.

Lola was highly moralistic in this lecture, pointing out that the only real secret of preserving beauty lay in three simple measures —temperance, exercise and cleanliness. Wines were "poisonous drugs." Late hours made women "fade as the leaf." Padding to give contour where there was none, stays to compress, paints of all hues were useless if "dissipation, late hours, immoderation, and carelessness have wrecked the loveliness of female charms."

It was obvious that Lola was tying up her lectures to the issues being pushed by the feminists—dress reform, sex hygiene, improved nutrition. But at the moment she was losing the battle herself. Although she kept up appearances for her lectures, she deplored the shams that many women of her age affected. Forty was old age to the woman of the 1850's. Lola had always devoted unlimited time to

278

her own toilet, and the texture of her skin, the firm line of her chin, and the curves of her figure were only now beginning to blur and sag. At forty the clear chiseling of her face was slightly impaired and she had the tired look of having seen too much, experienced too much. But she deplored in her lecture the "hoary-headed matron's attempts to equip herself to waken sentiments that could not be recalled," and said that she knew of no art that would atone for the defect of an unpolished mind and an unlovely heart. Better to seek for charm in the mental and social graces of Madame de Sévigné than in the meretricious arts of Ninon de Lenclos. Yet with fine irrelevance she advocated a beauty cream bearing Ninon's name, compounded of lemon juice, milk and white brandy, and recalled Madame de Staël's acknowledgment that she would exchange half her knowledge for personal charm.

Lola's prescriptions for cosmetics, washes, pastes and creams were slavishly followed by women who studied her own striking looks from hard benches in chapels, halls and auditoriums. The wash that gave the beauties of the Spanish court a "polished whiteness to the neck and arms"—one of her own great assets—could be achieved, she said, with a mixture of white bran, vinegar, egg yolks and two grains of ambergris, all distilled. She suggested cures for freckles, for pimples, chapped lips, yellow spots, wrinkles and all disorders of the skin, listing a fascinating mélange of herbs and molds and flowers—jessamine in rosewater; pimpernel soaked in rain; melon, pumpkin and cucumber with a dash of almond oil; musk and brandy. She warned against the excessive use of rouge and powder, and advocated icy sponge rubs, followed by hard friction with napkins, the usage of the beauties of Greece and Rome. She suggested binding thin slivers of raw beef tightly around the face to prevent wrinkles, but reminded busy housewives who had little time for such extravagances that bran and tepid water could do much for the skin, and the bathtub was best of all. Lola enlarged on the "delightful oriental fashion" of the bath, which every house and every gentleman of almost every nation except England and

America possessed. She found it as indispensable an article as the looking glass, and when she lived in Paris the fashionable beauties bathed in milk, she recalled.

As a lecturer and writer on beauty secrets Lola brought an inviting subject into the lyceum circuit that starred such women as the earnest-minded Margaret Fuller and Frances Wright. Rachel had just died in Cannes. Lucy Stone was refusing to pay taxes. Another revolution was in the making—this time between North and South. But Lola, in addition to her other subjects, was still carrying on her endless battle with the Jesuits, to the boredom of many, and the disgust of others.

Her lecture "Romanism" was a sharp irritant, since it brought all her old prejudices to the surface, and had her attacking the Roman Catholic Church with more zeal than sense. She argued that if the *Mayflower* had borne Catholics to America instead of Puritans, and they had brought with them the spirit of Rome instead of the Reformation, no progress would have been made. "America does not yet recognize how much she owes to the Protestant principle," said Lola. "It is that principle which has given the world the four greatest facts of modern times—Steamboats, Railroads, Telegraphs and the American Republic."

This widely quoted observation had a wild irrelevancy that confused her audiences as she toured Boston, Buffalo, Hartford and other centers where she had once appeared as a worldly and glittering star. Lola the lecturer had less appeal than Lola the dancer, and her audiences dwindled until no more than two hundred listeners turned up for one of her lectures in Boston. She resorted to holding receptions, charging a dollar for those who wished to shake hands with her, in the great American tradition. Weary and dazed, her face frozen and her eyes glazed, Lola was beyond bringing her natural wit and charm to bear on these encounters, as a series of faces rolled past her as if she were an exhibit in a zoo. She came to life briefly in an interview to show anger over Thackeray's *Vanity*

Fair, for she believed that he had modeled Becky Sharp after her. But Lola was now tilting at windmills.

However, she was her old dynamic and ridiculous self with the performance she staged in a New York courtroom just as she was about to begin her American lectures in 1858. She and David Wemyss Jobson, an old enemy from London, made sensational headlines in a suit brought in the United States Circuit Court to recover damages for infringement of a patent right. Jobson and Norman B. Griffin were the litigants and Lola injected herself into the case because she was smarting from a talk Jobson had given in Stuyvesant Hall on "Lola and Her Passion." Although the women in the audience had walked out on Jobson, calling him a humbug and a vulgarian for his attack on the Countess, she was determined to have her revenge. The battle raged through February, 1858, and it stimulated the sale of tickets for her lectures. Again she was suspected of making a bid for publicity but, if so, the results were two-edged and highly destructive to her already tarnished reputation.

Although she was not directly involved in the suit she became the star of the proceeding by insisting on testifying to the evil character of Jobson, thereby bringing on some unexpected revelations about herself. She had known him when she lived on Half-Moon Street on her return from Germany in 1849 and she remembered him as a rogue and jailbird who had blackmailed both her and her husband, George Heald. Each threw mud at the other, turning a routine court proceeding into a brawl, with Lola being alternately stately and vulgar on the witness stand, and the police finally arriving to calm things down. It was the kind of publicity that she always incurred, and although on her way to total penitence and humility she had not yet reached the stage of forgiving Jobson.

His lawyer, C. H. Schermerhorn, turned the tables on her with a savage attack on her morals based on what Jobson had told him. Lola was soon defending herself with candor and realism, and the papers were running columns of testimony and facts about her that

New Yorkers had not known before. The *Times* deplored the amount of irrelevant testimony introduced, apparently with no other object than to amuse the crowd that gathered to watch Lola's performance.

Jobson sat shivering in a corner of the room where the hearing was being held before Surrogate John W. Whiting. "Sit you between me and Lola," he whispered to one of the reporters. "She'll scratch my face before she's through."

The Countess made it clear before agreeing to testify that she must be assured she would not be insulted by "this person—Mr. Jobson, Attorney of London." She would not subject herself to insolence, violence or blackmailing, she said, and Schermerhorn assured her that she was in a land of law.

"Doctor Jobson," said Lola scornfully. "Who is *Doctor* Jobson? Are you a doctor, Jobson? How long since? You introduced yourself to me as Jobson, attorney-at-law, in London."

She recalled that when she was living on Half-Moon Street her maid told her one day that a man named Jobson wished to see her. He asked if he might write her memoirs. His card indicated that he was an attorney-at-law who also wrote for the newspapers. "He did not say he was a doctor," Lola pointed out. "He attempted to extort money from me in what you call blackmail. His general reputation at that time was of the very worst kind."

In fact, it had been so notorious that when Lord Brougham and the other nobles who had called on the Countess in Half-Moon Street learned that Jobson was bothering her, they had had two policemen assigned to protect her. Schermerhorn, who had been well primed on the witness's history by his client, icily remarked: "We'll see who *she* is."

But Lola would not be squelched, and after pointing out that Schermerhorn did not know how to pronounce "memoirs" properly she went on: "I would not believe him on his oath. He was known as a jail-bird in London; I knew him in Paris, too, and he asked my husband for two guineas blackmail. I have heard of him in New York from two or three persons whom he has very much annoyed."

Under cross-examination the Countess for once gave a reasonably accurate account of her early life, and made it clear that she was the stepdaughter of General Craigie, and the former wife of Captain James. Asked where she was born she snapped back: "I wasn't present when I was born. I have had two husbands and I am on the point of having a third—my first husband was Captain James."

"Were you married to Captain James?" Schermerhorn asked.

"The ring was put on my finger by a clergyman, but my spirit was never united to his."

Lola flared up like a rocket when asked how many intrigues she had had. "How many have you?" she demanded. "None. I resided at the Court of Bavaria for two years. . . . I knew the King of Bavaria. Mr. Wittelsbach he was called—that was his family name."

"Were you the mistress of the King?"

Lola jumped up with a sweep of skirts. "What!" she exclaimed. "No, sir. You are a villain for I'd take my oath on that book [indicating the Bible] which I read every night, that I had no intrigue with the old man. I knew the King, and moulded his mind to the love of freedom. He took me before the whole Court with his wife and presented me as his best friend. I was on the stage in Bavaria. It's easier to be a man's mistress than a dancer. I was in Bavaria in 1847 and 1848; in 1849 the Revolution occurred and liberty and I fled. The King and Queen supported me while I was there. I was engaged in political business. You might call me Prime Minister, if you please, or as the King said: I *was* the King. There was a man of straw there as prime minister . . . the memoirs that have been written about me are lies; that man was trying to get my memoirs, I suppose."

Lola said that she had been back in London from Switzerland for two months only when Jobson called on her. She laughed when

Schermerhorn asked if she had not summoned him first. "No, no," said Lola. "That is too funny. I was the Countess of Landsfeld and not Mrs. James then."

"Didn't Mr. Jobson subscribe a guinea to prevent you from being taken to the Watch House?"

"He hadn't a guinea."

"Did he not give you a guinea to keep you from taking to the streets for a livelihood?"

Lola rose indignantly. "Am I to be insulted?" she exclaimed. "Gentlemen, will you not protect me?"

"Mr. Schermerhorn should not have asked that question," said Surrogate Whiting severely.

The hearing was adjourned at this point, but when it was resumed a few days later Jobson arrived in court carrying a dark rattan cane, silver-mounted. Under further cross-examination Lola, looking tired and bored, laughed when asked if she had been known in London as Betsy Watson, Mary or Molly Watson, and if Jobson had known her as a chambermaid.

"I cannot tolerate a liar," she answered haughtily. "I should have considered myself a far greater woman if I *had* been born a chambermaid than I am today. You cannot make me out a chambermaid —not that it's dishonest to be a chambermaid."

The Referee reminded Lola that she had promised to keep quiet but when Schermerhorn called her a "woman" and quickly changed this to "lady" she told him scornfully: "Pray call me a woman. I am proud to be a woman. Your mother was a woman."

Jobson, however, objected to Lola's counsel, Frederick D. Seely, referring to him as a "fellow." "If you call me a fellow again, you vagabond shyster, I'll let you see," he shouted.

"You will," Seely shouted back. "Say another word and I'll drop you down three stories from this window."

After another interchange Seely jumped up and attempted to strike Jobson, but the stove intervened, and his blow did not land. Jobson raised his rattan cane and hit Seely on the head with it. Seely wrenched the cane from him, rushed past the stove, and pommeled him on the head until police pulled them apart. Surrogate Whiting kept running back and forth, wringing his hands, in a state of helplessness.

Lola, well away from the immediate area of battle, looked on, although the watching reporters noted that her expression showed she was all ready to strike a blow herself. The two men tangled a second time and were separated. As quiet was restored the Countess's voice suddenly echoed through the room, clear and insistent: "Oh, is there no law that can prevent a woman from being injured in her character, and in a false manner?"

The Referee announced that the hearing was adjourned but she had the last word. "I *will* say it, and I *will* speak, for I have been blackened and defamed here, sir, and I have a right to speak." She shook her fist at Schermerhorn: "I always take the part of women. If you want to learn about Jobson's character you have only to send to the magistrates in London and they will give you the papers. Take him off to the Tombs. He was there before. Mind, he is Jobson the jail-bird."

Both Seely and Jobson were charged with contempt of court, and on his way out Jobson whispered to Lola: "You are too low to be noticed."

"But it was 'My Lady' in London," she snapped back.

However, the Countess had got more than she had bargained for when she injected herself into the case to discredit Jobson. Her next appearance was in New York State Supreme Court, where the contempt proceeding was held. Spectators turned up as if for a Lola Montez opening night. The columns on the Surrogate's hearing, with fresh insight into the Countess's early history, promised further revelations.

Lola arrived with friends and sat by the stove, reading a newspaper and making sotto voce comments on Jobson and his counsel. Both Jobson and Seely admitted assault and battery. Lola was asked if she had used the expression: "Pommel him well. I would like to see him pommelled." She answered haughtily: "I never in my life made use of such an unladylike expression, and no witness will say that I did. I will tell you what I did say—'Never mind, Mr. Seely, he is not worth striking by a gentleman.' "

"I ask you whether Mr. Jobson was not assaulted?"

"I don't know what you call an assault but I think you make an assault on me all the time."

Seely apologized to the court for his conduct. Jobson would not yield an inch but continued to abuse the Countess. He said he had no apology to make, since a woman had been brought in to testify against him whose character he "would not pollute his lips by naming."

"Enough of this," said the Judge sharply.

Both men were found guilty of contempt of court and were taken to the Tombs. Seely was released at once by a writ of habeas corpus so that he walked out ahead of the persistent Jobson. One of the tangential consequences of these hearings was that Lola's lectures were well attended. Was this one more grandstand play for attention, or was her bitterness over Jobson an overwhelming motive to seek revenge in a courtroom? The testimony had thrown some retrospective light on Lola's more obscure days in London.

The *New York Times* editorialized at length on "The Great Jobson Case" which had made diverting reading and had brought Lola back into full focus with the public. But by mid-summer her lectures, her health and her morale were all in decline, and she had decided to try her luck once more in Europe.

SEVENTEEN

Lola, the Penitent, Dies in New York

All New York was *en fête* as Lola Montez made perparations in the autumn of 1858 to return to Europe—not as an actress and dancer this time, but as a lecturer. There was jubilation all around her in the streets for the successful laying of the transatlantic cable. It had taken years to forge this magic link that initiated the age of fast communication.

The noise, fluttering banners and pageantry seemed dim and distant to Lola. For her it had been a year of illness, of fading luster, of a growing sense of confusion. She was now moving away from her dissolute companions and worldly interests, and was plagued by a rising tide of self-loathing and remorse. Although only forty she was visibly burned out—her vitality gone, her brilliance fading, her bold spirit quenched at last. Never again would she pose as actress or dancer, the role that had brought her fame and applause as well as

287

defeat and scorn. She had been told too many times, in too many ways, by too many critics and friends that she lacked grace, rhythm and training as a dancer, to keep up the pretense any longer.

But Lola's constant need for attention and money drove her on. She had had sufficient success as a lecturer to feel that she might use this talent in Europe. For years her brief curtain speeches had interested her audiences, sometimes more than her dancing. She was well aware that her fame as a courtesan would again be exploited, but she now shrank from this image of herself, and showed none of her old flamboyance when she landed in Galway from the S.S. *America* on November 23, 1858. It was her first visit to Ireland since she left it as Mrs. James to sail back to India in 1838.

But the Irish did not warm to Lola Montez. Echoes of her struggles with the Jesuits in Bavaria only a decade earlier were still fresh, and the *Freeman* enlarged on Lola's influence over King Ludwig and her spectacular conduct on two continents. This was not the introduction she wished for her lecture tour, and she rushed into print in the old impulsive way to insist that she had never been the mistress of King Ludwig or of Dujarier. As always, her story was that she had merely been friend and adviser to the King and the fiancée of Dujarier, who had intended to marry her.

But it was to see Lola the courtesan, and not the sedate lecturer, that people flocked to the Round House in Dublin when she appeared there. She had abandoned the exhibitionist touch and was dressed without the usual pronounced emphasis on her curves. Her manner was quiet and persuasive and she skirted the Jesuit issue carefully, but somehow she left her audiences cold. They were used to snowy skin and lustrous blue eyes in their own women, and they did not view the Countess as a miracle of beauty. She somehow seemed pretentious on her semi-native soil, and her protestations of innocence were too insistent. Things went better with her when she crossed to England.

Her theatrical experience had shown her the importance of touring the provinces before tackling London, and she fared well as she lectured in Manchester, Sheffield, Nottingham, Leicester, Birmingham, Wolverhampton, Leamington, Worcester and Bristol. She appeared at the Free Hall in Manchester, but John Bright, who had disapproved of her political meddlings, refused to preside, a blow to her pride. When a man who accompanied her into a church in Chester was told to remove his hat she had a characteristic flash of anger, augmented by the fact that her dog, which had followed her down the aisle, was chased out. When she reached Bristol, the home of Elizabeth Blackwell and other well-known nonconformists who had sought freedom of worship in America, Barnum was lecturing and the Bible Society was having its quarterly meeting.

Lola adapted her lectures to her diverse audiences. One of her most popular dealt with the differences in American and British ways and character. She pictured America as looking to the future for its greatness, and Britain to the past. Her wit flashed out at times and she usually caused some laughter with her comment that Americans believed in the spittoon as a valuable institution, and speed as the great condition of success in all things. She avoided direct references to herself in her lectures, but used some of her own experiences in politics, love and the handling of men.

The *Era* noted on April 19, 1859, that those who had expected to see the "legendary bull-dog at her side and the traditional pistols in her girdle and the horsewhip in her hand" must have been disappointed. Nor was she in any way the "formidable-looking woman of Amazonian audacity, and palpably strong-wristed, as well as strong-minded" that the British public had expected to see. She was a great success in worldly Brighton, where the Pavilion was packed to the doors when she appeared, and the *Punch* cartoon showing her armorial bearings with a parasol for the sword, a bulldog for the lion and a pot of rouge for the rose brought her history clearly to mind.

But the air was distinctly chilly when the former Dolores or Eliza Gilbert returned to Bath as the Countess of Landsfeld. It was soon no secret that this famous woman, who had once been a schoolgirl in Bath, and had eloped from there with Thomas James, was Lady Craigie's daughter. The proud Georgian stronghold had lost track of her for years and had not associated the Gilbert girl with the notorious Lola Montez and the Countess of Landsfeld until Bath was mentioned in her bigamy trial. Now they also had the tale of her life in Bavaria unrolled for them in the incriminating Papon and Lola memoir that always seemed to arrive ahead of her and stir up trouble.

The people of Bath, always great book lovers, picked it up with interest and had their eyes opened to several aspects of Lola's career that they had not known. Although they crowded in to hear her lectures and studied her attentively through their opera glasses, she was fully aware of their disapproval. They were not unused to worldly living in Bath, but Lola was beyond the pale. Yet she was strangely moved to be back in this environment and to lecture in the Assembly Rooms which had once seemed so impressive to her. She visited the baths, with memories of many continental spas behind her, and she looked for the shops that she had known as a schoolgirl. But wherever she went she was conscious of scathing looks and contemptuous neglect. So marked was the chill in her reception that news of the snubbing she received was conveyed across the Atlantic to Mrs. Margaret Buchanan, wife of a New York florist named Isaac Buchanan. Small Eliza Gilbert and Margaret had attended school together and they would meet before long in New York, where their lives would be strangely intertwined in the closing months of Lola's life.

In the meantime she left Bath with a feeling of discouragement and futility. A flood of disturbing memories plagued her and there were no more scenes, although her temper still flashed out at times over trifles, and she quickly came to life to deny the canards that haunted her wherever she appeared. Like other sinners before her, Lola had come under the spell of the church and was a convert to Methodism. The nonconformist cause was gaining ground in England and was reaching all classes. She decided to proselytize, to distribute Bibles, and to give some of her lectures to raise money for the Methodist Church.

She made her own arrangements for four lectures she delivered in St. James's Hall in London in April, 1859. Her audience was not the kind that had gone to the theater to admire her as a dancer, but some of the men who had known her years earlier showed up to see how Lola Montez coped with religion. A number of titled women, whose interest swung at this time between religion and spiritualism, gave her their support and listened attentively to her various lectures while she discoursed on the Duchess of Sutherland, Lady Blessington and the Duchess of Wellington, as well as on Amelia Bloomer, who had introduced trousers for women in the United States.

The pomp and poverty that Lola had known in her brief life were recalled by some. She had lived in palaces and mining camps. At times she had performed in the great opera houses of Europe; more recently she had become familiar with the bare boards of a frontier town in Nevada. Her lovers had ranged from royalty to grooms, which made her unique among the reformed sinners caught up in the evangelical fervor of the mid-Victorian period. None was as beautiful as Lola; none could match the course she had run. In her black velvet gown, with her hair simply dressed from a center part, Lola suggested Mary Stuart to one of her newspaper observers. Her face, air, attitude and elocution were "thoroughly, bewilderingly feminine." The *Era* of April 10, 1859, described her as a good-looking lady in the bloom of womanhood . . . with easy, unrestrained manners, and speaking earnestly and distinctly, with the slightest touch of a foreign accent that might belong to any language from Irish to Bavarian." Her diamonds did not flash on this occasion, or any other symbol of her past. She was practicing simplicity and humility.

Some of her old friends were quoted in the newspapers day after day on issues that once would have been vital to her. Lord Malmesbury, a particular friend at one time, was taking a strong stand on the question of intervention in the war for the liberation of Italy from Austria, sparked by Cavour, the Turin statesman who battled for his country's freedom and was the voice piece of the Italian national government. The British were friendly to Cavour, who had formed an alliance with Napoleon III to drive the Austrians out of Italy. But the prospect of a great French army marching into Italy was too reminiscent of the conquest of Italy by Napoleon I. Czar Alexander II was as suspicious of Napoleon's moves as the British were, but after the defeat of the Austrians at the battles of Magenta and Solferino Napoleon deserted Cavour, made a private peace with the Austrians and took his army back to France.

The British Cabinet was in a ferment during this period. Lord Palmerston, John Bright and Lord John Russell were at odds over which course to follow. The public stood for nonintervention but Lord Malmesbury tried to persuade the French Emperor that the seacoast from Trieste to Cattaro should be declared neutral. In New York a *Tribune* editorial noted on June 17 that the "old organ of Despotism and Jesuitism, *The Augsburg Gazette*, clamors for war with France, dreams of conquering Paris and separating Alsatia and Lorraine from France—of course in favor of Bavaria." Metternich, back in Vienna but aloof from the echoes of a war that no longer touched him, died with his granddaughter, Pauline Metternich, at his bedside almost at the hour that the French made their entry into Milan.

Once all this would have been of intense interest to Lola, who had waged a bitter battle with the Augsburg paper, but her memories were faint and distant as she moved deeper into self-abstraction. She cared more now for the word of God than for the views of her old political friends Lord Brougham and Lord Malmesbury. Follin's death had unhinged her in some deep-seated way. She dwelled constantly on the violent deaths, the tragedy and disaster that seemed to follow her. It was just as Dumas had predicted, but at last she had lost her power either to fascinate or destroy. The process now was within herself—self-destruction. She was the epitome of the sinner who treads the sawdust trail of the evangelist, and there was still enough of the actress in her to feel the drama and the self-crucifixion of profound penitence.

The magdalens were running for cover as the Victorian influences grew stronger with the advancing century and the unabashed bawdiness and license of the Georgian period left fewer echoes in fashionable circles. But Lola was well aware that men of means lived as they had always done, except that their profligacy was now less openly flaunted. Charles H. Spurgeon was shaking up England with his lectures in the Metropolitan Tabernacle in London. This Baptist preacher was the Billy Graham of his day, drawing in huge crowds when he spoke. His collected sermons were bedtime reading along with the Bible in innumerable British homes.

Smoldering close to this bonfire of redemption was the public taste for animal magnetism, mesmerism and spiritualism. Sir William Crookes, the scientist, was investigating psychic phenomena, and Lord Brougham, in a state of despondency and eclipse at this time, was not above a little table rapping. He was in the best of company, for scholars, scientists, poets and statesmen were attempting to tamper with the beyond. The efforts of several charlatans to bring King Ludwig into communication with Lola at séances attended by her before she left America made her veer away from the professional spiritualists in England. Actually she had more knowledge of the techniques involved than most of the men and women who were then taking them up as cults. The King's interest in this field of investigation and her own dealings with Kerner had given her an expert understanding of the metaphysical elements involved. Andrew Jackson Davis had further enlarged her knowledge of animal magnetism and extrasensory perception.

So deeply was Lola involved in mystical lore that long after her death spiritualists on both sides of the Atlantic sought to invoke her presence at their séances. She had been sufficiently publicized as a believer to make her an intriguing figure to exploit. An Austrian named Rudi Schneider introduced her as "Olga" at gatherings of notables held in London. It was fashionable at the time to assemble in an atmosphere of rattling tambourines, floating mists and aerial voices, and the use of Lola's name always brought in some celebrities. Finally the National Laboratory of Psychical Research, studying the current phenomena in this field, invoked the help of Major Hervey de Montmorency, a nephew of Francis Leigh, the young English officer who had squired Lola in Paris in the early 1840's. "Olga" was expected to name Leigh and to answer specific questions about him. The test failed, but this was only one of many times that the spirits of Lola and King Ludwig were invoked at séances, both before and after their deaths.

Actually while Lola was in England on this last lecture tour her occult sensitivity merged into evangelical frenzy as consuming as the energy she had once poured into her love affairs. Sects meant little to her at this point. She had experienced Catholicism in Ireland and Bavaria, Calvinism in Montrose, the Anglican Church in India, and now the Wesleyan faith that had stirred up the people of Bath and spread all over England. She read Spurgeon's sermons as devoutly as she did Davis's *The Principles of Nature*, but she soon found her chief solace in close study of the Bible itself.

Lola continued to lecture to dwindling crowds through the spring but word reached New York in the summer of 1859 that she was wandering about in London, muttering to herself, reading the Bible to anyone who would listen. With Regent's Park flowering around her she sat meekly on park benches, a tired figure in black, with a big Newfoundland dog beside her, reading the New Testament. When a reporter recognized her and asked her if she were Lola Montez, her great blue eyes were momentarily veiled as she said to him: "Who I am is no matter. Once I was as ignorant as you, and very much more wicked. There was not a wicked thing that I did not do, and though I had plenty of money and friends, yet I was never happy until I found the beautiful truths of this little book."

She held up the New Testament that she had been reading to some children who had fled from her dog, but had been lured back when she showed them how harmless he was. She admitted to the reporter that she had finished with public appearances and would devote herself entirely to working for the poor. She now chose to wander in the parks, or through the slums, scattering Bibles. It pained her to think of Half-Moon Street and various haunts identified with her wilder years. But with some of the money she had made from her lectures she took a large house in Park Lane and rented out quarters in the fashionable style of the period. However, she was so disorganized that her tenants soon scattered. She talked in a rambling way about her sinful past and insisted on reading the Bible to them at odd moments. No longer her old imperious self, she found it impossible to handle servants, or to take care of the tasks that had always been done for her. Bills piled up. Creditors came to her door, and it was the old story of debts and insolvency. She no longer had Lord Brougham to help her when lawsuits developed, and her spirit was so broken that she collapsed altogether. By midsummer she was deep in a nervous breakdown diagnosed at the time as brain fever.

A philanthropic Methodist couple, who had met her through the work she was doing for their church, were touched by the plight of this ravaged woman. They took her back with them to their home in Derbyshire to convalesce in country surroundings, with gardens and fields on all sides, and an atmosphere of serenity and care that she had long lacked. As she improved they settled her by herself in the gatekeeper's cottage, and she took walks in these sylvan surroundings. But her gait was feeble now. She did not stride in the old Amazonian way. Her head was lowered, not flung back in pride. Her voice was almost inaudible. Nothing seemed to reach her from the outside world. She dreamed away the days in trancelike calm, imagining herself back in Bavaria as she watched swans gliding across a small pond near her cottage. In her schizophrenic state the miniature marble figures surrounding it assumed in her eyes the vast proportions of the statuary of Munich. At night she watched the heavens for Dujarier's star, a recurrent delusion.

As she recovered she kept a diary and her entry for September 10, 1859, mirrors her self-flagellant state of mind:

I only lived for my own passions. . . . What would I not give to have my terrible and fearful experience given as an awful warning to such natures as my own. . . . How many, many years of my life have been sacrificed to Satan, and my own love of sin. What had I not been guilty of, either in thought or deed, during these years of misery and wretchedness? What has the world ever given to me? (And I have known all that the world has to give —all!) Nothing but shadows, leaving a wound on the heart hard to heal— a dark discontent. . . . How manifold are my sins, and how long in years have I lived a life of evil passions without a check.

But trouble erupted even in the halcyon retreat in Derbyshire. Lola had a scene with her host. She resented something he said and her unregenerate self responded with anger. "Ought I to have resented what was said," she wrote in her diary. "No, I ought to have said not a word. The world would applaud me; but oh, my heart tells me that for His sake I ought to bear the vilest reproaches, even unmerited."

Lola realized that she must leave her comfortable resting place and go forth to fight her battle as a penitent. She talked of becoming a foreign missionary, a popular church ambition at the time. There was no better propaganda than the reformed sinner and Lola had the added qualities of fame, beauty and power in her past. But the break with her Derbyshire friends was a blow. "When last I wrote I was calm and peaceful—away from the world," was her diary entry at this point. "I must again go forth . . . my calm days of the cottage are gone—gone. But I will not look back. Onward! must be the cry of my heart. . . . Oh, give me a meek and lowly heart."

The rest from chain smoking and late nights, the gentle care and medical attention she had received had improved her condition to the point where she was able to sail back to the United States in November, 1859, after a year of almost total collapse and oblivion.

296

Again she was in need of money and she tried once more to lecture in America, but with calamitous results. Her final appearance was at the Melodeon in Boston, where she shocked her audience—not in the old way, but in the guise of a penitent. Those who had turned out with curiosity to hear her lecture were stunned to see the once-dashing Countess walk to the rostrum in flowing white robes, draped loosely around her in the Grecian manner, suggesting the vestments of biblical times.

Many remembered the old Lola, her figure sharply outlined in velvet. Now her robes helped to conceal the fact that she was little more than a wraith, with haunted eyes and feeble gestures. But her illness had not wholly marred the classical line of her profile, or quenched the deep blue glow of her eyes. She was half evangelist, half lecturer, and although she was politely applauded, everyone present knew that Lola Montez had reached the end of the road. But none dug up her past at this dark moment in her life.

Her condition was professionally appraised by Henry Chapman, a booking agent, when he ran into her on the Bowery soon after her return to America. He could not believe that she was the Lola Montez he had known. She sparkled for a moment and asked him if he would be her manager. As he studied her she talked of her lectures and of a book she was writing. To his amazement she told him that she was a firm believer in the hereafter, and was living across the river with a Christian family.

Chapman took her to Taylor's café on Broadway, run by John Taylor, New York's leading caterer. Some of the bolder women felt they could safely lunch in this chic haven, even when not escorted by men. He was famed for his ice cream, which Lola ate slowly as her mournful eyes seemed to plead for Chapman's help. He had always considered her a highly gifted woman—"a very brainy thinker"—but he had often observed that her quick and fiery disposition led to outbursts of violent temper. She got over them quickly, but she told him, on one occasion when he protested such free use of her whip, that swinging it around was the exercise she most desired after meals. Lola was always a wit, and many of her more light-hearted observations were taken quite literally; she rather enjoyed this form of badinage.

"At heart she was not such a very bad woman after all," Chapman noted. "But old Nick was in her at times and woe was it unto one who gained her disfavor. Lola was fond of her wine; alas too fond of it, and she enjoyed a strong cigar, too."

Chapman was one of the few commentators on Lola who made any mention of bibulous habits. For years she had been surrounded by carousers, but she was not conspicuously intemperate herself, although her violent outbursts often suggested that she was. Actually they were closer to madness. Chapman may have noticed that she did some drinking during her theatrical tour in America and her days in Grass Valley, but if so it all ended with her religious conversion. He had other engagements when he met her and he felt that he could not book her. But some months later she wandered into his office, a pitiful spectacle. "She was sick and wasting away," he recalled. "I shall never forget that interview."

In place of the old proud Lola, filled with charm and seduction, or angry and militant, was a meek, gentle figure, telling him in a feeble voice: "I have atoned for all and am not afraid to die." Chapman had known her as a great dissembler, but this time he was convinced of her sincerity. As she left his office, badly groomed and with trailing skirts, he felt that her end was near, and that she knew it.

Her decline was rapid after her return to America and her final fiasco in public. She was soon wandering about in Brooklyn and Manhattan much as she had done in London, talking to herself, singing snatches of hymns, sitting on park benches, feverishly reading the scriptures. She showed interest in children and animals, as of old, but her habits were so eccentric that passersby gave her a wide berth, thinking her demented. All through the summer of 1860 she lived in a boardinghouse in Brooklyn. Her fellow lodgers were Methodists, and when they gathered around the parlor organ in the evenings Lola led them in playing and singing hymns. She attended a nearby Methodist church and she was known as Fanny Gibbons, one of innumerable pseudonyms attached to her during her lifetime.

The anonymity to which she now clung was soon shattered by Mrs. Margaret Buchanan, who had been on her trail since hearing of her unfriendly reception in Bath. By some strategy she made connections with her as Lola walked along Broadway. Although Margaret Buchanan had known Lola only as a young girl she immediately assured her that she would have recognized her anywhere, which was understandable, since her pictures circulated widely. At first Mrs. Buchanan played a wholly protective role, helped her to bank her money, took over her possessions, and urged her to stay at her house in Astoria any time she wished. She swung Lola's interest from the Methodist to the Episcopal Church, and with this new evangelical connection Lola found a way to help the type of sinner she best understood. She was soon making weekly visits to the Magdalen Asylum to talk to the "fallen women" there, but this was the end of her obscurity.

The press quickly learned the identity of the heavily veiled figure in black who drove to Eighth Street regularly to fulfill this unlikely mission. The inmates were entranced when they learned that they were being lectured to by the uncrowned Queen of Bavaria, the most beautiful and interesting of all the philanthropically-inclined New York women who visited them. With mixed emotions they listened to the super-magdalen, a picture of faded beauty and intelligence, telling them how misguided they were. She read to them from the Bible, pointing the way to salvation. Lola did not accuse the sinners, but suggested that the love of God could save them.

With the press on her trail she now knew no peace. For once in her life she had sincerely turned her back on notoriety and had made every effort to drop from sight. But another chance encounter on Broadway was a savage shock to her deeply wounded spirit. When she recognized Caroline Follin, for whose education she had paid, she moved impulsively toward her, but was ignored by Noel Follin's daughter, who did not seem to know her. Lola's looks and manners were now so strange that passersby sometimes thought her drunk or mad, but Caroline's brush-off was so unexpected that when she returned that night to a room she had taken on Waverly Place after breaking her connection with the Methodists, she had a stroke and was found unconscious some hours later. Her speech was gone. Her left side was paralyzed, and her face was slightly distorted.

Mrs. Buchanan established her at her own home in Astoria, with a nurse named Mrs. Hamilton to care for her. News of her serious illness was published in Europe and her mother got in touch with Mrs. Buchanan through friends in Bath. There had been no communication between Lola and Lady Craigie in more than two decades, but now she announced that she would travel to America to see her daughter. When this news was conveyed to Lola in Astoria she panicked at the thought of her mother re-entering her life. She was in mortal fear, believing that she was coming only to see what estate she might inherit.

Lola was not altogether wrong about this. Lady Craigie was in touch with Count Blum, whom her daughter had known in Paris and who sometimes looked after her muddled business affairs when they had continental strings. When the Count, with one of his European colleagues, turned up with papers for Lola to sign, she felt sure that both men were working with Lady Craigie to ensure an inheritance. Count Blum made no secret of the fact that he would get a commission if she signed certain documents involving a claim for the restitution of revenues from the Landsfeld properties in Bavaria.

Lola looked vaguely at the papers, took the pen Blum held out to her and was about to sign her name when a flash of memory ran through her. She threw down the pen and exclaimed: "I won't do it because it's the price of sin." This was in keeping with the evangelicism that had her in its grip, but Count Blum had known the Countess in some of her highest moments and he was incredulous. Realizing how ill she was he helped her to get in touch with Dr. John Cooper, a judge's son who was a graduate of the University of Pennsylvania and had studied medicine in Paris.

Years later Dr. Cooper told his son, Dr. Harley B. Cooper, much that had happened in the days preceding Lola's death. He found her fatally ill and did not think that she would live long. He was struck by her intense hatred of her mother and her fear that Lady Craigie would reach her. She talked freely to Dr. Cooper about her past, and said that her mother had always been jealous of her, had never loved her, and could only be interested now in anything she might inherit, since they had had no communication for many years. Listening to her story Dr. Cooper came to the conclusion that Lola was a woman who had been greatly sinned against, and that she was truly penitent.

When he first saw her she was still at Mrs. Buchanan's but she begged to be hidden in some attic where her mother could not find her. She had called in the Reverend Francis L. Hawks of Calvary Episcopal Church to act as her clergyman and she sought his help, too, in hiding from her mother. The interest of Bishop Horatio Potter, head of the Episcopal Diocese of New York, was enlisted and he and Dr. Hawks helped to have her removed to a room at 194 West Seventeenth Street, where she was cared for by a practical nurse. Friends in California were convinced through newspaper reports sent west that Mrs. Buchanan was mistreating her and that she too was interested chiefly in Lola's worldly possessions. But the sparseness of the room in which she passed her last days did not trouble Lola. She was doing penance for her sins, and she no longer needed brocaded bedspreads, Persian carpets or cut-crystal perfume bottles. Her Bible was the only prop that mattered to her at this stage.

When Lady Craigie reached New York in November, 1860, she established contact with Mrs. Buchanan and Dr. Cooper, but there is no evidence that she was allowed to see her dying daughter, whom she referred to solely as Eliza Gilbert. The fashionable Lady Craigie, still effective-looking in her early sixties, with glinting green eyes and red hair only lightly dusted with gray, was assured by Mrs. Buchanan that her daughter was being well cared for, and that she was making progress. But she came nearer to learning the truth in a long talk she had with Dr. Cooper about the nature of Lola's illness and its hopelessness.

She quickly detected the air of penury and incurable disease attached to the daughter, whom she did not see. From Mrs. Hamilton and Blum she learned that there was no sign of property, money or jewels, although she was convinced that Lola must still have some of the diamonds and rubies that King Ludwig had given her. Frustrated and feeling that something was being withheld from her, Lady Craigie returned to England at once, leaving instructions that news of her daughter's condition should be sent to her. But when she heard nothing from Mrs. Buchanan she wrote to Dr. Cooper on January 14, 1861, three days before Lola's death: "I was well satisfied at your *judicious* treatment of her, and considered her progressing most favourably when I left New York. In a conversation I had with you one day, you said she had what is called softening of the brain. Is this still your opinion, or has she got over it, and what does she now suffer from?"

Lady Craigie asked Dr. Cooper to keep her letter confidential. She deplored not having seen him again the day before she left, for she had hoped to learn more about the true nature of her daughter's illness. As an Anglo-Indian the cold weather had upset her on the trip to America, she wrote, as well as what she had learned about her daughter's condition, and she had been unwell since returning to London, where she was staying at the home of Mrs. Scott Bell.

As she finished this letter a note from Mrs. Buchanan arrived which she sent on to Dr. Cooper. It had taken some time to cross the Atlantic but it was full of reassurance and it was also quite misleading. With Lola close to death in her miserable quarters her guardian wrote: "Your daughter is recovering her health. She is now able to walk alone with very little lameness, and looks in better health than I have ever seen her. Mrs. Hamilton is very attentive and she appreciates all the comforts she receives from her." Mrs. Buchanan added that she had called in another doctor for consultation.

The story of these last days was made public in a small book *The Story of a Penitent*, published by the Protestant Episcopal Society for the Promotion of Evangelical Knowledge. Dr. Hawks listened in amazement to Lola's history as she poured it out, with classical allusions and sundry bits of political history, all drowned now in her overpowering feeling of penitence. "In the course of a long experience as a Christian minister I do not think I ever saw deeper penitence and humility, more real contrition of soul, and more of bitter self-reproach, than in this poor woman," wrote Dr. Hawks. "If ever a repentant soul loathed past sin, I believe hers did. . . . She was a woman of genius, highly accomplished, of more than usual attainments, and of great natural eloquence."

Lola rambled on about her childhood in India, and said that her mother had exposed her to evil company early in life. She blamed Lady Craigie for the course her life had taken. Her experiences in Montrose caused Dr. Hawks to give distant assessment to their possible effect on Lola's character. "She was perverse and willful, though at the same time warm-hearted and impulsive and the severe treatment which was a part of the system of Scottish education of that day appears to have been most injudicious, and most unhappy in its effect upon such a temperament as hers."

"I would feel that she was the preacher and not I," Dr. Hawks said of these long sessions with Lola. "I listened to her sometimes with admiration, as, with the tears streaming from her eyes, her right hand uplifted and the singularly expressive features speaking almost as plainly as her tongue, she would dwell upon Christ, and the almost incredible truth that He would show mercy to such a vile sinner as she felt herself to have been."

Dr. Hawks was with her when she died on January 17, 1861. Her glorious blue eyes dimmed and, according to his recollection, her hand rested on the Bible as she uttered her last words: "Tell me, tell me more of my dear Saviour."

Since few people who had known Lola could reconcile this picture of her with her proud, reckless nature, Dr. Hawks's pamphlet was received with considerable skepticism when it appeared. But he personified the era when Bibles were being pushed and souls were thought to be "saved" by the most literal application of gospel teaching. Lola was a prime subject in this respect, having traveled from one extreme to the other. But there is no doubt that the Bible was her only solace in the last year of her life.

Mrs. Buchanan made the funeral arrangements and selected a plot in Greenwood Cemetery, overlooking a small pond. An Episcopal service was held at her house. Few were in the cortège that went to the cemetery on the bleak, icy day of her funeral, but Dr. Cooper was there, and observed with concern the unseemly haste with which the ceremony was pushed through. Isaac H. Brown, the famous sexton of Grace Church who managed the more fashionable weddings, funerals and receptions of New York, was in charge, and his tall figure towered over the open grave. He read the committal service with a practiced air, turning aside during a pause to hasten the work of the gravediggers. "Hurry up with that dirt, damn you," Brown muttered. Shivering, the little group scattered to their various carriages.

Lola's death left many echoes in distant countries. Another revolution was in the making, and all America was talking of the Civil War about to begin. The Prince of Wales, traveling as Baron Renfrew, visited George Washington's tomb, which was still unfinished, the verandah propped up with round poles. Ludwig was in Nice when the news reached him that Lola was dead. Her mother heard it in London, and old friends in Paris recalled the luminous and unforgettable Lola. She was sincerely mourned in

California, where she had many friends and had made a deep impression.

Brief sketches of her life history in papers around the world revived the story of her great loves—of Dumas, Dujarier, Liszt and Ludwig; of her political power; of her reputation as a dancer, actress and lecturer; of her strange life in California, and the spell she had cast over men wherever she went. The New York *Herald*, which had always cherished her, pointed out that she "had known society in all its varied forms—at one time greeted with applause from a multitude of votaries, and then again being obliged to flee in disguise from the enraged population." The New York *Tribune* said that she had the "elasticity of a Creole, and the gracefulness of a Spaniard, with the wit and vivacity of a native of Ireland."

Hers was a sordid end, her body ravaged by disease, her mind wandering, and her soul in quest of peace. Her riches and her jewels all were gone. She was thought to have kept a diamond necklace given her by Ludwig, but if she did it was never seen again, and in spite of the fortune that had come her way she died in comparative penury. She left two savings accounts in banks, amounting to $1,247, most of which was used for her funeral expenses. Her final gesture was a bequest of $300 to the Magdalen Asylum.

When Lady Craigie returned to America a month after her daughter's death, there was nothing for her and she quickly returned to England. But two of Lola's European admirers—both great stage names—took time to visit her grave and lay flowers close to the simple marble slab inscribed *Mrs. Eliza Gilbert. Died 1861.* They were Sarah Bernhardt and Adelaide Ristori. Both knew her European history well and they understood the forces that had driven her to such extremes. They thought it strange that she should not have been identified on her gravestone as Lola Montez or the Countess of Landsfeld, although this might have been her own wish—to shed her identity along with the burden of her sins.

But she lived on in the memory of innumerable men who had known and admired her. Snuff boxes and medallions with her picture were prized by the aging diplomats who had once danced with her at the embassy parties, and who remembered the flashing excitement that she seemed to exude.

A. Augustin Thierry, who had observed her in Paris as she absorbed political sophistication while bewitching men, had once said of Lola: "She was born a hundred years too late. In the eighteenth century she would have played a great Pompadour role, with taste in small matters and courage in big ones. She herself made a moment of history."

It might be said with equal truth that she was born a century too soon, for in spirit she resembled the Women's Liberationists of the 1970's. Her outlook on men took on a bitter edge after her course was run, and she then became the proponent of the free woman. It happened that she lived at a time when women were beginning to reach for a wider life. Submerged in the puritanism of the mid-Victorian era, smothered in restricting clothes, exhausted by constant childbearing, only the daring, the original, the women who flouted convention, came to public attention.

So invincible was her sex drive that Lola Montez might have emerged in any era. It was mere chance that her childhood in an exotic Indian setting gave her a touch of the imperious spirit that drove her from one excess to another. Her bitterness over these early years ran like a thread through her disorderly life. She had felt unwanted and a burden to her pleasure-loving mother, and she flowered into carnal knowledge early in life, maturing with tropical speed. The loss of her father had scarred her, too, although all these factors may have been excuses used by Lola to ease her remorse. Before the time of Freud she was adept at linking her history to an unnatural childhood.

She found her own rocky road to stardom, driving straight with a demanding spirit for the goal she sought, and never hesitating to use her great physical appeal and charm. In all areas of her life she was a rebel at heart, radical and determined, but ever mindful of the manners in which she had been trained when a show of pomp and circumstance was required. However democratic her professed views, she made full use of the privileges that might aid her in her climb, and she enjoyed playing the Countess, in spite of her whip, her cigars, her curses and her demented behavior when in one of her furies. Her blind spot was her bigotry about the Jesuits, and this became one of the most destructive forces in her stormy career. She was quick to forgive her enemies, but never the scholars of the church.

Lola's motto was: *Courage! And shuffle the cards.* She was prone to laugh when the house she had built came tumbling down. Her wit was often her saving grace, and clever men who set out to make love to Lola sometimes ended by having long political discussions instead, for she could hold them as convincingly with her brilliant conversation as with her alluring body. She had an unusual number of lawyer friends who swore by her logic and reasoning but most of all by her understanding of men.

When Charles Sumner, one of America's handsomest and most radical senators, met Lola in Rome he said that she was the most subtly beautiful woman he had ever looked upon. As a young man in Paris Sir John Millais wrote to John Ruskin that any artist would find it worth his while to journey from London to Paris to see Lola Montez. De Mirecourt, who compared her to Madame Pompadour and Du Barry, wrote: "Disaster after disaster left unexhausted her marvellous powers of recuperation. She could adapt herself to all men and all circumstances." Eduard Fuchs, whose collection of caricatures of Lola caught many aspects of her life, viewed her as "provocation incarnate," practicing eroticism in calculated fashion.

"There were few, indeed, if any, who really knew the depths of that wild Irish soul," said Charles Godfrey Leland of Lola with real perception. Known also as Hans Breitmann, a writer and humorist, Leland had seen a good deal of her while he was studying at Munich University. He practiced hypnotism and was a student of the occult and of gypsy lore. It was his boast that he was the only friend at whom she had "never thrown a plate or a brick, attacked with a dagger, poker, broom or other deadly weapon." Leland attributed this to the fact that he always treated her with respect and never made love to her. They preferred to study Apuleius together while she expounded her views on neo-platonism.

Candor was her best trait, according to Albert Dresden Vandam, an English writer who has left the most scorching comments on Lola. He belittled and derided her in his book *An Englishman in Paris*, published in 1892. He refused to concede any intellectual gifts on her part, although he admitted that better judges than he had been impressed by her wit, wide knowledge of men, and political understanding. Actually, she was usually most appreciated by men of stature, learning and style. Vandam dismissed her as a total fraud. He deplored her accent, considered her illiterate and wrote of her "pot-house wit" and "consummate impudence." Since this writer was not born until 1843 his knowledge of Lola was obviously derivative and secondhand, although he gave the impression of having known her well. He even wrote that she had asked him to help her with her memoirs, and his derogatory opinion of her has been widely and erroneously quoted.

The impression that she had a rare story to tell if she could bring herself to discuss the King hung over Lola for years. Ludwig lived for twenty years after his abdication, and once she was out of his life, and the political cares that irked him had been handed over to his son, he devoted himself freely again to the world of poetry, art and beautiful young women. His son, a serious, highly-educated young man, ruled without his father's dash or imagination. He was as lacking in the Wittelsbach charm as in the family's madness and follies.

In making a new life for himself Ludwig had regained the love of the Bavarian people. He was seen once more walking through the great boulevards he had planned, admiring the massive buildings, sometimes even lingering in the Barerstrasse, where he had passed golden hours with Lola. He lived for the most part in the Wittelsbach Palace, long occupied by his grandson, Ludwig II, the Mad King of Bavaria. These two monarchs had much in common, according to Princess Radziwill's estimate of their natures in *The Tragedy of a Throne*. "In character Ludwig was far more like his grandfather Ludwig I—whose eccentricities had culminated in his mad passion for the dancer Lola Montez, a passion that at last cost him his throne—than his own father, the sedate, stingy, and pedantic Maximilan," she wrote. "His inclinations were entirely artistic and, unfortunately for him, were never understood as they ought to have been."

Ludwig I watched the eerie development of his grandson with interest and understanding. He was in Sicily when news of Maximilian's death reached him, and he went back to Munich for the coronation of the "beautiful Swan-Prince," whose life would end mysteriously in Lake Starnberg. He lived to see his grandson fall under the spell of Richard Wagner, to watch Bavaria being crushed by Prussia under Bismarck's growing power, and to lament the fact that his son Otto was expelled from Greece, the country that had meant so much in his own life.

As the years went on Ludwig passed more and more time in the sunshine of the Riviera, a spirited old gentleman always surrounded by men of wit and knowledge and young women of beauty. When news of Lola's death reached him, he was having a light flirtation with a girl of sixteen. In 1867 he was unique among the royal figures at the Paris Exhibition, dining at the Tuileries with the Empress Eugénie and reminding her that he had been the guest of Josephine more than half a century earlier.

He died at Nice on February 29, 1868, seven years after Lola. On his deathbed he swore once more that she had never been his mistress, that theirs had been an innocent love, a communion of the spirit, but that their love had held joys second to none. Ludwig, the hedonist, had said that he would never die, but when the time came his coffin was exposed in the Glyptothek, with the archaeological finds he had treasured all around him. Celebrities of many interests traveled to Munich to honor this fallen monarch, this patron of the arts. Memorial services were held for him in Rome and Athens. He was laid to rest in the Basilica of St. Boniface with Queen Theresa.

The name of Lola Montez came to the fore again at the time of his death. It is alive in Munich today, where her portrait is the most admired in the gallery of beauties at the Nymphenburg Palace; where the site of her old home on the Barerstrasse is pointed out; where a night club bears her name; where it crops up in many of the city's landmarks. Mention Ludwig I and the name of the Countess of Landsfeld is recalled. Munich has forgiven Lola Montez but not forgotten her.

She had faced danger and disgrace so often in her lifetime that she was fatalistic at the end. In four decades the passion and ambition of her dual nature had ended in total ruin. In her autobiography she wrote that a woman, like a man of true courage, "should face the public deeds of her life rather than hide from her own historical presence." And with full realization of her own role she added: "Perhaps the noblest courage, after all, is to dare to meet one's self—to sit down face to face with one's own life, and confront all these deeds which may have influenced the mind or manners of society, for good or evil."

This was what Lola had tried to do as time ran out for her. The score against her seemed overwhelming when she finally reached this point, since she had lived with an intensity known to few women. "I must live before I die," she was apt to say in moments of rapture, or "I am subject to my whims and sensations alone." Her paradoxical nature encompassed the simple and the subtle, the ruthless and the tender, the generous and the rapacious, the imperious and the humble. Her penitence at the end was as extreme as the ecstasy that she had given and received, but before she lost all sense of identity, she floated on a golden cloud with diamonds for stars, believing that she had influenced the future of Bavaria, and would live forever in Ludwig's personal Walhalla as the ravishing presence, the unregenerate sinner, the uncrowned Queen.

Notes

1. A Calvinist Setting

Information supplied by Mrs. Anne Watson, of Holly House, Montrose, where Lola Montez spent part of her childhood as the ward of Sir Patrick Edmonstone Craigie, Provost of Montrose; and by John Lindsay, of Independent Television Authority, Glasgow, who grew up in Holly House; reminiscences of Major Colin Neish, of Tannadice, Forfar, a descendant of the Craigie family. Town records supplied by John S. Richardson, Town Clerk of Montrose; data from Miss Mary Smith, County Librarian, Montrose, and her associates; from Peter Pagan, Director, City of Bath Municipal Libraries; Thomas I. Rae, National Library of Scotland, Edinburgh; D. MacArthur, University Library, St. Andrews, Scotland; J. R. Barker, University Library, Dundee; H. J. H. Drummond, Aberdeen University Library, Aberdeen; files of the Montrose *Standard*, Montrose *Review* and Montrose *Chronicle* of the 1820's; *Montrose* by Duncan Fraser and *The History of Montrose* by

David Mitchell; *Historical Record of the Forty-fourth or the East Essex Regiment,* compiled by Thomas Carter; Richard Rush, *Memoranda of a Residence at the Court of London;* Arthur Bryant, *The Age of Elegance, 1812–1822;* Lola Montez, *The Lectures of Lola Montez with a full and complete autobiography of her life;* R. W. Frazer, *British India.*

2. *From Bath to Simla*

Robert E. M. Peach, *Bath, Old and New;* Alfred Barbeau, *Life & Letters at Bath in the XVIIIth Century;* John Earle, *A Guide to the Knowledge of Bath;* Lewis S. Benjamin, *Bath under Beau Nash;* The Hon. Emily Eden, sister of Lord Auckland, *Up the Country, Letters written to her sister from the upper provinces of India;* the Hon. W. G. Osborne, *The Court and Camp of Ranjit Singh;* R. W. Frazer, *British India;* Hugh Murray, *Historical and Descriptive Account of British India from the Most Remote Period to the Present Time,* vol. 3; James Howard Harris (Earl) Malmesbury, *Memoirs of an Ex-Minister;* Geoffrey T. Garratt, *Lord Brougham;* Jasper Ridley, *Lord Palmerston;* A. J. P. Taylor, *Bismarck, the Man and the Statesman;* Emil Ludwig, *Bismarck;* Otto Pflanze, *Bismarck and the Development of Germany;* Horace Wyndham, *The Magnificent Montez;* Philip Walsingham Sergeant, *Dominant Women;* Edmund B. d'Auvergne, *Lola Montez;* W. R. H. Trowbridge, *Seven Splendid Sinners;* Lola Montez, *The Lectures of Lola Montez with a full and complete autobiography of her life;* London *Times,* December 16, 1842; London *Morning Herald,* December 18, 1842.

3. *The Spanish Dancer*

London *Times,* December 16, 1842, and June 5, 1843; London *Morning Herald,* December 16 and 18, 1842, and June 3 and 8, 1843; Files of *Illustrated London News,* 1843; Files of *Era,* 1843; Charles G. Rosenberg (Q), *You Have Heard of Them;* Benjamin

Lumley, *Sirenia, or Recollections of a past existence;* George Augustus Sala, *The Life and Adventures of George Augustus Sala written by himself;* James Howard Harris Malmesbury, *Memoirs of an Ex-Minister: an Autobiography of the Rt. Honourable the Earl of Malmesbury;* Henry Lord Brougham, *The Life and Times of Henry Lord Brougham written by himself,* vol. 3; Jasper Ridley, *Lord Palmerston;* Harriet Elizabeth (Cavendish) Leveson-Gower Granville, *Letters of Harriet, Countess Granville, 1810–1845;* Sacheverell Sitwell, *Liszt;* James G. Huneker, *Franz Liszt;* Ethel Colburn Mayne, *Enchanters of Men;* Ignaz Moscheles, *Life of Moscheles, with selections from his diary and correspondence,* ed. by his wife, Charlotte (Embden) Moscheles; Guy de Pourtalès, *Franz Liszt;* Ernest Newman, *The Man Liszt;* Lina Ramann, *Franz Liszt, als künstler und mensch,* vol. 2; W. R. H. Trowbridge, *Seven Splendid Sinners;* Philip Walsingham Sergeant, *Dominant Women;* Horace Wyndham, *The Magnificent Montez;* Edmund B. d'Auvergne, *Lola Montez;* Eleanor Stimson Brooks, *Franz Liszt;* William Bolitho, *Twelve Against the Gods;* Frances A. Gerard, *Some Fair Hibernians;* Lola Montez, *The Lectures of Lola Montez with a full and complete autobiography of her life;* T. Everett Harré, "Lola Montez—the Heavenly Sinner," *Dance Magazine,* March to October, 1930.

4. *The Boulevards of Paris*

Lola Montez's lecture *Wits and Women of Paris;* Lola Montez, *The Lectures of Lola Montez, with a full and complete autobiography of her life;* Eugène de Mirecourt, *Les Contemporains;* vols. 1, 3 and 5; Gustave Claudin, *Mes Souvenirs. Les Boulevards de 1840–1870;* A. Augustin Thierry, *Lola Montès, Favorite Royale en Bavière, Revue des Deux Mondes,* December, 1935; Julie de Marguerittes, *The Ins and Outs of Paris: or Paris by Day and Night;* Edmonde de Amicis, *Studies of Paris;* Alfred Barbou, *Victor Hugo and His Time;* René Benjamin, *Balzac;* Léon Séché, *Del-*

phine Gay, Mme. de Girardin, dans ses rapports avec Lamartine, Victor Hugo, Balzac, Rachel, Jules Sandeau, Dumas, Eugène Sue et George Sand; Frances Winwar, *The Life of the Heart. George Sand and Her Times;* Albert Dresden Vandam, *An Englishman in Paris, Notes and Recollections,* vol. 1; Marie (Jenney) Howe, ed. and trans., *George Sand. The Intimate Journal of George Sand;* Charlotte Haldane, *The Passionate life of Alfred de Musset;* Théophile Gautier, *Histoire de l'art dramatique en France, Famous French authors* and *Souvenirs romantiques;* Edgar A. Dolph, *The Real 'Lady of the Camellias' and Other Women of Quality;* Henriette Ceralié, *La Vie Vagabonde Tumultueuse de Lola Montès;* Anne Mariel, *Lola Montès, la scandaleuse;* Alfred Delvau, *Les Lions du Jour;* Alfred Asseline, *Victor Hugo, Intime Mémoires, Correspondance, Documents inédité facsimile de lettre;* Sir John Hall, *The Bravo Mystery and Other Cases;* Auguste Ehrhard, *Fanny Elssler, Une Vie de Danseuse;* Edmund B. d'Auvergne, *Lola Montez. An Adventuress of the Forties;* Helen O'Donnell Holdredge, *The Woman in Black; the Life of Lola Montez;* T. Everett Harré, *The Heavenly Sinner. The Life and Loves of Lola Montez.*

5. *A Duel in the Bois*

Testimony taken in Rosemond de Beauvallon trial in Rouen, March 26–30, 1846, for murder of Alexandre Henri Dujarier, from Armand Fouquier's *Beauvallon et d'Ecquevillez, Dujarier duel,* vol. 2 of *Causes Célèbres de Tous les Peuples;* "Trial for Murder in France—Lola Montez," *The American Law Journal,* July, 1848; Horace Wyndham, *The Magnificent Montez;* Geoffrey T. Garratt, *Lord Brougham;* Sir John Hall, *The Bravo Mystery and Other Cases;* Albert Dresden Vandam, *An Englishman in Paris, Notes and Recollections,* vol. 1; Edmund B. d'Auvergne, *Lola Montez;* Julie de Marguerittes, *The Ins and*

Outs of Paris; or Paris by Day and Night; Gertrude Aretz, *The Elegant Woman. From the Rococo Period to Modern Times;* Erich Pottendorf, *Lola Montez, Die Spanische Tänzarin;* Lola Montez, *The Lectures of Lola Montez with a full and complete autobiography of her life.*

6. *Adviser to the King*

Karl Wilhelm Vogt (pamphlet), *Das Nächtlager in Blutenburg oder der Lola Montez;* "Aus den Tagen der Lola Montez," *Neue Deutsche Rundschau,* 1901; Karl Bosl, *Geschichte der Bayern;* Heinrich von Treitschke, *Deutsche Geschichte im 19. Jahrhundert,* vol. 5; Ernest Posse, "Lola Montez, Metternich und der Weinsberger Geistersturm," *Historische Zeitschrift,* 1929; Georges Bordonove, *Les Rois Fous de Bavière;* Henry Channon, *The Ludwigs of Bavaria;* Wilfrid Blunt, *The Dream King, Ludwig II of Bavaria;* Luise von Kobell, *Unter den Vier Ersten Königen Bayerns;* George Henry Francis, "The King of Bavaria, Munich and Lola Montez," *Fraser's Magazine,* January, 1848; *Allgemeine Zeitung,* March, 1847; *Illustrated London News,* March 20, April 3, 1847; London *Morning Herald,* March 3, 1868; London *Times,* March 18 and April 9, 1847; G. A. C. Sandeman, *Metternich;* Prince Metternich, *Memoirs of Prince Metternich,* vols. 4 and 5; William Bolitho, *Twelve Against the Gods;* Ferdinand Bac, *Louis I de Bavière et Lola Montès;* Horace Wyndham, *The Magnificent Montez;* W. R. H. Trowbridge, *Seven Splendid Sinners;* Erich Pottendorf, *Lola Montez, die Spanische Tänzerin;* Eduard Fuchs, *Ein Vormärzliches Tänz-Idyll; Lola Montez in der Karikatur;* William Leonard Langer, *Political and Social Upheaval, 1832–1852;* Theodore S. Hamerow, *Restoration, Revolution, Reaction: Economics and Politics in Germany 1815–1871;* Jasper Ridley, *Lord Palmerston;* Lola Montez, *The Lectures of Lola Montez with a full and complete autobiography of her life.*

7. *A Woman Rules*

Text of Cabinet remonstrance to King Ludwig against naturalization of Lola Montez, February 11, 1847; Lola Montez's own version of her ancestry, London *Times*, April 9, 1847; *London Illustrated News*, March 20, 1847; London *Times*, March 2, 8, 9, 11, 12 and 18, 1847; *Augsburg Zeitung* and *München Zeitung*, March and April, 1847; *Metternich Diary*, April 6 and September 26, 1847; George Henry Francis, "The King of Bavaria, Munich and Lola Montez," *Fraser's Magazine*, January, 1848; Otto Pflanze, *Bismarck and the Development of Germany;* A. J. P. Taylor, *Bismarck;* Erich Pottendorf, *Lola Montez, die Spanische Tänzerin;* Philip Walsingham Sergeant, *Dominant Women;* Gertrude Aretz, *The Elegant Woman. From the Rococo Period to Modern Times;* Ferdinand Bac, *Louis I de Bavière et Lola Montès;* Karl Bosl, *Geschichte der Bayern;* Henry Channon, *The Ludwigs of Bavaria;* Edmund B. d'Auvergne, *Lola Montez;* Horace Wyndham, *The Magnificent Montez* and *Feminine Frailty;* Paul Erdmann, *Lola Montez und die Jesuiten;* August Fournier, "Lola Montez und der Regierungswechsel im Bayern," *Deutsche Revue,* October, 1909; Edward Fuchs, *Ein Vormärzliches Tänz-Idyll: Lola Montez in der Karikatur;* August Fournier, *Lola Montez und die Studeten;* W. R. H. Trowbridge, *Seven Splendid Sinners;* Cameron Rogers, *Gallant Ladies;* Marquess of Salisbury, *Essays by the late Marquess of Salisbury. Foreign Politics;* Lola Montez: *The Lectures of Lola Montez with a full and complete autobiography of her life.*

8. *Student Revolt*

City Chronicle. The part which the Magistrate and the population of the community and citizenship in Munich played on February 10 and 11, 1848, hour by hour account of city insurrection preserved in Munich State Archives; London *Times*, March 8 and 9, 1847; George Henry Francis, "The King of Bavaria,

Munich and Lola Montez," *Fraser's Magazine,* January, 1848; August Fournier, "Lola Montez und der Regierungswechfel im Bayern, 1847," *Deutsche Revue,* October, 1909; *Lola Montez und die Studeten,* Eine Monatschrift von Richard Fleischer, 1914; Joseph Ignaz Döllinger letter to Elise Marie (Madame Rio), dated Munich, February 25, 1848, and published by Dom L. Gougaud in the *Irish Ecclesiastic Record,* 1914, vol. 3; Horace Wyndham, *The Magnificent Montez* and *Feminine Frailty;* Edmund B. d'Auvergne, *Lola Montez;* Cameron Rogers, *Gallant Ladies;* W. R. H. Trowbridge, *Seven Splendid Sinners;* Philip Walsingham Sergeant, *Dominant Women;* William Bolitho, *Twelve Against the Gods;* Dr. Paul Erdmann, *Lola Montez und die Jesuiten;* Isaac Goldberg, *Queen of Hearts;* Erich Pottendorf, *Lola Montez, die Spanische Tänzarin;* Eduard Fuchs, *Ein Vormärzliches Tänz-Idyll; Lola Montez in der Karikatur;* P. J. Proudhon, *Idée Générale de la Révolution au XIX Siècle;* Veit Valentin, *1848: Chapters of German History.*

9. *Flight and Abdication*

Auguste Papon correspondence with King Ludwig and intermediaries, Joel Cherbuliez, Joseph Hirsch and M. Rossman, regarding projected book about King and Lola Montez, in Staats Bibliothek, Munich: Papon to King, December 1, 1848, and January 13, 1849; Joel Cherbuliez, January 15, 1849; Auguste Papon, *Lola Montès Mémoires accompagnés de lettres intime de S.M. Le Roi de Bavière et de Lola Montès;* Lola Montez, *Lola Montez, or a reply to the "Private History and Memoirs"* of that celebrated lady recently published by the Marquis Papon, formerly secretary to the King of Bavaria and for a period the professed friend and attendant of the Countess of Landsfeld; Ernest Posse, "Lola Montez, Metternich und der Weinsberger Geistersturm," *Historische Zeitschrift;* correspondence of Andreas Justinus Kerner and Theobald Kerner regarding Lola Montez—J.K. to Emma

Niendorf, February 19, 1848, and to Sophie Schwab, April 2, 1848; Heinrich Huber, "Zum Fall Lola Montez," *Monatscheft*, January, 1901; R. G. M., "Das erste Austreten von Lola Montez in Deutschland," *Monatscheft*, January, 1901; Metternich Diary, February 14, 1848; George Henry Francis, "The King of Bavaria, Munich and Lola Montez," *Fraser's Magazine*, January, 1848; Lola Montez scrapbooks in State Archives, Munich; Erich Pottendorf, *Lola Montez, die Spanische Tänzerin;* A. Augustin Thierry, *Favorite Royale en Bavière;* Georges Bordonove, *Les Rois Fous de Bavière;* Henry Channon, *The Ludwigs of Bavaria;* Lyndon Orr (Harry Thurston Peck), *Famous Affinities of History;* William Bolitho, *Twelve Against the Gods;* August Fournier, "Lola Montez und der Regierungswechsel im Bayern, 1847," *Deutsche Revue*, October, 1909; *The American Law Journal*, July, 1848; Richard Fleischer, *Lola Montez und die Studenten*, Stuttgart and Leipzig, 1914.

10. *Marries Wealthy Englishman—Flees Bigamy Charge*

Benjamin Disraeli's letters to his sister Sarah, May 2, 1849, and July, 1848, *Lord Beaconsfield's Correspondence with His Sister, 1832–1852;* Prince Metternich, *Memoirs of Prince Metternich,* vols. 4 and 5; G. A. S. Sandemann, *Metternich;* Daria Khristoforovna Lieven, *Letters of Dorothea Princess Lieven, during her residence in London, 1812–1834;* James Howard Harris (Earl) Malmesbury, *Memoirs of an Ex-Minister; an autobiography of the Rt. Honourable the Earl of Malmesbury;* Edward F. Leveson-Gower, *Bygone Years, Recollections;* Harriet Elizabeth (Cavendish) Leveson-Gower Granville, *Letters of Harriet, Countess Granville, 1810–1845;* Charles Cavendish Fulke Greville, *The Greville Memoirs* (third part), *A Journal of the Reign of Queen Victoria from 1852–1860;* Geoffrey T. Garratt, *Lord Brougham;* Henry Lord Brougham, *The Life and Times of Henry Lord Brougham written by himself,* vol. 3; George Augustus Sala, *The*

Life and Adventures of George Augustus Sala, vol. 1; Horace Wyndham, *The Magnificent Montez* and *Feminine Frailty;* Edmund B. d'Auvergne, *Lola Montez;* Gertrude Aretz, *The Elegant Woman. From the Rococo Period to Modern Times;* A. Augustin Thierry, *Lola Montez, Favorite Royale en Bavière;* Erich Pottendorf, *Lola Montez, Die Spanische Tänzarin;* Eduard Fuchs, *Ein Vormärzliches Tänz-Idyll: Lola Montez in der Karikatur;* Lola Montez, *The Lectures of Lola Montez with a full and complete autobigraphy of her life;* London *Times,* August 7, 1849; New York *Herald,* November 24, 1848, and December 25, 1851; San Francisco *Examiner,* August 18, 1849; Raoul Auernheimer, *Prince Metternich, Statesman and Lover;* Jasper Ridley, *Lord Palmerston;* Victor A. G. R. Bulmer-Lytton, *The Life of Edward Bulmer, first Lord Lytton, by his grandson,* vol. 1.

11. *Love and War*

London *Times,* August 7, 10 and 11, September 12 and October 23, 1849; New York *Herald,* November 12, 24 and 29, 1849, January 28, April 12, 22 and 24, 1850; May 20, 1850; July 2, 1850, September 9 and 20, 1850, October 3 and 7, 1850, December 5, 23, 1850, February 8, 17 and 21, 1851, June 5 and 24, 1851, August 29, 1851, October 12, 1851; *Illustrated London News,* April 29, 1848, November 26, 1848, September 22 and October 27, 1848; *Le Siècle,* August 10, 1850, March 20, June 23 and July 3, 1851; *Le Pays,* December, January and February, 1851; Morris R. Werner, *Barnum;* Henry A. Beers, *Nathaniel Parker Willis;* Edmund B. d'Auvergne, *Lola Montez;* Helen O'Donnell Holdredge, *The Woman in Black; the Life of Lola Montez;* Horace Wyndham, *The Magnificent Montez; Musical World,* August, 1851; Eugène de Mirecourt, *Les Contemporains,* vol. 3; Julie de Marguerittes, *The Ins and Outs of Paris; or Paris by Day and Night;* Alfred Barbou, *Victor Hugo and His Time;* Gustave Claudin, *Mes Souvenirs. Les Boulevards de 1840–1870;*

Théophile Gautier, *Histoire de l'Art Dramatique en France depuis Vingt-cinq Ans; Assemblée Nationale,* November, 1849; Auguste Papon, *Lola Montès Mémoires accompagnés de lettres intime de S.M. Le Roi de Bavière et de Lola Montès;* "Lola Montez and Her Agent," *Galagnani's Messenger,* November 2, 1851; *Albion,* May 15, 1847, and November, 1851; *Courrier des États Unis,* May 14, 1847.

12. *A New Land*

New York *Herald,* December 4, 6, 23, 25 and 30, 1851, January 15, February 9 and 13, March 20, April 3, 27 and 30, 1852; New York *Daily Times,* September 30 and December 6, 1851, January 15 and August 26, 1852; New York *Tribune,* August 26, 1852; Boston *Transcript,* March and April, 1852; Lola Montez Manifesto, April 1, 1852, published in Boston *Transcript* and New York *Herald;* Lola Montez papers in Harvard Theater Collection; Scrapbooks in Lincoln Center; *Dance Magazine,* March to October, 1930; *Musical Courier,* July 28 to September 1, 1909; *Musical World,* August, 1851; "The Jesuits and Lola Montez," *Living Age,* vol. 13, and "Lola Montez," *Living Age,* vol. 28; M. M. Marberry, "How New York Greeted King Ludwig's Girl Friend," *American Heritage,* February, 1955; *The Pick,* August 28, September 4 and 11, 1852; *Albany Atlas and Argus,* February 8, 1851; George C. D. Odell, *Annals of the New York Stage,* vols. 5 and 6; H. P. Phelps, *Players of a Century;* New York *Clipper,* September 16, 1911; Auguste Papon, *Lola Montès Mémoires accompagnés de lettres intime de S.M. Le Roi de Bavière et de Lola Montès;* Eugène de Mirecourt, *Les Contemporains;* Henry Scott Holland and W. S. Rockstro, *Memoir of Madame Jenny Lind-Goldschmidt;* Helen O'Donnell Holdredge, *The Woman in Black; the Life of Lola Montez;* M. R. Werner, *Barnum;* Allis M. Hutchings, "The Most Famous Vamp Who Ever Lived," *The Magazine for Collectors,* April, 1945.

13. *The Golden West*

California *Democratic State Journals*, June and July, 1853, September 22, October 12 and December 13, 1853, and January 3, 1856; San Francisco *Herald*, May, June and July, 1853; San Francisco *Alta*, May, June and July, 1853; *The Illustrated London News*, October 1, 1853, January 26 and May 17, 1856; *The Golden Era*, May, June, July and August, 1853; March, April and May, 1854; *The Californian*, July 30 and September 24, 1864; *The Letters of Miska Hauser, 1853*, in W.P.A. *History of Music in San Francisco Series*, May, 1939, vol. 3; Edwin Franklin Morse, "The Story of a Gold Miner," dictated to his daughter, Mary Phipps Morse, *California Historical Society Quarterly*, December, 1927; Idwal Jones, "Plumes and Buskins," *The American Mercury*, March, 1928; Oscar Lewis, *Lola Montez. The Mid-Victorian Bad Girl in California;* Edmond M. Gagey, *The San Francisco Stage;* B. E. Lloyd, *Lights and Shades in San Francisco;* Amelia Ransome Neville, *The Fantastic City;* Mrs. Frank Leslie, *California: A Pleasure Trip from Gotham to the Golden Gate;* Ishbel Ross, *Rebel Rose* and *Charmers and Cranks;* George Rupert MacMinn, *The Theater of the Golden Era in California;* Constance Rourke, *Troupers of the Gold Coast;* Zoeth Skinner Eldredge, *The Beginnings of San Francisco*, vols. 1 and 2; *Gleason's Pictorial Drawing Room Companion*, vols. 2 and 3, 1852; *California Historical Society Quarterly*, September, 1928, vol. 7, and March, 1929, vol. 8.

14. *Grass Valley*

Ronald Isetti, "Lola Montez in Grass Valley," *The Pacific Historian*, May, 1960; Andy Rogers, *Rough and Ready, A Hundred Years of Rip and Roarin';* Edwin Franklin Morse, "The Story of a Gold Miner," *California Historical Society Quarterly*, December, 1927; *Grass Valley Telegraph*, March 9, 1854 and December, 1855; *The Golden Era*, March 19, April 30, May 28, June 4, August 6 and October 2, 1854; *Illustrated London News*, October 1, 1853; James Winchester to Captain E. Winchester, August 14, 1853, California State Library; Sacramento *Union*, February, March and August 1854, and November 22, 1854, September 17 and 18, 1856; S. Dickson, "Lola Montez," *San Franciscan*, April, 1929; Gene Coughlin, "Romantic Rebels," *San Francisco Examiner* (*American Weekly*) September 4, 1949; Ralph Friedman, "Lola Montez in Grass Valley," *Prairie Schooner*, Spring, 1951; John Considine, "The King's Favorite Comes to Camp," *Sunset*, 1922; W. J. Davis, "Lola Montez," *Themis*, December 6, 1890; Idwal Jones, "The Dona of Sawmill Flat," *Westways*, November, 1944; *Nevada Journal*, August 3, 1853; Joseph Henry Jackson, *Anybody's Gold, the Story of California mining towns;* Carl B. Glasscock, *The Big Bonanza;* Duncan Aikman, *Calamity Jane and the Lady Wildcats;* Constance Rourke, *Troupers of the Gold Coast;* Helen O'Donnell Holdredge, *The Woman in Black; the Life of Lola Montez;* Stephen C. Massett, *"Drifting About," or what "Jeems Pipes of Pipesville," Saw—and—Did;* Andrew Jackson Davis, *Principles of Nature;* David Dempsey with Raymond P. Baldwin, *The Triumphs and Trials of Lotta Crabtree;* Nolie Mumey, "Lola Montez, 1818–1861," *The Denver Westerners Monthly Roundup*, September, 1960; Edwin F. Bean, *History and Directory of Nevada County.*

15. *Off to the Antipodes*

Melbourne *Morning Herald*, May 7, 1856; *Illustrated London News*, January 26 and May 17, 1856; "Lola Montez in Australia," *Deutsches Theater-Album*, January, 1856; *The Golden Era*, July 27 and August 3, 1856; Sacramento *Union*, September 8 to 18, 1856; San Francisco *Alta*, September 1 and November 20, 1856; Lola Montez to editor of *Estafette*, picked up by Émile de Girardin in *La Presse*, from St. Jean de Luz, September 2, 1856; Jean Mauclerc's reply from Bayonne, September 9, 1856; Hildegarde Ebenthal (Princess Catherine Radziwill), *It Really Happened;* Helen O'Donnell Holdredge, *The Woman in Black; the Life of Lola Montez;* Horace Wyndham, *The Magnificent Montez;* Edmund B. d'Auvergne, *Lola Montez;* William Bolitho, *Twelve Against the Gods;* Henry Channon, *The Ludwigs of Bavaria;* Frances A. Gerard, *Some Fair Hibernians;* H. P. Phelps, *Players of a Century. A Record of the Albany Stage;* Albany *Atlas and Argus,* February 2 and 10, and June 26, 1857; Albany *Morning Times,* February 4 and 7, 1857; *Providence Journal,* February 12–13 and 16–17, 1857; Madeleine B. Stern, *Purple Passage;* Ishbel Ross, *Charmers and Cranks;* Bernard Falk, *The Naked Lady: or Storm over Adah;* David Dempsey with Raymond P. Baldwin, *The Triumphs and Trials of Lotta Crabtree;* Lola Montez, *The Lectures of Lola Montez with a full and complete autobiography of her life.*

16. *Champion of Her Sex*

New York *Daily Times,* February 19, 20 and 27, 1858; New York *Tribune,* May 25 and 27, and November 18, 1858; New York *Herald,* September 5, November 23, December 20 and 29, 1858; San Francisco *Alta,* November 18, 1858; *Illustrated London News,* June 4, 1858 and August 22, 1859; Lola Montez, *The Lectures of Lola Montez with a full and complete autobiography of her life;* Lola Montez, *The Arts of Beauty, or, Secrets of a Lady's Toilet with hints to gentlemen on the art of fascinating;* Gertrude Aretz, *The Elegant Woman. From the Rococo Period to Modern Times.*

17. *Lola, the Penitent, Dies in New York*

Era, April 10, 1859 and February 10, 1861; New York *Tribune,* November 23, 1859 and January 21, 1861; New York *Herald,* December 20 and 29, 1860, and January 20, 1861; correspondence between Lady Craigie, Dr. John Cooper and Mrs. Margaret Buchanan in Andy Rogers' *Rough and Ready, A Hundred Years of Rip and Roarin',* prepared by the staff of the Public Library of

Fort Wayne and Allen County, February, 1953; Scrapbooks in
Theater Collection, Lincoln Center; New York *Clipper*, September,
1911; Francis Lister Hawks, *Lola Montez. The Story of a Peni-
tent;* Andrew Jackson Davis, *Principles of Nature;* Princess Pauline
Metternich, *The Days That Are No More;* Jasper Ridley, *Lord
Palmerston;* Horace Wyndham, *The Magnificent Montez;* Helen
O'Donnell Holdredge, *The Woman in Black; the Life of Lola
Montez;* Albert Dresden Vandam, *An Englishman in Paris;* Henry
Channon, *The Ludwigs of Bavaria;* Princess Catherine Radziwill,
The Tragedy of a Throne; Gustave Claudin, *Mes Souvenirs;*
Charles Godfrey Leland, *Memoirs;* A. Augustin Thierry, *Lola
Montès, Favorite Royale en Bavière;* Lyndon Orr (Harry Thurston
Peck) , *Famous Affinities of History.*

Bibliography

AIKMAN, DUNCAN. *Calamity Jane and the Lady Wildcats.* New York: Henry Holt & Company, 1927.

AMICIS, EDMONDE DE. *Studies of Paris.* New York: G. P. Putnam's Sons, 1879.

ARETZ, GERTRUDE. *The Elegant Woman. From the Rococo Period to Modern Times.* Translated with a preface by James Laver. New York: Harcourt, Brace & Company, 1932.

ASSELINE, ALFRED. *Victor Hugo.* Paris: C. Marpon et E. Flammarion, 1885.

AUERNHEIMER, RAOUL. *Prince Metternich, Statesman and Lover.* New York: Alliance Book Corporation, 1940.

BAC, FERDINAND. *Louis I de Bavière et Lola Montès. L'Allemagne Romantique.* Paris: Louis Conard, 1928.

BARBEAU, ALFRED. *Life & Letters at Bath in the XVIIIth Century,* with a preface by Austin Dobson. New York: Dodd, Mead & Company, 1904.

BARBOU, ALFRED. *Victor Hugo and His Time.* New York: Harper & Brothers, 1882.

BEAN, EDWIN F. *History and Directory of Nevada County.* 1867.

BEERS, HENRY A. *Nathaniel Parker Willis.* Boston: Houghton, Mifflin and Company, 1885.

BENJAMIN, LEWIS S. *Bath under Beau Nash.* London: E. Nash, 1907.

BENJAMIN, RENÉ. *Balzac.* New York: Alfred A. Knopf, 1927.

BLOS, WILHELM. *Der Prinzipienreiter.* Eine Geschichte aus dem Jahre 1848. Berlin: Buchhandlung Vörwarts Paul Singer. 1912.

BLUNT, WILFRID. *The Dream King. Ludwig II of Bavaria.* A Studio Book. New York: The Viking Press, 1970.

BOLITHO, WILLIAM. *Twelve Against the Gods.* New York: Simon & Schuster, 1929.

BORDONOVE, GEORGES. *Les Rois Fous de Bavière.* Paris: Robert Laffont, 1964.

BOSL, KARL. *Geschichte der Bayern.* Darmstadt: Wissenschaftliche Buchgesellschaft, 1965.

BRETT, OLIVER. *Wellington.* Garden City, N.Y.: Doubleday, Doran and Company, 1928.

BROOKS, ELEANOR STIMSON. *Franz Liszt.* New York: Henry Holt & Company, 1926.

BROUGHAM, HENRY LORD. *The Life and Times of Henry Lord Brougham, written by himself.* Vol. 3. New York: Harper & Brothers, 1872.

BRYANT, ARTHUR. *The Age of Elegance, 1812–1822.* New York: Harper & Brothers, 1950.

CARTER, THOMAS. *Historical Record of the Forty-fourth or the East Essex Regiment, compiled by Thomas Carter.* Chatham: Gale & Polden, Brompton Works, 1887.

CERALIÉ, HENRIETTE. *La Vie Vagabonde Tumultueuse de Lola Montès.* Paris: Librairie Arthème Fayard, 1950.

CERTIGNY, HENRI. *Lola Montès. D'un trône à un cirque.* Paris: Gallimard, 1960.

CHANNON, HENRY. *The Ludwigs of Bavaria.* New York: E. P. Dutton & Company, 1933.

CLAUDIN, GUSTAVE. *Mes Souvenirs. Les Boulevards de 1840–1870.* Paris: Calmann Lévy, editeur Ancienne Maison Michel Lévy Frères, 1884.

D'AUVERGNE, EDMUND B. *Lola Montez. An Adventuress of the Forties.* New York: John Lane Company, 1909.

DAVIS, ANDREW JACKSON. *Principles of Nature.* New York: S. S. Lyon & William Fishbough, 1851.

DELVAU, ALFRED. *Les Lions du Jour.* Paris: E. Dentu, Éditeur Librairie de la Société des Gens de Lettres, 1867.

DEMPSEY, DAVID, with BALDWIN, RAYMOND P. *The Triumphs and Trials of Lotta Crabtree.* New York: William Morrow & Company, 1968.

DISRAELI, BENJAMIN. *Lord Beaconsfield's Correspondence with His Sister, 1832–1852.* London: John Murray, 1886.

DOLPH, EDGAR A. *The Real 'Lady of the Camellias' and Other Women of Quality.* London: T. W. Laurie, 1927.

DUMAINE, ALFRED. *Ambassadeur de France. Choses d'Allemagne.* Paris: Arthème Fayard & Cie, 1925.

EARLE, JOHN. *A Guide to the Knowledge of Bath.* London: Longman, Green, Longman, Roberts and Green, 1864.

EDEN, HON. EMILY. *Up the Country. Letters written to her sister from the upper provinces of India.* London: Richard Bentley, 1966.

EHRHARD, AUGUSTE. *Fanny Elssler, Une Vie de Danseuse.* Paris: Librairie Plon-Nourrit et Cie, 1909.

ELPHINSTONE, MOUNTSTUART. *History of India.* London: J. Murray, 1841.

ERDMANN, DR. PAUL. *Lola Montez und die Jesuiten.* Hamburg: Hoffman und Campe, 1847.

FALK, BERNARD. *The Naked Lady: or Storm over Adah.* London: Hutchinson & Company, 1934.

FOLEY, DORIS. *The Divine Eccentric. Lola Montez and the News-*

papers. Los Angeles: Westernlore Press, 1969.

FOUQUIER, ARMAND. *Causes Célèbres de Tous les Peuples. Beauvallon et d'Ecquevillez, Duel Dujarier*. Vol. 2. Paris: Leburn & Cie, 1858–74.

FOURNIER, AUGUST. *Lola Montez und die Studenten*. Eine Monatschrift herausgegeben von Richard Fleischer. Stuttgart und Leipzig: Deutsche Verlags-Anstalt, 1914.

———. "Lola Montez und der Regierungswechfel im Bayern, 1847." *Deutsche Revue*, October, 1909.

FRASER, DUNCAN. *Highland Perthshire*. Montrose: Standard Press, 1969.

———. *Montrose (before 1700)*. Montrose: Standard Press, 1967.

FRAZER, R. W. *British India*. New York: G. P. Putnam's Sons, 1901.

FUCHS, EDUARD. *Ein Vormärzliches Tanz-Idyll: Lola Montez in der Karikatur*. Berlin: Ernst Fernsdorff, 1904.

GAGEY, EDMOND M. *The San Francisco Stage*. New York: Columbia University Press, 1950.

GARRATT, GEOFFREY T. *Lord Brougham*. London: Macmillan and Company, 1935.

GAUTIER, THÉOPHILE. *Famous French Authors*. New York: R. Worthington, 1879.

———. *Souvenirs Romantiques*. Paris: Garnier Frères, 1929.

GERARD, FRANCES A. *Some Fair Hibernians*. London: Ward & Downey, 1897.

GLASSCOCK, CARL B. *The Big Bonanza. The Story of the Comstock Lode*. Indianapolis: Bobbs-Merrill Company, 1931.

GOLDBERG, ISAAC. *Queen of Hearts*. John Day Company, 1936.

GRANVILLE, HARRIET ELIZABETH (CAVENDISH) LEVESON-GOWER. *Letters of Harriet, Countess Granville, 1810–1845*, edited by her son, Hon. F. Leveson-Gower. London, New York: Longmans, Green and Co., 1894.

GREVILLE, CHARLES CAVENDISH FULKE. *The Greville Memoirs*

(third part). *A Journal of the Reign of Queen Victoria, from 1852–1860*. London: Longmans, Green and Co., 1887.

HALDANE, CHARLOTTE. *The Passionate Life of Alfred de Musset*. New York: Roy Publishers, 1960.

HALL, SIR JOHN. *The Bravo Mystery and Other Cases*. New York: Dodd, Mead and Company, 1925.

HAMEROW, THEODORE S. *Restoration, Revolution, Reaction; Economics and Politics in Germany 1815–1871*. Princeton, N.J.: Princeton University Press, 1958.

HARRÉ, T. EVERETT. *The Heavenly Sinner. The Life and Loves of Lola Montez*. New York: Macaulay Company, 1935.

HAUSER, MISKA. *The Letters of Miska Hauser, 1851*. San Francisco: W.P.A. History of Music in San Francisco Series, 1939. Vol. 3.

HAWKS, THE REV. FRANCIS LISTER. *Lola Montez. The Story of a Penitent*. New York: Protestant Episcopal Society for the Promotion of Evangelical Knowledge. Bible House, 1867.

HENNINGSEN, CHARLES F. *Révélations sur la Russie*. Paris: J. Labitte, 1845.

HOLDREDGE, HELEN O'DONNELL. *The Woman in Black; the Life of Lola Montez*. New York: G. P. Putnam's Sons, 1955.

HOLLAND, HENRY SCOTT, and ROCKSTRO, W. S. *Memoir of Madame Jenny Lind-Goldschmidt; Her Early Life and Career*. London: J. Murray, 1891.

HORNBLOW, ARTHUR. *A History of the Theater in America*. Philadelphia: J. B. Lippincott Company, 1910.

HOWE, MARIE (JENNEY.) *George Sand. The Intimate Journal of George Sand*, edited and translated by Marie Jenney Howe. New York: John Day Company, 1929.

HUNEKER, JAMES. *Franz Liszt*. New York: Charles Scribner's Sons, 1911.

HUNT, ROCKWELL D., and VAN DE GRIFT ZANCHE, NELLIE. *A Short History of California*. New York: Thomas Y. Crowell Company, 1929.

JACKSON, JOSEPH HENRY. *Anybody's Gold, the Story of California Mining Towns*. New York: D. Appleton-Century Company, 1941.

KISSINGER, HENRY A. *A World Restored. Metternich, Castlereagh and the Problems of Peace, 1812–22*. Boston: Houghton Mifflin Company, 1957.

KOBELL, LUISE VON. *Unter den Vier Ersten Königen Bayerns*. Munich: C. H. Becksche Verlagsbuchhandlung, 1894.

LANGER, WILLIAM LEONARD. *Political and Social Upheaval, 1832–1852*. New York: Harper & Row, 1969.

LELAND, CHARLES GODFREY. *Memoirs*. New York: D. Appleton & Co., 1893.

LESLIE, MRS. FRANK. *California: A Pleasure Trip from Gotham to the Golden Gate*. New York: G. W. Carleton Company, 1927.

LEWIS, OSCAR. *Lola Montez. The Mid-Victorian Bad Girl in California*. San Francisco: The Colt Press, 1938.

LIEVEN, DARIA KHRISTOFOROVNA (BENKENDORFF). *Letters of Dorothea Princess Lieven, during Her Residence in London, 1812–1834*, edited by Lionel G. Robinson. London: Longmans, Green, and Co., 1902.

LLOYD, B. E. *Lights and Shades in San Francisco*. San Francisco: A. L. Bancroft & Company, 1876.

LONGFORD, ELIZABETH (Harman) PAKENHAM. *Queen Victoria: Born to Succeed*. New York: Harper & Row, 1964.

——. *Wellington; the Years of the Sword*. New York: Harper & Row, 1969.

LUDWIG, EMIL. *Bismarck. The Story of a Fighter*. Boston: Little, Brown and Company, 1927.

LUMLEY, BENJAMIN. *Sirenia, or Recollections of a past existence*. London: R. Bentley, 1862.

MACMINN, GEORGE RUPERT. *The Theater of the Golden Era in California*. Caldwell, Idaho: Caxton Press, 1943.

MALMESBURY, JAMES HOWARD HARRIS (Earl). *Memoirs of an Ex-*

Minister; an autobiography of the Rt. Honourable the Earl of Malmesbury. London: Longmans, Green and Co., 1885.

MARGUERITTES, JULIE DE. *The Ins and Outs of Paris: or Paris by Day and Night.* Philadelphia: William White Smith, 1855.

MARIEL, ANNE. *Lola Montès, la scandaleuse.* Paris: Les Éditions du Scorpion, 1955.

MASSETT, STEPHEN C. *"Drifting About," or what "Jeems Pipes of Pipesville" Saw—and—Did.* New York: G. W. Carleton Company, 1863.

MAUROIS, ANDRÉ. *The Titans.* New York: Harper & Brothers, 1957.

MAYNE, ETHEL COLBURN. *Enchanters of Men.* Philadelphia: George W. Jacobs & Company, 1909.

METTERNICH, PRINCE. *Memoirs of Prince Metternich,* edited by Prince Richard Metternich. Vols. 4 and 5. New York: Charles Scribner's Sons, 1881.

METTERNICH, PRINCESS PAULINE. *The Days That Are No More.* New York: E. P. Dutton Company, 1921.

MIRECOURT, EUGÈNE DE. *Les Contemporains.* Vols. 1, 3 and 5. Paris: J. P. Roret et Compagnie, 1854 and 1855.

MITCHELL, DAVID. *The History of Montrose.* Montrose: George Walker, 1866.

MONTEZ, LOLA, COUNTESS OF LANDSFELD. *Anecdotes of Love: Being a True Account of the Most Remarkable Events Connected with the History of Love, in all Ages and Among All Nations.* New York: Dick & Fitzgerald, 1858.

———. *The Arts of Beauty, or, Secrets of a Lady's Toilet with hints to gentlemen on the art of fascinating.* New York: Dick & Fitzgerald, 1858.

———. *Lola Montez, or a reply to the "Private History and Memoirs" of that celebrated lady recently published by the Marquis Papon, formerly secretary to the King of Bavaria and for a period the professed friend and attendant of the Countess of Landsfeld.* New York: Sold by all booksellers, 1851.

——. *The Lectures of Lola Montez with a full and complete autobiography of her life.* Edited by the Rev. Charles Chauncey Burr. Philadelphia: T. B. Peterson & Bros., 1858.

MORSE, EDWIN FRANKLIN. "The Story of a Gold Miner," dictated to his daughter, Mary Phipps Morse. *California Historical Quarterly*, December, 1927.

MOSCHELES, IGNAZ. *Life of Moscheles, with selections from his diary and correspondence*, by his wife, Charlotte (Embden) Moscheles. London: Hurst and Blackett, 1873.

MURRAY, HUGH. *Historical and Descriptive Account of British India from the Most Remote Period to the Present Time.* 3 vols. New York: J. & J. Harper, 1832.

NEVILLE, AMELIA RANSOME. *The Fantastic City. Memoirs of the Social and Romantic Life of Old San Francisco.* Boston: Houghton Mifflin Company, 1932.

NEWMAN, ERNEST. *The Man Liszt.* New York: Charles Scribner's Sons, 1935.

ODELL, GEORGE C. D. *Annals of the New York Stage.* Vols. 5 and 6. New York: Columbia University Press, 1931.

ORR, LYNDON (HARRY THURSTON PECK). *Famous Affinities of History.* New York: Harper & Brothers, 1914.

OSBORNE, THE HON. W. G. *The Court and Camp of Ranjit Singh. The Punjab Series.* Vol. 1. Lahore: Punjab Economical Press, 1895.

PAPON, AUGUSTE. *Lola Montès Mémoires accompagnés de lettres intime de S.M. Le Roi de Bavière, et de Lola Montès.* Nyon: A. M. Desoche, 1849.

PFLANZE, OTTO. *Bismarck and the Development of Germany.* Princeton, N.J.: Princeton University Press, 1968.

PHELPS, H. P. *Players of a Century. A Record of the Albany Stage.* Albany: Joseph McDonough, 1880.

POTTENDORF, ERICH. *Lola Montez, die Spanische Tänzerin.* Zurich: Leipzig, Vienna: Amalthea-Verlag, 1955.

POURTALÈS, GUY DE. *Franz Liszt.* Translated from the French by

Eleanor Stimson Brooks. New York: Henry Holt & Company, 1926.

PROUDHON, P. J. *Idée Générale de la Révolution au XIX Siècle.* Paris: Garnier Frères, 1851.

RADZIWILL, PRINCESS CATHERINE (Ebenthal, Hildegarde). *Germany Under Three Emperors.* New York: Funk & Wagnalls Company, 1917.

———. *It Really Happened.* New York: Dial Press, 1934.

———. *The Tragedy of a Throne.* New York: Funk & Wagnalls, 1917.

RAMANN, LINA. *Franz Liszt, als kunstler und mensch.* Vol. 2. Leipzig: Breitkopf & Hartel, 1880–1894.

RIDLEY, JASPER. *Lord Palmerston.* London: Constable, 1970.

ROGERS, CAMERON. *Gallant Ladies.* New York: Harcourt, Brace & Company, 1928.

ROSENBERG, CHARLES G. (Q). *You Have Heard of Them.* New York: Redfield, 1854.

ROSS, ISHBEL. *Charmers and Cranks.* New York: Harper & Row, 1965.

———. *Rebel Rose.* New York: Harper & Brothers, 1954.

ROURKE, CONSTANCE. *Troupers of the Gold Coast.* New York: Harcourt, Brace & Company, 1928.

RUSH, RICHARD. *Memoranda of a Residence at the Court of London.* Philadelphia: Carey, Lee & Blanchard, 1833.

RUSSELL, WILLIAM HOWARD. *My Diary in India in the Year 1858–9.* London: Routledge, Warne, and Routledge, 1869.

SALA, GEORGE AUGUSTUS. *The Life and Adventures of George Augustus Sala.* Vol. 1. New York: Charles Scribner's Sons, 1895.

SALISBURY, MARQUESS OF. *Essays by the Late Marquess of Salisbury. Foreign Politics.* New York: E. P. Dutton & Company, 1905.

SANDEMAN, G. A. S. *Metternich.* London: Methuen & Company, 1911.

SÉCHÉ, LEON. *Delphine Gay, Mme de Girardin, dans ses rapports avec* Lamartine, *Victor Hugo, Balzac, Rachel, Jules Sandeau, Dumas, Eugène Sue et George Sand.*

SERGEANT, PHILIP WALSINGHAM. *Dominant Women.* London: Hutchinson & Company, 1930.

SITWELL, SACHEVERELL. *Liszt.* Boston: Houghton Mifflin Company, 1934.

STERN, MADELEINE B. *Purple Passage. The Life of Mrs. Frank Leslie.* Norman, Oklahoma: University of Oklahoma Press, 1953.

TAYLOR, A. J. P. *Bismarck, the Man and the Statesman.* London: Hamish Hamilton, 1955.

THIERRY, A. AUGUSTIN. *Lola Montès, Favorite Royale en Bavière.* Paris: Editions, Barnard-Grasset, 1936.

TREITSCHKE, HEINRICH VON. *Deutsche Geschichte im 19. Jahrhundert.* Vol. 5. Leipzig: Verlag von G. Hirzel, 1894.

———. *Germany, France, Russia and Islam.* New York: G. P. Putnam's Sons, 1915.

TROLLOPE, MRS. FRANCES. *Paris and the Parisians in 1835.* New York: Harper & Brothers, 1836.

TROWBRIDGE, W. R. H. *Seven Splendid Sinners.* New York: Brentano's, 1910.

VALENTIN, VEIT. *1848: Chapters of German history,* translated by Ethel Talbot Scheffauer. London: G. Allen & Unwin, 1940.

VANDAM, ALBERT DRESDEN. *An Englishman in Paris. Notes and Recollections.* New York: D. Appleton & Company, 1892.

WINWAR, FRANCES. *The Life of the Heart. George Sand and Her Times.* New York: Harper & Brothers, 1945.

WYNDHAM, HORACE. *Feminine Frailty.* London: Ernest Benn, Ltd., 1920.

———. *The Magnificent Montez.* London: Hutchinson & Company, 1935.

INDEX

Abell, Alexander, 221
actress, Montez as, 26–7, 206, 223, 230, 264, 269–70, 287–8
  see also Dancing and dances
Adelaide (Australia), 260–1
Adelbert, Prince, 132
Adler, Kirke, 239, 243, 245–7
Adventures of Mrs. Seacole, The (Seacole), 217–18
affairs and liaisons, of Montez, 1–2, 13, 25, 59, 151–3, 187
  see also Dujarier, Alexandre Henri; Follin, Augustus Noel; Liszt, Franz; Ludwig I of Bavaria; Marriage; names
Afghan War, 19–21
Aiglon, L' (Rostand), 61
Albany (New York), 269–71
Albert, Madame, 66, 70, 80
Albert, Prince, 47–8, 159, 165, 174
Albion, 197
Alemannia, 124–30, 133, 135, 137–9, 141, 157
Alexander II of Russia, 292

Alston, Rev. A., 166
Amalia, Queen of Greece, 120
ambition, of Montez, 37
American Law Journal, 155
Anglicanism, 294
animal-magnetism cult, 253–4, 293
animals, Montez's interest in, 4, 97, 153, 166, 186, 240–1, 252–3, 259, 263
anticlericalism, 58–9, 111, 148
  see also Religion
Antony and Cleopatra, Montez in, 264
appearance and dress of Montez, 19–20, 25, 45, 84, 88–9, 95, 97, 99, 101, 158, 164–7, 169, 175–6, 182, 185–6, 192, 205, 215, 217–19, 228, 234, 242–3, 245–6, 254, 265, 273, 279, 291, 297, 307
Arco, Count Louis, 138
Arco-Valley, Count, 98
Arts of Beauty, or Secrets of a Lady's Toilet with hints to gentlemen on the art of fascinating (Montez), 277

337

Index

Index

Index

348

72 73 74 75 10 9 8 7 6 5 4 3 2 1